Spectrum Auctions and Competition in Telecommunications

Spectrum Auctions and Competition in Telecommunications

Gerhard Illing and
Ulrich Klüh, editors

CES

The MIT Press
Cambridge, Massachusetts
London, England

This book was set in Palatino on 3B2 by Asco Typesetters, Hong Kong, and was printed and bound in the United States of America.

Library of Congress Cataloging-in-Publication Data

Spectrum auctions and competition in telecommunications / Gerhard Illing and Ulrich Klüh, editors.
    p.   cm. — (CESifo seminar series)
Includes bibliographical references and index.
ISBN 0-262-09037-6 (hc : alk. paper)
    1. Telecommunication—Case studies. 2. Trade regulation—Case studies.
3. Competition—Case studies. I. Illing, Gerhard. II. Klüh, Ulrich. III. Series.
HE7631.S63   2004
384'.041—dc22   2003059262

Contents

Contributors

Klaus Abbink, University of Nottingham, School of Economics, Centre for Decision Research and Experimental Economics, University Park, Nottingham NG7 2RD, United Kingdom

Paul de Bijl, Ministry of Finance, Financial and Economic Policy Directorate, P.O. Box 20201, 2500 EE The Hague, The Netherlands

Tilman Börgers, University College London, Department of Economics, Gower Street, London WC 1E6BT, United Kingdom

Eric van Damme, Tilburg University, Center for Economic Research, P.O. Box 90153, 5000 LE Tilburg, The Netherlands

Christian Dustmann, University College London, Department of Economics, Gower Street, London WC 1E6BT, United Kingdom

Christian Ewerhart, Universität Bonn, Economic Theory III, Adenauerallee 24-26, 53113 Bonn, Germany

Veronika Grimm, Humboldt Universität zu Berlin, Institut für Wirtschaftstheorie I, Spandauer Straße 1, 10178 Berlin, Germany

Steffen H. Hoernig, Faculdade de Economica, Universidade Nova de Lisboa, Travessa Estêvão Pinto, 1099-032 Lisboa, Portugal

Gerhard Illing, Universität München, Volkswirtschaftliches Institut, Seminar für Makroökonomie, Ludwigstraße 28, 80539 München, Germany

Bernd Irlenbusch, Universität Erfurt, Lehrstuhl für Mikroökonomie, Nordhäuser Str. 63, 99089 Erfurt, Germany

Paul Klemperer, Nuffield College, Oxford, OX1 1NF, United Kingdom

Ulrich Klüh, Universität München, Volkswirtschaftliches Institut, Seminar für Makroökonomie, Ludwigstrasse 28, 80539 München, Germany

Benny Moldovanu, Universität Bonn, Chair of Economic Theory II, Lennestrasse 37, 53113 Bonn, Germany

Martin Peitz, Faculty of Economics and Business Administration, University of Frankfurt, Uni-PF 77, 60054 Frankfurt, Germany

Ray Rees, Universität München, Volkswirtschaftliches Institut, Lehrstuhl für Versicherungswissenschaft, Ludwigstraße 28, 80539 München, Germany

Frank Riedel, Humboldt Universität zu Berlin, Institut für Wirtschaftstheorie I, Spandauer Straße 1, 10178 Berlin, Germany

Bettina Rockenbach, Universität Erfurt, Lehrstuhl für Mikroökonomie, Nordhäuser Str. 63, 99089 Erfurt, Germany

Abdolkarim Sadrieh, Department of Economics and CentER, Tilburg University P.O. Box 90153, 5000 LE Tilburg, The Netherlands

Klaus M. Schmidt, Universität München, Volkswirtschaftliches Institut, Seminar für Wirtschafttheorie, Ludwigstraße 28, 80539 München, Germany

Reinhard Selten, Universität Bonn, Institut für Gesellschafts- und Wirtschaftswissenschaften, Adenauerallee 24-42, 53113 Bonn, Germany

Tommaso M. Valletti, Management School, Imperial College, Exhibition Road, London SW7 2PG, United Kingdom

Ingo Vogelsang, Boston University, Department of Economics, 270 Bay State Road, Boston, MA 02215, United States

Elmar Wolfstetter, Humboldt Universität zu Berlin, Institut für Wirtschaftstheorie I, Spandauer Straße 1, 10178 Berlin, Germany

Series Foreword

This book is part of the CESifo Seminar Series in Economic Policy, which aims to cover topical policy issues in economics from a largely European perspective. The books in this series are the products of the papers presented and discussed at seminars hosted by CESifo, an international research network of renowned economists supported jointly by the Center for Economic Studies at Ludwig-Maximilians-Universität, Munich, and the Ifo Institute for Economic Research. All publications in this series have been carefully selected and refereed by members of the CESifo research network.

Hans-Werner Sinn

1   Spectrum Auctions and Competition in Telecommunications: An Introduction

Gerhard Illing and Ulrich Klüh

During the last decades, the telecommunications sector has been characterized by an amazing scale of innovation and by substantial institutional and regulatory change. Triggered by technological advancements, privatization, and liberalization, these changes have stimulated competition and driven down prices substantially. Currently, telecommunications is going through a new period of major transformations, in particular the transition from second generation mobile telephony (2G) to third generation technologies (3G), or universal mobile telephone services (UMTS). In most countries, this new era was initiated by spectrum auctions held in 2000 and 2001. Some of these auctions, especially those in the United Kingdom and in Germany, were widely considered to be outstanding success stories. Others, like the ones conducted in Austria, Switzerland, and the Netherlands, were harshly criticized. This discrepancy has puzzled many observers, mainly because similar rules had been applied in both groups of countries. It has also stimulated a lively debate about the conditions under which a particular design delivers the desired result. As Eric van Damme puts it in chapter 16: *"a license auction ... is not an isolated event; it takes place in a certain context and this context should be taken into account when designing the auction rules. Second, auction design is an art in itself of which the difficulty should not be underestimated"* (289).

The purpose of this book is to combine the insights of many of the most renowned experts from various fields to add to our understanding of this art. As van Damme's statement indicates, a careful evaluation of auctions has to take into account the context of an auction. This context includes the political, regulatory, and technological environment as well as the characteristics of the relevant industry. The single most important characteristic of a formerly monopolized sector is the intensity of competition it displays. Most of the contributions to this book therefore view the auction game as a relatively small, yet important, stage of a complex market game: The auction takes place in an already existing environment of imperfect competition. Many important features of the auction game are thus determined beforehand. Furthermore, bidding behavior is strongly influenced by expectations about the future interaction among winners, losers, the government, and consumers. At the same time, the auction subgame is of immense importance since it is at this stage that the number of players and their identity is determined. It follows that license auctions and competition issues are closely related. This interconnectedness of two important and highly productive areas of modern economics—auction theory and industrial organisation—was the working basis of a CESifo conference held in November 2001, where all but one of the chapters collected here were initially presented as conference papers.[1] It is inevitable that a conference volume partly forfeits the atmosphere of productive conflict that was present during the event. However, by publishing comments and responses, the editors hope to preserve some of the most fascinating controversies. Emphasizing the main lines of disagreement, this introduction serves a similar purpose.

1.1 Competition and Efficiency in Telecommunication: Trade-Offs, Issues, and the Role of Auctions

The final objective of any policy for and regulation of a specific industry is to support a high degree of static and dynamic efficiency or, respectively, to trade off the two optimally. As the case may be, other social objectives have to be taken into account. Whereas this proposition is a truism everybody would agree to, fierce controversies exist about how to define efficiency, how to weigh different objectives in the face of potential trade-offs, and how to achieve efficiency given a set of social objectives. What are the main drivers of efficiency? Among a multitude of candidates, this book identifies competition as the single most important determinant of static and dynamic efficiency. Economists are often accused to blindly rely on competition and of sometimes even confusing it with efficiency. However, with regard to telecommunications, economists are in a comfortable position to build on ample empirical evidence for the benefits of a competitive environment (see, e.g., Boylaud and Nicoletti 2001). Nevertheless, one has to be careful not to overuse competition or ignore the trade-offs involved: With technologies requiring substantial fixed costs (such as broadband or UMTS), static efficiency may first increase with additional competition. At a certain point, however, the social losses from duplicating fixed costs will outweigh these gains. The same holds true for dynamic efficiency: An increasing number of entrants as well as a higher intensity of measures against anti-competitive behavior will certainly force companies to improve technology and customer service. From a certain point on, however, rents from innovative behavior will shrink, reducing incentives to invest in quality. Furthermore, other policy objectives such as equity (as in the case of Universal Service obligations) or the promotion of technologies that may foster economic growth (such as broadband services) may be related to measures of competition policy.

Auction theorists often have to abstract from many of these trade-offs and policy problems. In fact, their job is not to analyze the game in its totality and in full detail. Their goal rather is to identify the major mechanisms relating the auction to the rest of the game. Analyzing the policy problem "at the gate of the market," namely the determination of market participants, they can legitimately restrict themselves on the grounds of the following argument: Whereas there is widespread progress in understanding the efficiency of different auction designs theoretically, it is very difficult to tell whether a real-world auction leads to the efficient outcome. It is literally impossible to quantify the degree of efficiency, neither ex ante nor ex post. Therefore, it is better to trust some basic empirical results of industrial organization and rely on a rule of thumb: "Coin a license auction 'efficient' when it has encouraged entry and has successfully prevented collusion" (see, e.g., chapter 10) or simply: when it leads to more competition. Increased competition is likely to deliver an increase in consumer surplus, and this, in turn, implies higher efficiency. On such grounds, many complicated trade-offs and policy problems can be excluded from the analysis. Nonetheless, auction theorists should be aware that they analyze merely a stage in a much larger and complex market game. In fact, all of the contributions to this book recognize this in one or more of the following dimensions:

• The outcome of an auction depends on the characteristics of bidders. These characteristics are largely determined beforehand—for example, by the structure of related markets (such as 2G networks in the case of UMTS), by the valuation of company stakeholders not directly involved in bidding, or by financing constraints.

• Before and after the auction, regulators and companies are involved in an ongoing relationship. Before the event, companies will try to exert pressure on the regulator to adapt auction rules that serve their particular interests. During the auction, expectations of the nature of future regulation are of great importance in companies' valuation models. For example, competitors closely monitor the way the regulator deals with potential asymmetries between entrants and incumbents.

To summarize, the auction is embedded in a dynamic interplay among consumers, firms, legislation, and regulation. Economists working in areas outside auction theory have developed sophisticated tools to analyze this interplay. They also have added substantially to the understanding of the trade-offs mentioned earlier. A one-dimensional discussion that looks at a single policy problem (the appropriate allocation of spectrum) and a specific instrument alone (the auctioning of licences) runs the risk of squandering these important insights. The first part of this book is therefore dedicated to their exploitation.

1.2 Setting the Stage: (New) Competition, (New) Challenges, and Regulatory Innovation

In the light of rapid changes in technology, company behavior, and industry environment, regulators are permanently forced to straighten up their toolboxes. The purpose of a book such as this one is in fact to support regulators in doing so. However, the process of regulatory progress in telecommunications is complicated for a variety of reasons.

First, regulation does not advance in the way the public interest theory of regulation predicts. To give valuable recommendations, economists have to have an idea about the way innovative solutions diffuse in the political arena. In particular, it would be important to know under what conditions welfare-enhancing innovations are likely to be implemented, how pressure groups influence the outcome, and what role scientific advice can play in a world of imperfectly informed voters, optimizing politicians, and interest groups. The recent past contains numerous examples of regulatory change in telecommunications that can be extremely valuable in answering these questions. Ingo Vogelsang (chapter 2) sets the scene for this book by taking these experiences seriously. He discusses the international diffusion of regulatory approaches and asks under what conditions useful reforms in one country help to improve competition policy internationally. He looks at the design of regulatory institutions, price caps, universal service policies, network competition, proxy cost models, and spectrum auctions in different countries as potential areas of such a "cross-fertilization." He concludes that the evidence for efficient cross-country learning is rather mixed. In some cases such as price cap regulation it has taken place; in other cases, useful policy innovations were not adopted. In assessing the conditions for the transfer of ideas, Vogelsang highlights the importance of the political economy of regulation. He reminds us that academic advisors should always bear in mind that the proper policy solution still has to be marketed to politicians and the public.

Second, telecommunications is not a mature industry with an oligopolistic structure. The main challenge is therefore not to prevent collusion among a known set of market players, but to generate *new competition* and to deal with its consequences. The generation of new competition, in turn, can be achieved by a variety of instruments, such as auction rules that favor entrants, mandatory roaming or asymmetric access pricing. But which policies should a regulator adopt, and how do these policies interact? Central to the understanding of these questions are potential asymmetries between entrants and incumbents. Asymmetries affect auctions in a variety of ways, for example, through the prevention of a value-maximizing outcome within the auction (see chapter 13). It is therefore important to understand their regulatory implications thoroughly. The contribution of Paul de Bijl and Martin Peitz (chapter 4) draws interesting conclusions in this respect. De Bijl and Peitz ask how competition can be achieved when new entrants are characterized by an initial lack of track record. This situation is typical to newly liberalized telecommunications markets. It also tracks closely the nature of asymmetries between different participants in spectrum auctions, an issue of major concern for regulators during the design stage. The authors show that an asymmetric access pricing policy in the wholesale market is the appropriate answer to initial heterogeneity, leaving entrants and consumers better off. Furthermore, they analyze the interrelation between different policies in terms of incentives for entry and consumer surplus. Among others, they investigate the combination of different access pricing regimes with price caps on the incumbent's subscription fees and per-minute prices. The ambiguous welfare effects of such a policy are driven by trade-offs and mechanisms highly relevant to regulatory attempts to level the playing field. For example, a price cap favoring consumers in the short run may induce a more aggressive pricing policy of the incumbent operator, possibly deterring entry by lowering profits. This, in turn, may violate the long-run objective of stimulating competition. When discussing ways to level the playing field using auctions, one should bear in mind these and other considerations mentioned in chapter 4 and in the inspiring remarks by Ingo Vogelsang (chapter 5).

Finally, the telecommunications industry operates in a highly dynamic environment in terms of technology and preferences. As a result of the fundamental uncertainty surrounding any decision, regulation is not a one-shot game; all regulation is followed by unforeseen consequences in terms of the competitive behavior of firms. These reactions, in turn, require a constant modulation of policy measures. A complex interplay between regulation and competition emerges. Steffen H. Hoernig and Tommaso M. Valletti (chapter 6) use the experiences in the area of universal service obligations (USOs) to study this interplay. They touch important issues, such as the problem of cream skimming, the importance of network externalities, and the contribution of telecommunications to overall economic growth. Besides being inspiring on its own, their analysis is closely related to license auctions in various ways. We name only two. First, licenses are typically assigned with the obligation to reach a certain part of the population within a prespecified period of time. Service obligations in 3G markets are thus not universal, neither in the sense of geographic availability, nor in the sense of "affordability" of prices. Nevertheless, some of the findings of Hoernig and Valletti concerning the strategic implications of USOs may still apply to service obligations in 3G markets. The current lobbying activities of European license holders for (in the case of small firms) and against (in the case of large players) a suspension of service obligations contain interesting case studies in this respect. Second, the authors advocate the use of auctions to assign USOs together with a certain level of subsidies. The problems involved in implementing such a procedure (e.g., bidder participation and asymmetry of information concerning market attractiveness) closely track those described in the remaining parts of this book.

1.3   European Spectrum Auctions: A British Success Story and Continental Failures?

These remaining parts focus on the design and outcome of specific spectrum auctions in different European countries. A number of crucial questions are addressed: What is the optimal, efficient design of a spectrum auction? How should auction design be related to competition policy? Should designers focus on raising government revenue or on stimulating competition? Was the auction design in some countries fatally flawed? Does traditional game theory help little to predict the outcome of these auctions, simply because participants do not pursue rational bidding behavior? The contributions use the ample empirical evidence provided by the European experience to answer these and other important questions.

The most astonishing feature of European 3G auctions in 2000 and 2001 is undoubtedly the huge variation in revenues: Whereas the U.K. and the German auction generated revenues in excess of 600 Euros per capita, revenues for all the other countries range from 20 (Switzerland) to 170 (Netherlands) Euros per capita. Differences in market size and attractiveness are by no means able to explain these variations. In chapter 7, Paul Klemperer takes up this phenomenon and offers some very convincing explanations. His starting point is the difference between ascending (English) and sealed-bid (Dutch) auctions. Whereas ascending auctions minimize the probability that a player with lower valuations outbids a player with higher valuations, they have considerable disadvantages in encouraging entry and preventing collusion. In particular, they allow bidders to signal their willingness to collude and to punish non-cooperative behavior. Furthermore, participation of potential entrants may be deterred, since a weaker player knows with certainty that a stronger rival can always top his bid. Arguing on the same grounds, sealed-bid auctions are suitable for preventing tacit collusion and encouraging entry. However, they bear the danger of awarding the license to players with lower valuations. For these reasons, it might be useful to combine the two designs in a so-called Anglo-Dutch auction. In a first stage, an ascending format guarantees a high degree of value efficiency, since strong bidders drive out the lowest valuations. The ascending auction continues until the number of active bidders is slightly higher than the number of available licenses. The remaining players then submit a sealed bid. This second stage is intended to inject enough uncertainty into the game to make participation attractive and to deter collusion. In summary, Klemperer advocates an English design when new entry and competitive bidding can be guaranteed otherwise. He favors a Dutch design when encouraging entry is the main concern. In intermediate situations, a hybrid design might be the best solution.

The various experiences of countries using a straightforward ascending auction (the United Kingdom, the Netherlands, Italy, and Switzerland) serve as evidence for this line of reasoning. The U.K. auction was widely considered to be a success in terms of revenues and a competitive market structure. In contrast, all three other auctions failed, even though they had chosen a very similar design. In Klemperer's view, this discrepancy is easily explained by the fact that the Radicommunication Agency of the United Kingdom had chosen to allocate more licenses than there were incumbents. This convinced many potential entrants to participate, making arrangements to cooperate more difficult and risky. Participation was encouraged and, given a good chance of entry, collusion was effectively prevented: Everybody had to bid up to his or her true valuation, leading to revenues of 39 billion Euros. In contrast, the Netherlands, Italy, and Switzerland failed to convince entrants that they had a reasonable chance to win. Therefore, small companies entered joint-bidding agreements or attempted to close deals with powerful incumbents. As a result, bidders managed to coordinate on the low revenue equilibrium. Klemperer concludes that the respective governments simply failed to understand the advantages of a Dutch or Anglo-Dutch regime in their specific situation. In his view, the Danish experience with a sealed-bid design provides some evidence for such a claim. Klemperer also discusses the German and Austrian variant of the ascending setup. The main dimensions of his heavy criticism are taken up in part IV of this book, where the German auction is analyzed in detail. Pointing to the Austrian experience, he states that the German government was simply "lucky" that similar problems did not arise there. He concludes that the U.K. design was much more immune against possible inefficiencies.[2]

Tilman Börgers and Christian Dustmann (chapter 8) critically review the empirical evidence for such a claim. Their contribution is one of the first attempts to take the data seriously. Furthermore, it is highly innovative in the way the existing data is used to produce interesting results. Börgers and Dustmann first ask whether observed bids in the United Kingdom are compatible with the idea that bidders (a) form values ex ante and (b) bid rationally given their private valuations. If this had been the case, Klaus Schmidt (chapter 9) writes, the "claim that the outcome of the British UMTS auction was efficient would be on much safer grounds" (159). However, the authors' findings do not point in that direction; most companies' behavior cannot be reconciled with straightforward bidding on the basis of fixed private valuations. This does not necessarily mean that the U.K. outcome was inefficient, as explained by the authors themselves and detailed by Schmidt and by Paul Klemperer (chapter 10). In particular, straightforward bidding with fixed valuations is only a narrow characterization of rational behavior in auctions. Introducing common values or allocative externalities alters rational strategies significantly (see the next paragraph). Moreover, as stressed by Schmidt, even if the authors had found evidence for straightforward bidding, efficiency could still have been inhibited by factors related to the environment of the auction. Examples include a technically inappropriate division of spectrum, principal-agent problems inside companies, or credit constraints. It is open to questioning whether these issues should have been incorporated into the auction format, as it has been partly the case in Germany.

Though an interesting application of their analysis, assessing the efficiency of the British auction is not the main purpose of Börgers and Dustmann. They attempt rather to look for "footprints" in the data that may help discriminate between alternative explanations for the observed violation of straightforward bidding with fixed valuations. These include allocative externalities, social learning, shareholders' opinion, budget constraints, or management disagreements. Unfortunately, neither of the hypotheses considered is strongly supported. However, while some of the explanations, including allocative externalities, are clearly refused by the data, other rationalizations simply do not leave any footprints and thus cannot be confirmed or rejected. Therefore, budget constraints, social learning and attempts to conceal true valuations might have played a role in shaping the outcome.

Chapter 8 raises another extremely important point. As reviewed by Ewerhart and Moldovanu (chapter 13), most results concerning the efficiency of specific auctions in different (informational) environments are based on strong rationality assumptions. Additionally, research that explains puzzling auction outcomes tries to "rationalize" them in the traditional sense: It is asked how actual bidding behavior can be reconciled with rational decision making.[3] This is an important research project, as the chapters in this volume impressively illustrate. However, a discussion of license auctions is incomplete without tackling another set of issues: Do bidders form their valuations in line with our standard assumptions? Do we observe departures from rational bidding behavior? Are concepts like straightforward bidding (Milgrom 2000) appropriate as a descriptive device? How do social learning and managerial desires to "be the winner" enter the picture? Questions of that kind are not only important to improve our understanding of bidding behavior in license auctions, but also a necessary condition for the future advancement of auction theory in general. While it will take a huge research effort to incorporate behavioral aspects in current modeling practices, economists should at least scrutinize harum-scarum statements about the efficiency of a particular design.

1.4   The Behavioral Approach to Auctions: Further Insights from Experimental Economics?

A behavioral enrichment of auction theory needs guidelines in the form of empirical regularities concerning systematic departures from standard assumptions. Typically, experiments are conducted to explore these phenomena. Additionally, one could look at the way firms actually prepare their bidding strategy. In an interesting case study, Klaus Abbink, Bernd Irlenbusch, Bettina Rockenbach, Abdolkarim Sadrieh, and Reinhard Selten (chapter 12) combine these two approaches. They report on their experiences as consultants for a company involved in the German DCS-1800 auction and describe the steps conducted to formulate a bidding strategy using experiments: After the collection of relevant information on the value of a license to the company and its competitors, game-theoretic experiments inspired by behavioral considerations were conducted with students and managers. The results obtained were used to formulate bidding strategies (in the game-theoretic sense) for different scenarios. These strategies were finally applied in training sessions. A striking result was the obvious discrepancy between experimental results and the outcome of the real world auction: Whereas experiments were highly competitive, the real auction was characterized by quasi-instantaneous collusion. During the conference, this result induced a controversial discussion on the value added by laboratory experiments, a subject significantly underresearched in our view.

1.5   The German Auction Design

Part IV discusses the German and the Austrian auction. Both governments had chosen to use a modified version of the simple ascending design. In particular, the number of licenses and their size was not predetermined. Each bidder could collect either two or three out of twelve blocks of spectrum; the number of licenses could thus range from four to six. This approach was heavily criticized on the grounds of these arguments:

• Consumer interests are not adequately represented in such a design: The regulator should not leave the decision about the number of entrants in the hands of those who are interested in a concentrated market structure.

• The design does not generate sufficient entry. In fact, only seven bidders competed for a maximum of six licenses. One reason for this might have been the ascending nature of the German auction.

• The design is vulnerable to collusive behavior. Indeed, there is evidence that players tried to signal their willingness to stop bidding at a certain stage. Additionally, there were rumors of collusive offers between two new entrants. It might have been the case that the existence of many small blocks made collusion especially attractive.

• The auctions complexity generates a number of potential inefficiencies. In particular, bidders might get stuck with a license that they do not want in the resulting market environment or might be the winner of just one block that is not sufficient to generate a license (see chapter 13 on exposure and regret problems).

In spite of all these arguments, the German design proved to be very successful. Revenues per capita reached British levels and two new entrants won a license. As a result of its puzzling outcome and unconventional design, the German auction has stimulated an intense discussion among academics and practioners.

The German experience helps clarify the major trade-offs and policy problems that keep regulators busy during the design stage. It also illustrates the manifold linkages between competition policy and auction design: What is the optimal number of market participants and new entrants and what is the best way to discover it? What is the optimal size of a license, taking into account the need for nationwide services, technological constraints, and dynamic efficiency? In the German case, the fundamental uncertainty surrounding most of these issues convinced regulators to leave a great deal of these decisions to the market, endogenizing block size and the number of licenses finally allocated. This approach raises a highly important, yet often neglected aspect of auction design. Specifically, a regulator not only has to decide upon an efficient allocation procedure given a ready set of allocative problems to be solved within the auction (e.g., identifying the market participants that assign the highest value to a license). An auction also has the potential to address a variety of regulatory problems (e.g., identifying the "right" players and determining market size, encouraging entry and supporting new entrants actively) and conflicting or complementary objectives (e.g., value maximization, efficiency and revenue maximization). In chapter 13, Christian Ewerhart and Benny Moldovanu nicely pick up these concerns. They stress that "the outcome of any allocation procedure influences the future interaction among winning firms, regulator (i.e., government), and consumers" (203). Thus, an appropriate auction design has to incorporate elements of industrial organisation and mechanism design, taking into account the complex trade-offs between revenue maximization, value maximization and efficiency. After reviewing the current state of auction-theoretic literature on these issues, Ewerhart and Moldovanu investigate the German and the Austrian auction. They conclude that the efficiency gains obtained through a very flexible design have probably been overcompensated by the negative consequences of exposure and regret problems and the risks of ending up with excessively high license prices. Emphasising the exposure problem within multi-object auctions (i.e., bidders pay too much for individual items or bidders with preferences for certain combinations drop out early to limit losses) the authors also find some convincing explanations for its puzzling outcome. In particular, they argue that a strong bidder (typically the incumbent) that tries to eliminate a potential competitor suffers from regret when she fails to do so. This may result in prices well above the level of a less flexible setting, with adverse consequences on participation and the financial health of the industry.

Veronika Grimm, Frank Riedel, and Elmar Wolfstetter take a quite different stance in chapter 14. In their view, the idea to let bidders aggregate their own licenses had its specific merits, especially when compared to the English rules.[4] Specifically, they argue that the endogeneity of block size and the number of assigned licenses was able to produce more competition and more revenue at the same time. To support their argument, they have to show that the successful outcome of the auction was not as "bizarre" (Jehiel and Moldovanu 2001, 16) as many other observers have claimed. In particular, they have to rationalize the behavior of the two large incumbents in the crucial phase of the auction, when both players unexpectedly give up attempts to crowd out the sixth bidder. We do not want to repeat their argument, since this is nicely done in the chapter. We would rather emphasize that Grimm, Riedel, and Wolfstetter find an interesting strategic explanation for the German "puzzle" by including a small detail of the actual design: the possibility of one spectrum block being leftover in the first auction. This detail can create incentives for players to ensure the existence of such a leftover, leaving them in the position to purchase it for less in the following second round. The mere possibility of such an outcome may significantly alter incentives to play a predation strategy or to bid straightforwardly. Since the other strong bidder now has the chance to free-ride on predation while receiving a third block cheap, there are strong incentives to resign relatively early. In addition to this surprising explanation, the authors find further advantages of the German design. In particular, they take up Klemperer's point of the importance of bidder participation and turn it upside down. They argue that the attraction of participation and entry was particularly tricky after the U.K. auction. Valuations and the strength of bidders had already been revealed, so weak bidders were extremely pessimistic about their chances to win in a British setting. In contrast, the flexibility of the German setting might have added enough incentives to participate.[5]

1.6   Closing the Circle: The Dutch Auction and the Interplay among the Political Process, Market Structure, and Strategic Behavior in Auctions

The contributions by Eric van Damme (chapter 16) and Christian Ewerhart (chapter 17) conclude the book. They analyze the hotly debated failure of the Dutch auction in July 2000 and provide another captivating view on the difficulties in designing an efficient auction. In doing this, they take up many issues discussed earlier. In its three main sections, chapter 16 in fact summarizes the main lines of research and debates consolidated in this volume. Section 16.2 studies the appropriate specification of goals. Discussing the factors that influence efficiency, it again highlights the importance of asymmetries between incumbents and entrants, an aspect that received much attention in chapters 4 and 6. Section 16.3 describes the process leading to the Dutch auction design, stressing the role of lobbying activities of incumbents. This section explains the failure of the Dutch government to attract new entry, demonstrating the importance of the political-economy perspective advocated by Ingo Vogelsang. Section 16.4 describes the developments occurring simultaneously inside and outside the auction room; it provides a detailed discussion of strange bids, (tacit) collusion, insider information, and predation, issues frequently addressed in the chapters on specific auctions.[6] The author draws important conclusions, and we name only a few. First, one of the main insights of the Dutch experience is that the Dutch regulator failed to deliver a level playing field in terms of information sets. In fact, the auctioneer did not intervene at all when it became clear that one of the entrants submitted important insider information to one of the incumbents, distorting bidding behavior. Van Damme concludes that letting an independent and knowledgeable agent conduct the auction could have prevented these and other politico-economical problems during the design stage. Second, there was considerable confusion with respect to the specification of goals and their relation to each other. Different concepts of efficiency (value versus cost versus market efficiency) were not adequately distinguished and the role of revenue motives was by no means clear. Without a proper specification of goals, however, it is not possible to design a license auction adequately. It is therefore necessary to define a transparent set of objectives that may explicitly include a revenue motive. Recognizing the benefits of high revenues in the presence of distortionary taxes might be superior to an incredible and inconclusive declaration to pursue pure efficiency motives. Third, the close interlacing between the auction and the overall market game has implications not yet sufficiently incorporated in the thinking of either politicians or academics. Both have to recognize that the participation in an auction may not signal a willingness to win but an attempt to improve ones position "elsewhere in the game."

1.7   Epilogue: The Current Situation

This book documents the considerable progress made in understanding the interplay between competition policy and auction theory. It also contains numerous examples for the achievements of a formerly monopolized industry and its regulators in increasing economic welfare. In spite of these achievements, a seemingly very different subject currently attracts the attention of the public and the press, namely, the financial problems of telecommunication firms. After having praised them to the skies, many observers now blame European license auctions as being at the root of current problems. Greedy governments, so the argument goes, had chosen to award licenses in a manner inconsistent with a smooth introduction of the new technology, thereby violating consumer interests. Companies, in turn, were infected by the fatal disease of "bidding fever," whose side effects are now borne by shareholders. The same companies now knock on the doors of regulators, lobbying for an attenuation of the strict rules obliging them to build up networks within a relatively short period of time.

We do not want to overstate these developments and the sometimes overheated debates surrounding them. However, we believe that recent experiences highlight two important avenues for future research. At the same time, they illustrate that this book already covers aspects whose relevance was not foreseen by many other observers beforehand. First, recent months have shown that financial considerations may play a far more important role than previously expected—all the more so since they are closely related to competition issues. For example, it is open to question to what extent strong companies bid up prices in an attempt to weaken the financial position of small ones, thus crowding them out of the market. While it is certainly true that the mechanisms relating finance and license auctions await explorations that go far beyond the scope of this book, we believe that such research can be perfectly conducted along the lines already envisioned here. For example, the exposure problem raised by Ewerhart and Moldovanu provides us with a promising starting point for the analysis of many important topics. The same holds true for Börgers and Dustmann's assessment of the impact of shareholders' opinion[7] and budget constraints on bidding behavior. As Klemperer notes in chapter 7, "the area seems ripe for research" (109).[8] Second, we again cite Ewerhart and Moldovanu, who stress in chapter 13 that the "outcome of any allocation procedure influences the future interaction among winning firms, regulator (i.e., government), and consumers" and that "this obvious effect should be taken into account for applications of auction theory" (203). Whereas we believe that this book has added impressively to our understanding of firm interaction and auctions, much work remains to be done in incorporating the incentive effects of future regulation. In this respect, many exciting aspects (e.g., the tradability of licenses or the dynamic consistency of regulatory decisions) await incorporation into our treatment of spectrum auctions and their relation to competition.

Notes

1. The paper by Paul Klemperer (chapter 7) first appeared in the *European Economic Review* 46(4–5) (2002): 829–845. It has been included in this volume to give a comprehensive picture of the debate. All other articles in this volume first appeared in *ifo studien* 48(1) (2002). They were originally presented at a CESifo conference in November 2001, marking the relaunch of *ifo studien* as *CESifo Economic Studies* (www.

cesifoeconomicstudies.de). *CESifo Economic Studies* publishes thoroughly refereed papers by top-level academic economists, written in a style accessible to all economists regardless of their specialization.

2. Klemperer (chapter 15) also interprets the evidence for falling revenues over time. In his view, the sequencing had the effect of aggravating the problems of insufficient entry and tacit collusion. In particular, bidders seem to have learned to play auctions of a specific type and to have gained experience in how to cooperate. Furthermore, incoming information about the values assigned by opponents might have facilitated attempts to share the cake outside the auction room.

3. It is worth mentioning that all authors of this book take a pragmatic stance, underscoring aspects outside the scope of auction theory. For example, Klemperer mentions the difficulties of figuring out optimal strategies in complex and opaque settings and managerial concerns about relative performance.

4. For a critical assessment of the British auction rules, see Wolfstetter (2003).

5. Grimm, Riedel, and Wolfstetter (chapter 14) also raise some new and important policy topics, proposing to (a) replace the current regime by one which allocates the entire spectrum to different types of users in one auction and (b) free spectrum space by abandoning air transmission of other services.

6. Christian Ewerhart (chapter 17) takes up van Damme's description (chapter 16) of strange bids during the Dutch spectrum auction. These strange bids closely resemble those described in Börgers and Dustman (chapter 7). The author rationalizes this outcome by introducing uncertainty about one's own valuation, correlated net present values of expected revenues, and a common value element.

7. Closely related, incentive structures within the firms seem to be another fruitful research area. Again, we could directly refer to one or another chapter of this book to identify exciting avenues for further studies. For example, Klaus M. Schmidt (chapter 9) mentions principal-agent and collective decision making problems and states that "it is not clear whether the auction format could or should be used to solve these internal problems of the involved companies" (160).

8. Specifically, economists tend to look for binding budget constraints. In Germany and the United Kingdom, however, the problem might have been an *excessive* amount of funds due to overvalued telecom shares. Expecting the bubble to burst, managers might have decided to spend the money before it was gone.

References

Boylaud, Olivier, and Giuseppe Nicoletti. 2001. "Regulation, Market Structure and Performance in Telecommunications." *OECD Economic Studies* 32(1): 99–142.

Jehiel, P., and Benny Moldovanu. 2001. "The European UMTS/IMT-2000 license auctions." Working paper, University College London and University of Mannheim.

Milgrom, P. 2000. "Putting Auction Theory to Work: The Simultaneous Ascending Auction." *Journal of Political Economy* 108: 245–272.

Wolfstetter, E. 2003. "The Swiss UMTS Spectrum Auction Flop: Bad Luck or Bad Design?" In *Regulation, Competition, and the Market Economy. Festschrift for C. C. V. Weizsäcker*, 281–294. Göttingen: Vandenhoeck & Ruprecht.

I

Setting the Stage: (New) Competition, (New) Challenges, and Regulatory Innovation

2

Cross-Fertilization between U.S. and European Telecommunications Regulation

Ingo Vogelsang

2.1 Introduction

One of the most important tasks for a regulation economist is to help improve regulation. While theory can offer guidance and serve as a source of inspiration, the practical demonstration of new policies is generally more convincing. In order for this to happen, someone has to take the lead and implement genuinely new policies. Throughout most of the history of the telephone, the United States was considered the leader in the telecommunications sector development, and, for the last few decades, it also became the leader in regulatory reform and liberalization of the sector. This certainly was the case in most areas of telecommunications. However, more recently, the United States has been losing some of its leadership role and has become a follower in areas, such as price cap regulation. In addition, according to Elixmann et al. (2001), the United States in 1999 occupied only a middle rank in terms of liberalization and competition compared to eight European countries. In this chapter, I try to characterize the recent era of cross-fertilization and draw some lessons for better policies. The analysis roughly covers the time after the watershed year 1984, when AT&T was divested in the United States and British Telecom (BT) was privatized in the United Kingdom.

Surprisingly little economic analysis seems to exist on cross-country learning of policies. To my knowledge this policy aspect has neither been incorporated in economic theories of regulation nor has it been used as an explanatory variable in empirical analyses of regulatory reform.

In section 2.2 we try to place cross-country learning in the context of the prevalent explanations of regulatory behavior and reform. Section 2.3 looks at specific examples of cross-country learning. Section 2.4

concludes with normative policy consequences from the positive analysis and with suggestions for research.

2.2   Conditions for the Transfer of Regulatory Reform Ideas

2.2.1   Introduction

Why is regulatory reform done in the first place? Under what conditions will regulatory innovations and learning from experiences travel from one country to another? It travels (a) because the conditions for reform are similar in different countries in the same industry and (b) because the reform was successful in at least one country. Item (b) implies that there is a lag between leading and following. Unsuccessful reform can also lead to cross-fertilization by preventing bad policies (the California electricity disaster).

Similar external conditions that can potentially lead to similar regulatory outcomes and to regulatory reform include changes in market conditions and technological changes. Since such changes occur worldwide and have been very pronounced in the telecommunications sector, parallel regulatory changes in many countries would not be surprising. However, in addition, there continue to exist leads and lags as well as paper trails that show influences of established policies in one country on the new policies in another country.

An example of a technical and market change of this kind is the introduction of ADSL in the local loop. In combination with the strong unbundling policy established by the U.S. Telecommunications Act of 1996 (1996 Act), this led to a regulatory policy of line sharing at the end of 1999. This policy provides access to new entrants to the high frequency part of the local loops owned by incumbent carriers. It is now being copied and, to some extent, adapted in Europe. The U.S. solution showed that line sharing was physically and organizationally feasible in combination with collocation, which the United States had pioneered earlier. It is quite obvious in both line sharing and collocation that cross-country learning has been taking place.[1]

Policies that come from different conditions and therefore do not travel easily include the U.K. approach to local telephony by cable TV companies. The United Kingdom was in the unique position of having a small and expanding cable TV network when it opened the local telephone market to cable TV companies. In contrast, countries like the United States and Germany had a large installed base in cable TV that did not easily lend itself to conversion to a hybrid television/telephone system.

2.2.2 Political Economy

The economic theory of regulation, originally developed by Stigler (1971), is based on the optimizing behavior of politicians and interest groups. Regulators in his framework would be subsumed under politicians, who would maximize votes by pleasing some interest groups and burdening others. Peltzman (1976) developed the approach further by introducing imperfect information of voters and organizing costs for interest groups. The imperfect information is never made explicit in his models, but it is a prerequisite for the success of interest group propaganda in convincing voters to vote in favor of a politician, who places a net burden on them.

In my view, imperfect information is at the heart of Peltzman's approach. This is precisely where cross-country learning can come in. The experiences of other countries provide information about possible or likely policy outcomes. This information is strong because it is based on actual observations, but it is tainted by the differences between countries. The information is publicly available, but it is even more visible to experts—policymakers and interest groups. Thus, we may expect that experience in other countries would not wipe out the information problem in Peltzman's model. However, it is likely to influence the outcome. In particular, I conjecture that cross-country learning would bend the outcome more in the direction of efficiency and away from voting against one's own interests. This could come about both by following a good foreign example and by rejecting a bad one. Without reference to cross-fertilization, a move in this direction is already anticipated by Becker (1983).

In a way, Becker explains why economists have been fooled so long by the public interest theory of regulation. His observation is that, even in an interest group environment, more efficient policies have a better chance of being implemented than less efficient policies, because the former create more surplus to be distributed than the latter do. In other words, the winners win more and the losers lose less under efficient than under inefficient policies. Given the limited resources of politicians and regulators, they would therefore concentrate more on efficient policies. Foreign examples, in this context, act as public goods without exclusion. They reduce the costs of learning about such policies and increase the scope for efficiency improvements. These effects come about because policymakers would gain an edge by having this information and thereby would have an interest in acquiring it.[2] The same holds for interest groups. However, interest groups also want to suppress information that is unfavorable to them.[3] Under imperfect information, the winning groups would be the main beneficiaries of inefficient regulation. If information costs are lowered, cross-country learning would then benefit the burdened and initially less powerful interest groups and thereby make information-suppressing tactics less successful. Cross-country learning could, however, also help the winning groups avoid making mistakes that would cost them support in the future.

2.2.3 Institutional Endowment

Learning from experience within a country should be easier than learning from other countries with different political, legal, and economic institutions and different populations, standards of living, and geography. For that reason, learning between countries would occur primarily in sectors, where only a single policy is applied in a country. The United States differs from the European countries by having fifty states, each of which has its own regulatory policies. This has created the laboratory of the states, from which all of them and the federal regulatory authorities can learn, and that should reduce the incentive to learn from other countries.

Learning between countries requires that their institutional and economic conditions not be too different.[4] Europe and the United States have many things in common: a high standard of living, Western culture, a federal structure, and moderate climate. There are also substantial differences: The heterogeneity between countries in Europe is stronger than between states in the United States, for example, language, political and legal system, and history. There are also differences in political attitudes toward the market system and social responsibilities of firms and governments. Antitrust traditionally plays a stronger role in the United States than in European countries, although Europe has been catching up recently.

Specific differences between the United States and Europe in telecommunications result largely from the history of public enterprise and recent privatizations in Europe as opposed to a one hundred-year-old tradition of regulation of private utilities and regulatory reform in the United States. They include the degree of vertical integration of the dominant national carriers, and the due process rules applied to regulation and the independence and position of the regulators. The due process rules in American regulation influence the way information enters the regulatory process. A large part of the information is provided by the affected parties. Due process rules help avoid capture of the regulator by the regulated firms. In part they do that by allowing other interested parties to present evidence, which could be the foreign experience.

The long history of U.S. regulation was accompanied by the establishment of regulatory compacts that gave the parties some right to the status quo. Change in regulation has therefore become difficult if, in particular, the regulated firm would likely become a major loser. The avoidance of losers explains, for example, why price rebalancing has been so difficult. In contrast, the history of public enterprises required less due process and fewer formal assurances, because the government represented both the regulator and the owner. Privatization in the United Kingdom resulted, among others, because public enterprise reforms had failed. In fact, the presence of public enterprises, for a long time, prevented the adoption of regulatory innovations generated in the United States, for example, in connection with long-distance liberalization.[5] However, once privatization occurred, there was no burden with regulatory traditions. This also implies that privatization, while hard to achieve in itself, enabled a fresh start.

All these differences provide for different starting positions for regulatory reforms and for individual policy measures. From the commonalities arise important factors that make similar regulatory solutions optimal. For example, both the United States and the European countries have the institutional capabilities to implement sophisticated regulations, such as price caps or interconnection rules, which require some regulatory discretion and the ability to commit. At the same time, differences in geography and national backgrounds may prevent the same regulations from being implementable or optimal in both regions. Nevertheless, policies may be copied wrongly, in spite of institutional differences.[6]

International bargaining could play a role in cross-fertilization in cases where one country has an interest in its regulatory policy being applied in other countries as well. This most naturally holds in the case of international telephone traffic that is based on rules of reciprocity for the ruling access charge regime (called accounting rates or settlement rates). It also holds for market liberalization in case a country has strong telecommunications companies that want to become global players. This has been one of the main reasons for U.S. pressure in the World Trade Organization (WTO) context.

2.3   Examples of Transfers of Regulatory Reforms

In this section, I concentrate on some select examples of cross-fertilization. I leave out the original case for learning from the United States, the drive to competition in long-distance markets. This showed that small firms were viable in an environment characterized until then by natural monopoly. Although that competition was undoubtedly helped if not triggered by AT&T's cross-subsidized price structure, it ultimately proved that network competition worked. It also showed how cross-subsidization is undermined by competition, forcing regulators either to preserve cross-subsidization through high access charges and other universal service policies or to rebalance end-user prices.[7]

2.3.1   Independence of the Regulator

Regulatory institutions in the telecommunications sectors of European countries are generally young. They were created as a result of privatization of the incumbent carrier and/or liberalization of the sector. Europeans without regulatory tradition (caused by the prevalence of public enterprises) have adopted some of the regulatory institutional features from the United States, including independence, publicity, and process orientation.

The U.S. regulatory institutions could have provided examples for both specialized regulatory agencies like the Federal Communications Commission (FCC) and for more general agencies like the state public utility commissions (PUCs) or antitrust authorities. To my knowledge, all European countries followed the specialized model. In part, this can be explained by successive privatization, starting with BT in the United Kingdom. BT was the first utility to be privatized. So, the first regulatory agency was tailored to it and did not quite fit for the next privatization. However, the United Kingdom could have chosen to attach regulation to competition policy. The task was probably viewed as too overwhelming and specialized to be handled by the somewhat improvising Monopolies and Mergers Commission. Thus, the federal U.S.

example probably was quite decisive in choosing a specialized regulator. The United Kingdom, however, deviated from the U.S. model in many other aspects, including the installation of a director general instead of a commission and the embedding of the agency in a ministry rather than giving it a setup of its own. Nevertheless, Oftel and its director general received at least part of the decision-making powers and the independence from the day-to-day operations of the government that the FCC enjoys.

The U.S. example was crucial for any early European regulatory reform efforts in telecommunications simply because the United States had a long tradition of regulating private telecommunications carriers and because the United States was the first major country to experiment with competition in the telecommunications sector. Since privatization appeared to be a prerequisite for competition, the European countries had to find a new governance system for the sector if they wanted effective competition. The U.S. regulatory model was the only one to look for. The U.S. model, however, was not ideal. This was known well enough to the Americans, who had introduced competition, inter alia because their regulation was less than perfect. It is thus no surprise that the British, the first Europeans to privatize their telephone monopoly, rejected many of the U.S. regulatory features. They saw that privatization gave them a chance that the United States did not have. They could learn from the U.S. experience better than the Americans themselves because they had started with a clean slate, not having to bother with stranded costs. Thus, the Europeans could pick and choose at the time of their sector reforms. In this respect, one has to differentiate clearly between the United Kingdom, which privatized BT at the time of the AT&T breakup, and other European Union (EU) countries like Germany, which privatized their domestic dominant carriers more than ten years later. The latter countries could learn both from the United States and from the United Kingdom.

In summary, the United States has been quite influential for Europeans in choosing specialized, somewhat independent regulators, but hardly in the specific regulatory setups.

2.3.2   Price Caps

Price caps are the classic and best-documented case of cross-fertilization between the United States and Europe. Aside from some experimentation with an early form of price caps in Michigan in

1981–1983, price caps in their established form are a British invention. Littlechild (1983) suggested them to the British government for the regulation of BT after privatization. Although Littlechild's suggestion built on earlier academic work, which was partly U.S. based, it is an original policy contribution. Its main American influence came from the sound rejection of the American rate-of-return regulation model. Thus, in this case, the outcome of cross-fertilization was a negative one. Littlechild's suggestion was implemented in 1984 with some modifications and became known as RPI-X regulation.

About two years later, the first state PUCs in the United States started with their own versions of price caps. These were not usually modeled after the U.K. approach. Rather, the U.S. PUCs experimented with all kinds of incentive regulation approaches, including profit sharing, banded rate-of-return regulation, price moratoria, and price caps. PUCs had ample experience with fuel adjustment clauses in electricity and gas regulation, and were probably influenced more by Baumol's (1982) suggestions for inflation and productivity adjustments than by the U.K. experience. Thus, cross-fertilization is doubtful in these cases. This changed in 1987, however, when the FCC initiated price cap proceedings for AT&T and for access prices charged by local exchange carriers. In its notice of proposed rule making the FCC then was referring, among others, to the British experience. In fact the suggestion and the schemes implemented bore large resemblance to the U.K. model. It was clear that, in this case, the United States was learning from the United Kingdom. However, the price caps adopted for AT&T deviated from BT's RPI-X in a number of features, such as the introduction of bands for price increases and price reductions of individual services. These changes resulted from the partisan process of U.S. regulation and from the fact that AT&T was already facing strong competition in its regulated long-distance markets, something that was lacking in the United Kingdom at the beginning of BT's regulation. Consumer groups wanted to be protected from individual price increases, while competitors wanted to be protected from exclusionary behavior through excessive price reductions. It is interesting that these new features do not appear in price cap regulation adopted later, for example, in Germany. Either the new competitors did not yet see the issue or, in 1997, they did not yet have the political clout to effect such changes.

Another difference between the U.K. model of price caps and the U.S. model comes from the U.S. tradition in rate-of-return regulation.

When price caps were introduced, the U.S. carriers had a right to a fair rate of return. Therefore much care needed to be taken in determining the X factor, which was done through productivity estimates. In contrast, the British started with a clean slate during privatization of BT. Thus, the original X factor could be determined more freely and the methodology for its adjustment developed en route. This led to a more pragmatic and forward-looking approach in the United Kingdom than in the United States.[8]

By their very nature, price caps are a very flexible instrument. Flexibility has the advantage that price caps can be tailored to specific situations and therefore easily adapted to the local circumstances of a particular country. It has the disadvantage that commitment to a specific practice is hard to make. Also, price caps can be bent toward the interests of particular groups. It appears that price caps initially were almost always bent in favor of the incumbent firms. This was true in the United Kingdom, in the United States (both at the federal and at the state level), and in Germany.[9] Thus, cross-country learning could have proceeded by lowering the incumbents' opposition to price caps. To summarize, price caps are probably one of the best-documented cases of cross-country fertilization.

2.3.3   Universal Service and Rate Rebalancing

The United States has had implicit and explicit universal service policies at least since 1970. The policies were used primarily to keep local residential telephone rates low. The declared aim was high penetration throughout the country. The means of achieving the low rates included cross-subsidization through interstate access charges and business rates and, more recently, explicit subsidies raised as surcharges on long-distance rates and on monthly charges. The main subsidy flow today occurs from high-density to low-density states and, within states, from high-density to low-density areas. This policy has become very costly in terms of allocative distortions, and it includes substantial amounts of redistribution. The policy is administratively cumbersome and is likely to retard and distort competition. To some extent, the European countries have copied the United States by introducing universal service policies. However, their policies are usually much weaker and, as a result, potentially less distorting. In particular, in contrast to the United States, the European policies have not stood in the way of rebalancing of end-user prices. While European countries generally have geographically uniform rates within each country, the United States has local service rates that tend to vary inversely with costs (Rosston and Wimmer 2001).

In her discussion of universal service and rebalancing in Europe as opposed to the United States, Cherry (2000) brings out the conditions that would prevent the (inefficient) U.S. policy from being adopted in Europe and the (more efficient) European policy from being adopted in the United States. These factors are largely institutional. The first is that the European Commission could simply delegate the rebalancing and universal service decisions to the national regulatory authorities (NRAs), because there existed no transnational subsidy mechanism. In contrast, the FCC had to get involved in redistributional issues between the states. Dismantling the implicit redistributions in the pre-1996 Act universal service schemes would have created a number of losers sure to oppose such a move. Thus, state regulators would have been unable to rebalance rates. The 1996 Act in principle allowed for rate rebalancing through explicit subsidy mechanisms. However, the implicit transfers had been so high that they could not all be converted into explicit transfers. Thus, the new mechanisms would not fully enable rebalancing and would create winners and losers among states. In order not to reveal the latter, the provisions were left opaque, and expressions like rebalancing were left out of the Act. Congress left the universal service provisions for the FCC to implement, and the FCC chose to do part of that by limiting the ability to rebalance.

In contrast to the FCC, the European regulators faced much less organized groups opposing their policies. Regulators here were new institutions, and competitors and consumer groups had not yet established themselves to the same extent as in the United States with its one hundred years of regulatory tradition. Interestingly, the European solutions to rebalancing and universal service differ substantially between countries, although none comes close to the U.S. universal service policies. The United Kingdom is probably farthest in terms of rebalancing. It therefore needs virtually no universal service policy. France has an expensive universal service policy, preventing some rebalancing. Germany has neither rebalanced nor had an intrusive universal service policy. Some rebalancing is allowed by the German telecommunications law (TKG). However, increasing competition could then force the universal service issue.

In the United States the universal service policy has a strong backing both from traditional cross-subsidies and from the extreme variation in telephone network densities and therefore costs. Thus, rather than reducing the scope of universal service, the 1996 Act has increased it. The Europeans certainly were aware of the U.S. policy but decided not to copy it. Besides the institutional reasons given earlier the geography has played a major role. For example, calculations for the United Kingdom showed that the costs to BT for providing universal service were negligible and probably counterbalanced by advantages from being the universal service provider and from having geographically unified tariffs. The calculation may have been helped by the rebalancing that BT had undertaken since 1984, which resulted in real increases in line rentals. Similarly, in Germany the Deutsche Telekom AG (DTAG) seems not to have approached the Regulatory Authority for Telecommunications and Post (RegTP) yet in order to gain geographic deaveraging of monthly line charges. Thus the European learning from the United States on universal service policy has largely been that of avoiding the U.S. mistakes in this area.

2.3.4 Access/Interconnection and Unbundling

Interconnection and access charges have become the key issues in network competition in telecommunications. Much of the approach to interconnection and bottleneck access granted to new telecommunications competitors is originally based on the U.S. essential facilities doctrine. This doctrine first emerged in an antitrust concept in a U.S. court in the early 1900s. It found its way into regulated industries again first through antitrust and then through regulatory commissions, the FCC in particular. Application of the essential facilities doctrine requires behavioral control over time, something that is better accomplished under regulation than under antitrust (Areeda 1990).

The FCC and courts granted discriminatory access to new long-distance carriers to the local networks of incumbents during the 1970s. Equal access was then implemented in the course of AT&T's divestiture in 1984. At that time, it was well established that long-distance competition required local access. So, when BT was privatized in 1984, interconnection of its network with the emerging Mercury was part of it.[10] However, the British provisions were based on private negotiations with Oftel as the arbitrator in case of disagreement. In fact, Oftel was called in and subsequently de facto regulated conditions of access and access charges. Included in these were long-distance connections that never were regulated in the United States.

In the area of interconnection a large number of problems needed to be solved, since competition was progressing from long-distance to local networks and into more and more services. In the course of this, the United States and United Kingdom came to represent two fairly distinct models. The United States was generally more open to the choice between infrastructure and service competition. By facilitating interconnection and other ways of helping entry, such as resale, the United States in fact allowed for service competition without major facilities. In contrast, the United Kingdom heavily favored infrastructure competition. As a result, Oftel did not force BT to offer unbundled parts of the network and collocation that would enable entrants to pick and choose which parts of the network they would provide themselves and which they would get from the incumbent. Rather, Oftel concentrated on interconnection charges as a means to direct investment. In contrast, the United States forced the incumbents to make all parts of the network available to entrants. This policy was developed first in progressive states, such as New York and Illinois, and by the FCC in the Open Network Architecture (ONA) and Expanded Interconnection Proceedings.[11] Solving the problems of unbundling and collocation required regulatory, organizational, and technical problem solving that was pioneered in the United States. The European countries could thus take advantage of the U.S. footwork and its good and bad experiences. None of the European countries followed the full unbundling that the United States pursued. However, they also did not follow the U.K. approach of no unbundling. For example, the U.S. practice had shown that, among the unbundled network elements, only local loops were really in demand. Supplying them required collocation. Thus, the Europeans largely restricted unbundling to the loops and introduced collocation. By EU directive, even the United Kingdom is now forced to follow suit. While access and interconnection policies were originally conceived in the United States, cross-fertilization is now starting to take place, especially outside the United States.

2.3.5 Proxy Cost Models

While the United States pioneered the right of access, based on the essential facilities doctrine, it was the United Kingdom that pioneered the price of access, first, by unsuccessfully trying out a version of the efficient component pricing rule (ECPR) called "access deficit contributions," and, second, by including the use of the first incremental cost models (first developed by Mitchell (1990) in the United States). It is not clear that the U.S. cost models benefited much from the U.K. example. They turned out to be much different. Both the U.S. and the U.K. access and interconnection prices have become yardsticks for European countries not depending on cost models.

Long-run incremental costs have become a widespread standard used by telecommunications regulators for access and interconnection charges and for prices of unbundled network elements. In the United States they have also become the basis for calculations of universal service subsidies. Long-run incremental costs are by definition efficient. Regulating by long-run incremental costs is therefore very different from cost-plus or rate-of-return regulation. Long-run incremental costs were found in engineering cost models rather than in accounting data. Such models were first developed in the United States at the RAND Corporation (Mitchell 1990) and the National Regulatory Research Institute (NRRI). The use of such costs for interconnection pricing was then proposed in an EU-sponsored study in 1994 (WIK/EAC 1994), which included U.S. participation and experience. It was taken up in practice by U.S. PUCs in the mid-1990s and in the 1996 Act as well as by Oftel in the United Kingdom around the same time. The use of such models was thus pioneered on both sides of the Atlantic.

In the United Kingdom the model development occurred as an Oftel initiative, bringing together industry experts from BT and its competitors. Since BT favored an accounting-based top-down modeling approach in contrast to a bottom-up engineering approach, the British effort resulted in two models that were reconciled with the help of NERA, a firm of consulting economists. The U.S. cost modeling started with industry-sponsored engineering models with heavy inputs from consulting firms. The models were more technical, more geographically disaggregated, and more detailed than the British models. At that time, the U.S. industry had large modeling capabilities in organizations, such as Bellcore, the consulting and research arm of the Regional Bell Operating Companies (RBOCs) at the time. The competing U.S. models reached vastly different conclusions. Thus, the FCC had to find the "correct" model. Rather than deciding on a single one of the competing models, it developed its own hybrid model. Nevertheless, the other models were used in state PUC determinations of interconnection charges, and the know-how was exported to other countries. The German WIK cost model, for example, was based on a later version of the original NRRI model. The current WIK models have substantially advanced from there and contain many new features. However, it is clear that a lot of cross-fertilization has taken place in this area, and it is not just restricted to the U.S. and Europe but extends to countries like Australia.

The use of model-based rather than firm-based costs in regulatory proceedings has been highly controversial and has been challenged in court. In the United States, this happened shortly after the FCC had issued its monumental Local Competition Order in August 1996. In 2000, a federal U.S. appeals court found that costs, though forward-looking, have to be based on actual firm data. This decision was overturned by the U.S. Supreme Court in 2002, so that cost models continue to be used. However, in Germany, a court issued a similar decision in 2001 with the result that the RegTP based its subsequent order on international benchmarks (which themselves are probably based on the efficient firm cost standard). Thus, a new round of learning can be expected.

2.3.6 Spectrum Auctions

Spectrum auctions were suggested in the academic literature at least four decades before being first applied in 1989. While New Zealand was the actual innovator, the New Zealand second price, sealed bid auction design contained major flaws, because the second price was often ridiculously low (Mueller 1993). The United States followed in 1994 with an innovative design. Since auctions played a major role in the application of game theory to economic issues and since spectrum auctions posed challenging theoretical problems, it was not surprising that the approach used by the FCC to spectrum auctions was heavily influenced by academic consulting input (Kwerel and Rosston 2000). In collaboration with those consultants, the FCC developed a sophisticated simultaneous multiple round auction design that allows for bidding on many geographic spectrum licenses at the same time and permits several winning bidders in each area. Bidders can simultaneously bid on licenses in all geographic areas. The auction is over if no increased bids are recorded for any area. The amounts of leading bids are known at any moment in time. The simultaneity allows bidders to accumulate complementary licenses without being stuck with a single one and not being able to acquire the other. The completely new item in this auction design was the activity rule proposed by Milgrom and Wilson for the purpose of progressing in an auction with potentially many bids and potential complementarity between licenses.

The U.S. auctions were highly successful in raising revenues and allocating licenses in consistent ways. Analysis of the outcomes shows that they were quite efficient (Cramton 2002). However, some problems appeared and had to be solved, and there were unanticipated flaws. Problems arose with collusion, because the FCC initially allowed for unrestricted bid increments that enabled signaling collusion via the last digits of the bid amounts. Other problems included the conflicts between local and nationwide licenses and the collection of auction revenues. The last of these was due to a design flaw. Small-firm bidders were allowed to stretch payments into the future. They could therefore compete without having the necessary financing and would be induced to bid too high. When these bidders could not raise the money for build out and for the licenses, they declared bankruptcy. A related flaw resulted from bidder preferences for small firms in the form of discounts on the bid price. This was done in a separate auction for small bidders. The result was that these bidders bid away the discounts among each other. Having resolved these problems, the U.S. auction methodology emerged as a successful model that was exported by consulting firms to other countries.[12] However, these countries did not blindly copy the U.S. approach but rather added their own features. Noteworthy is, for example, the British approach of reserving one license to newcomers or the German approach of endogenizing the number of winning bidders between four and six.

Spectrum auctions, even more so than price caps, are noteworthy for the strong involvement of academic economists. In this case, they were the inventors and took a major part in developing the innovation and in the dissemination.

2.4 Conclusions and Outlook

Telecommunications has for a long time been an innovative sector, characterized by technical change, new products, and substantial growth. It has also undergone institutional reform in most parts of the world. The institutional reform started in the United States, making it the leader in liberalization and deregulation policies. The characterization as a leader implies that there are followers, and the U.S. example certainly influenced reforms in other countries. However, that did not mean the other countries copied the U.S. model. Rather, U.S. policies were adapted. In addition, other leaders, such as the United Kingdom, emerged with reform efforts more suited to European countries. In some respects, these reformers overtook the United States and made the United States look abroad for better solutions. Our examples show that clear cases of cross-fertilization exist, such as price caps and proxy cost models. There are other cases where the influence of another country is less apparent, so that common causes may have led to similar outcomes. This could, for example, hold for regulatory institutions. Having a clear leader acts as a focal point that facilitates information gathering and thereby cross-country learning. Now that the United States has fallen behind, several competing sources of regulatory reform have emerged so that cross-country learning, while richer, may also have become informationally more demanding.

What is the verdict on cross-fertilization in terms of improved efficiency? What are the patterns? Does one find that efficient policies are copied/adapted and inefficient policies rejected? In order to answer these questions conclusively, one would need empirical studies that demonstrate the efficiency of a chosen instrument compared to those that were not chosen. Such studies are hardly available at all. The only area that is fairly well researched is that of price and profit regulation. In particular, price cap regulation has been compared to rate-of-return regulation and profit sharing in the U.S. context. Somewhat weaker than empirical evidence is a comparison by use of theoretical models, such as the Averch-Johnson model for rate-of-return regulation. Such models, however, only exist for very few policies and are themselves full of controversies. For example, for access pricing the ECPR is promoted by theoretical arguments as is the Ramsey pricing rule or the marginal cost-pricing rule. It is not that these theories contradict each other. Rather, they differ in their views on empirical regularities to which they are applied.

My subjective assessment of some of the cross-country learning is as follows:

a. New Zealand had, in the 1980s, decided to leave telecommunications issues in the hands of its general competition policy. Problems occurred when bottleneck issues could not be resolved, and the case ended up in court for several years. This experience suggests that a specialized agency is probably superior, as long as competition is not fully viable. The reason is that competition depends on interconnection of essential facilities. It is, however, well known that the provision of essential facilities is better regulated by a specialized agency than by antitrust authorities (Areeda 1990).[13] Following the United States in terms of establishing a specialized agency was thus efficient. The result of even limited European learning from the U.S. regulatory institutions is that the institutional setups in the United States and Europe are now much more compatible than they were before privatization and regulatory reform in Europe. As a result of this institutional rapprochement, one can expect that cross-fertilization in regulatory contents should be facilitated for the future.

b. Price caps seem to be genuinely a superior regulatory mechanism (Newbery 2000). In spite of that, the quantitative empirical evidence on price reduction, cost reduction, and investment compared to conventional regulation, while significant, is not impressive (Sappington 2002). The early experience in the United Kingdom of price caps for BT shows strong rebalancing and overall cost reductions that allowed for successive increases in the X factor. The claimed superiority of price caps holds not only for monopoly regulation but also, in particular, for the transition to full competition. Price caps allow for rebalancing and competitive responses and, at the same time, protect consumers and provide incentives for cost reductions. The United States has been substantially more restrictive than Europe in limiting rebalancing, which has reduced some of the incentive effects of price caps.

c. The difficulties in making U.S. universal service policies compatible with market competition shows the policy dilemma in correcting inefficient policies. The fact that Europe did not copy these policies shows differences in the institutional settings and that inefficient examples may have deterring effects.

d. In contrast, access, interconnection and unbundling policies demonstrate cross-fertilization that is efficient with respect to the general principles of these policies, but may be overly bureaucratic and restrictive when it comes to specific rules.

e. This also comes out in the proxy cost models that are highly sophisticated with great technical and geographic details. Cross-fertilization has led to much improved models, but certain crude factors remain that account for large differences between models. These can lead to inefficient policy outcomes as can the application of these models to an inefficient policy, such as the U.S. universal service policy.

f. Auctions are theoretically the most efficient way to distribute scarce spectrum. They allocate it to the bidders with the highest prospective value and lead to government revenues that can replace distortionary taxes. However, practical application of auctions does not always assure this outcome, as shown in the early New Zealand auctions. Cross-country fertilization with academic input, in this case, provided major improvements, although the road to success continues to be bumpy. This shows that auctions are complex institutions.

Nevertheless, the record suggests that auctions have been superior to other mechanisms in speeding up allocation and getting the spectrum into the hands of users with high values.

Examples where cross-fertilization did not take on include the following: Nobody followed the U.K. duopoly policy, which was a disaster, because it prevented further entry for seven years without assuring a strong duopoly. Nobody followed the U.K. access deficit contribution, because they were too cumbersome to administer and were ineffective. Nobody followed the U.K. dispute resolution process, although it provides strong stability and commitment power (Spiller and Vogelsang 1997). The reason here is probably that such a process requires the preexistence of a trusted institution. The lesson from these negative examples is that learning is either prevented by geographic/institutional differences or it takes the form of rejecting policies deemed unsuccessful.

From the examples, can one learn anything more general about the efficiency of cross-country learning? Certainly more empirical analysis of the efficiency effects would be required to answer this question. These would have to be guided by more specific and more elaborate theoretical hypotheses from the institutional and political economy literature than those developed earlier in section 2.2. Specifically, from the previous examples one might expect that cross-fertilization would be quite successful in transferring difficult technical tools (such as auction design or cost models). This is likely to be efficient if the tools are applied to an efficient policy, but they might not be. There is, in particular, the danger that a tool might be transferred to an inadequate institutional setting. However, if an efficient solution is implemented in country A and if country B is institutionally very similar, one also expects a transfer. The empirical question therefore is if the relevant actors correctly perceive the efficiency of foreign policies and their applicability to the domestic situation.

Since learning from foreign experience is a form of free riding, the question arises, How does a country become a leader in the first place? An example among the U.S. states provides one answer. In this instance the states of New York and Illinois were the definite leaders in the introduction of local telephone competition before passage of the 1996 Act. The explanation appears to be that they have the largest and densest metropolitan areas among U.S. states. In these metropolitan areas the pressure for entry and the feasibility of entry was the greatest.[14] So, they became natural leaders. In such cases, there exists compensation for first-mover disadvantages, such as making mistakes by moving into uncharted territories and incurring large setup costs for new policies. It is harder then to explain why the United States and the United Kingdom became leaders in telecommunications regulation. This is particularly difficult because of the direction of causality. Definitely, the United States has traditionally been the country with the largest telecommunications demand. But was that due to the geography and economic strength of the country or to the way its telecommunications sector was organized? Thus, is the reason the private ownership of AT&T (with a mission for universal service) as opposed to the public ownership of the PTTs in Europe? Did the United Kingdom become a leader in the 1980s because it was the first (among large European countries) to privatize its PTT (postal, telegraph and telephone)?

Where can one expect the exchange of new regulatory ideas and practices to become most important in the future? Two big problems, in particular, need solutions in Germany: which parts of the telecommunications sector to deregulate and how to expand competition in the local network. For both, no ready-made foreign solution is available at this time. Deregulation was spearheaded in New Zealand, but its radical approach showed more failures than success. In contrast long-distance competition was successfully deregulated in the United States, in part due to the vertical separation of AT&T in 1984. Such separation would be a hard sell in Germany at this time. Local competition has been introduced quite successfully in the United Kingdom, but this is based on cable TV networks, starting from a small base that is no longer available in Germany. Here, the U.S. approach may be more doable. It is based on a combination of alternative networks, unbundled local loops, and service resale. The success of local competitors in terms of market share in the United States is substantially higher than in Germany, but it is still quite moderate. So, a quick solution may not exist in this area.

Notes

1. Collocation at the federal U.S. level built on learning from earlier state experience, particularly in New York and Illinois. See Vogelsang and Mitchell (1997).

2. They also come about through the interest of "informants" like myself, who want this knowledge to spread.

3. Newbery (2000, 143) argues that interest groups put much effort into concealing unfavorable information and that that is likely to increase the inefficiency of regulation.

4. Such differences could themselves be the result of different policies so that cross-country fertilization could nevertheless be in order.

5. In contrast, Knieps (1985) hypothesizes that the federal regulatory structure as opposed to the more unitary policy structure of European countries was responsible for the lack of European liberalization at the time. The explanation for subsequent liberalization in Europe then would have to be that the federal structure in Europe emerged through the EU. This would not, however, explain the British example of liberalization way ahead of the EU.

6. I owe this information to Barbara Cherry.

7. See Newbery (2000, 153–160) for more on the introduction of long-distance competition.

8. For these differences between the United States and the United Kingdom, see Beesley and Littlechild (1989) and Crew and Kleindorfer (1996).

9. Germany also has no financial model of the DTAG, as Oftel does for BT, or total factor productivity measurements, as are available to the FCC.

10. Mercury received a network license already in 1982, but the interconnection issues took some time to emerge.

11. For details, see Vogelsang and Mitchell (1997).

12. In the course of this, it turned out that some of the features that were successful in the U.S. contained some hidden flaws. The activity rule, for example, could be used as a commitment device to restrict bidding in the future. See Grimm, Riedel, and Wolfstetter (2003).

13. Nevertheless, Australia has integrated the regulation of network utilities in the Australian Competition and Consumer Commission (ACCC), which is a general competition authority.

14. In empirical work, Zhuang (1999) has shown that U.S. states with higher population density adopted incentive regulation earlier than states with less dense populations.

References

Areeda, P. 1990. "Essential Facilities: An Epithet in Need of Limiting Principles." *Antitrust Law Review* 58: 841ff.

Baumol, W. J. 1982. "Productivity Adjustment Clauses and Rate Adjustment for Inflation." *Public Utilities Fortnightly* (July 22): 11–18.

Becker, G. 1983. "A Theory of Competition among Pressure Groups for Political Influence." *Quarterly Journal of Economics* 98: 371–400.

Beesley, M., and S. C. Littlechild. 1989. "The Regulation of Privatized Monopolies in the United Kingdom." *Rand Journal of Economics* 20: 454–472.

Cherry, B. A. 2000. "The Irony of Telecommunications Deregulation: Assessing the Role Reversal in U.S. and EU Policy." In I. Vogelsang and B. M. Compaine, eds., *The Internet Upheaval*, 355–385. Cambridge, MA: MIT Press.

Cramton, P. 2002. "Spectrum Auctions." In M. Cave, S. Majumdar, and I. Vogelsang, eds., *Handbook of Telecommunications Economics*, chap. 14. Amsterdam: Elsevier Scientific Publishers.

Crew, M., and P. Kleindorfer. 1996. "Incentive Regulation in the United Kingdom and the United States: Some Lessons." *Journal of Regulatory Economics* 9: 211–225.

Elixmann, D., G. Kulenkampff, U. Schimmmel, and R. Schwab. 2001. "Internationaler Vergleich der TK-Märkte in ausgewählten Ländern—ein Liberalisierungs-, Wettbewerbs- und Wachstumsindex." WIK Diskussionsbeitrag Nr. 216, February.

Grimm, V., F. Riedel, and E. Wolfstetter. 2003. "Low Price Equilibrium in Multi-Unit Auctions: The GSM Spectrum Auction in Germany." *International Journal of Industrial Organization*. Forthcoming.

Knieps, G. 1985. *Entstaatlichung im Telekommunikationsbereich*. Tübingen: J. C. B. Mohr (Paul Siebeck).

Kwerel, E. R., and G. L. Rosston. 2000. "An Insider's View of FCC Spectrum Auctions." *Journal of Regulatory Economics* 17: 253–289.

Littlechild, St. C. 1983. "Regulation of British Telecommunications' Profitability." Report to the Secretary of State, Department of Industry. London: Her Majesty's Stationery Office.

Mitchell, B. M. 1990. "Incremental Costs of Telephone Access and Use." Report R-3909-ICTF, RAND Corporation, Santa Monica, July.

Mueller, M. 1993. "New Zealand's Revolution in Spectrum Management." *Information Economics and Policy* 5: 159–177.

Newbery, D. M. 2000. *Privatization, Restructuring, and Regulation of Network Industries*, Cambridge, MA, and London, UK: MIT Press.

Peltzman, S. 1976. "Towards a More General Theory of Regulation." *Journal of Law and Economics* 19: 211–240.

Rosston, G. L., and B. S. Wimmer. 2001. "From C to Shining C: Competition and Cross-Subsidy in Communications." In B. M. Compaine and S. Greenstein, eds., Communications Policy in Transition," 241–261. Cambridge, MA, and London, UK: MIT Press.

Sappington, D. E. M. 2002. "Price Regulation." In M. Cave, S. Majumdar, and I. Vogelsang, eds., *Handbook of Telecommunications Economics*, chap. 7. Amsterdam: Elsevier Scientific Publishers.

Spiller, P. T., and I. Vogelsang. 1997. "The Institutional Foundations of Regulatory Commitment in the UK—The Case of Telecommunications." *Journal of Institutional and Theoretical Economics* 153: 607–629.

Stigler, G. J. 1971. "The Theory of Economic Regulation." *Bell Journal of Economics* 2(1): 3–21.

Vogelsang, I., and B. M. Mitchell. 1997. *Telecommunications Competition: The Last 10 Miles.* Cambridge, MA, London, UK, and Washington, DC: MIT Press and AEI Press.

WIK/EAC. 1994. "Network Interconnection in the Domain of ONP." Final Report of Study for the European Commission, Brussels (J. Arnbak, B. Mitchell, W. Neu, K.-H. Neumann, and I. Vogelsang), November.

Zhuang, S. 1999. "The Adoption of Incentive Regulation Schemes and Its Impact on the Local Telecommunications Industry." Unpublished Ph.D. diss., Boston University.

3

"Cross-Fertilization between U.S. and European Telecommunications Regulation": A Comment

Ray Rees

There is virtually nothing in this stimulating and wide-ranging chapter with which I disagree, and so my comments will mainly be concerned with adding my own observations on some of the main points Ingo Vogelsang has made.

The underlying nature of tastes and technological possibilities in the telecommunications markets of the European countries and the United States in the 1970s was inherently similar. What differed hugely was the economic organization of these markets, and this is what made the United States the leading source of innovation. The postal, telegraph and telephone (PTT) structure of the leading European telecommunications markets was a major obstacle to progress. Starved of the investment funds required to expand services and carry out technical innovations by the forced cross-subsidization of inefficient and highly labor intensive postal services, organized as public bureaucracies rather than commercial enterprises, the telecommunications suppliers in Europe lagged seriously behind those in North America. Perhaps the most profound single innovation in the USA was the introduction of competition in the long-distance telephone market. The cosy assumption that telecommunications was a natural monopoly in all its markets was invalidated in a stroke.

In the United Kingdom in the late 1970s, more so than in the other major European countries, attempts were being made to change the structure and organization of telecommunications supply to remedy the situation, but problems were still created by subjection to public-sector borrowing constraints. Then came privatization. Privatization was a central element in the ideological position of the new Thatcher government, part of the general commitment to "roll back the public sector" and break the power of the trade unions. By those concerned with trying to reorganize telecommunications supply, it was seen as the way to solve the funding problems of telecommunications as well as to create a modern and dynamic enterprise, while the privatization policy itself derived strength and impetus from the existence of such a suitable and relatively unproblematic candidate.

At this point U.S. experience again exerted an important influence, but this time in terms of what *not* to do. There was considerable U.S. literature on the perverse incentive effects of "rate-of-return regulation," the problems of capture inherent in the American regulatory system, and its generally adverse effects on economic efficiency. Thus the price cap regulation system was devised (largely by Steven Littlechild) in a conscious attempt to achieve something better. It was to provide positive incentives for cost reduction, maximize the possibilities of the development of effective competition, and minimize the dangers of capture.

Ingo Vogelsang's chapter mentions economists being "fooled" by the public interest theory of regulation, but in fact this theory receives a good deal of support from the formulation of the price cap regulatory system. As conceived by Littlechild, this system was not the outcome of some interest group equilibrium, but an attempt to provide an economically efficient framework of regulation. Of course, something like this was required to "sell" the privatization policy to a doubtful electorate. Moreover, there is an interesting difference between the system as Littlechild conceived it and the one that was actually implemented, which may give Chicago some comfort and is relevant to the rest of the story. Littlechild proposed that long-distance markets would be exempt from the price cap regulation, since they would be subject to competition, and regulation was only required for markets where there would be no competition. That is, long-distance services should not be included in the basket of charges to which a price cap was to be applied. In fact, they were included, and this had important implications, both for the profitability of the newly privatized concern and for the issue of "rebalancing." British Telecom (BT) was able to meet competition in the long-distance market, while maintaining overall profitability, by raising prices sharply in the local domestic market, in a way that would not have been possible if the local charges alone had been subject to the price cap. This meant that the problem of rebalancing, or reducing the large cross-subsidies from long-distance to local services, a problem that still bedevils telecommunications pricing in the United States, was solved relatively quickly and comprehensively in the United Kingdom. Since on efficiency grounds such rebalancing is certainly defensible, it must be counted as a welcome achievement of price cap regulation, though it probably had more to do with concern for BT's profitability than for economic efficiency as such.

In the U.S. context, "universal service provision" seems to be code for the rebalancing problem—that is, the provision of local telephone services to virtually all domestic consumers at highly subsidized prices—while in Europe it means something quite different. Here it means the provision of access to telecommunications services in sparsely populated rural areas, or to low-income consumers, and the provision of public call boxes, at prices less than cost. In short, forms of income redistribution that could just as well be achieved by explicit subsidies from the public purse, except that governments prefer that the true costs are buried in the accounts of the enterprise and the true nature of the income redistribution involved is thereby hidden. Vogelsang's comment that the costs of this to BT are negligible would certainly be disputed by them, and his remark probably rests on a study by the regulator (Oftel) that purported to show that. It was only able to do this, however, by setting the costs against such dubious benefits as the advertising value to BT of rural telephone boxes, or the gratitude felt by currently low income subscribers who eventually would become higher income and would repay BT by loyally buying its services, regardless of how its prices compared to those of its competitors. The root problem is of course that of cream-skimming, that is, that competitive entry takes place only into profitable markets, leaving the incumbent to finance loss-making services from a shrinking profit base. The Oftel study was essentially an attempt to avoid having to find a way to deal with this problem, at least for the time being.

European consumers should be grateful for the impact developments in the United States have had on the structure and performance of their telecommunications markets, just as European taxpayers, at least those in the United Kingdom and Germany, should be grateful for the example provided by the American spectrum auctions. It is not so clear to me, even accepting the example of price cap regulation, that so very much has flowed in the opposite direction as to warrant use of the term *cross-fertilization*. But Ingo Vogelsang's attempt to make the case for that has made for very interesting and informative reading.

4

New Competition in Telecommunications Markets: Regulatory Pricing Principles

Paul de Bijl and Martin Peitz

4.1 Introduction

It has become conventional wisdom that competition in telecommunications (possibly subject to regulation) serves welfare and consumers better than the former state monopoly, both from a static as well as from a dynamic perspective. The British regulatory authority Oftel states: "Competition is the means to best protect consumers interests. Competitive markets with incentives to innovate are fundamental to meeting consumer needs. Regulation must not undermine such incentives but instead should be directed towards achieving effective competition and, as necessary, protecting consumers before it is achieved or where there is a need for additional protection" (2000, 1.2–1.4). Regulation (shortly after liberalization) can thus be seen as a means to promote competition in the short and the long run. It promotes competition in the short run if, for given entry, the pressure on prices is increased; it promotes competition in the long run if entry into the market is facilitated.

Shortly after liberalization, the regulator possibly has to intervene to avoid the exploitation of the consumers by the former state monopolist who still enjoys a dominant position. Such regulation must bear in mind that the incentives to enter and invest in infrastructure must not be undermined by such regulation. Ideally, regulatory pricing policy is designed such that it fosters competition and makes consumers better off.

Competition in asymmetric markets—and this is what "new" competition implies—and regulatory policy in such markets is the topic of this chapter. Asymmetric market environments may ask for asymmetric regulation. In the policy debate the desirability of asymmetric regulation has been recognized (European Commission 2000; Oftel 2000).[1] Recent market liberalization in Europe has allowed new competitors into the market, some of whom are busy to build up their own networks. Central to the success of an entrant is its access to the end users. If entrants are to build their own consumer base, they have to either build up their own access network (local loop) or engage in unbundling agreements with the owner of the local loop, in the former case one speaks of facilities-based competition, in the latter of local loop unbundling.

In this chapter we present a simple model of competition in the telecommunications market in which entrants have already made the necessary investments (or contractual arrangements) to compete in a particular telecommunications market. An entrant operator has access to consumers either by its own facilities or through local loop unbundling. Hence, we consider a situation of two-way interconnection. Our main question is, How should one design regulation with the purpose of stimulating competition, ensuring that consumers benefit from entry and operators have sufficient interests to be active in the market?

Different from most of the literature, our focus is on asymmetric initial market conditions and asymmetric regulation. Papers by Armstrong (1998), Laffont, Rey, and Tirole (1998), and Carter and Wright (1999) have initiated the literature on the economic theory of two-way interconnection. This work and follow-ups have been reviewed by Laffont and Tirole (2000) and Armstrong (2002); see also de Bijl and Peitz (2002). In de Bijl and Peitz (2002, 2001) and Peitz (2001), we develop models that allow us to address some of the asymmetries that have received little attention in the existing theoretical literature.[2] We draw heavily on this earlier work. In this chapter our focus is on policy relevant conclusions that emerge from access price regulation in an evolving industry.

In our market, the entrant initially lacks a track record of quality whereas the incumbent already has such a track record. This captures the reliability of the networks and the reputation for quality. Given that the entrant is active, its track record improves exogenously over time and the asymmetry between the operators becomes smaller as the entrant gains experience and reputation. Operators compete in two-part tariffs, that is, they set a price per call minute and a monthly subscription fee. In this chapter we present and discuss some of the results within a particularly simple setting.

The main insight of this chapter is that asymmetric access price regulation is a powerful policy instrument that benefits the entrant and consumers.[3] This provides a policy recommendation for the regulation of the wholesale market.

To the extent that wholesale price regulation on its own still leaves room for the former state monopolist to exploit consumers, regulation of retail prices may be desirable: Since the incumbent initially enjoys substantial market power, a price cap regime in the retail market may be needed in addition to asymmetric access regulation to protect consumers from excessive retail prices. However, binding price caps on the incumbent's subscription fee make the incumbent operator more aggressive, which possibly reduces or eliminates the incentives for an entrant to undertake the necessary investments to compete in the market. Hence, such retail price regulation has to be applied very carefully.

Section 4.2 presents the model, the solution procedure, and a short discussion of the first-best outcome (including a discussion of the costs and benefits of liberalization). Based on Peitz (2001), section 4.3 analyzes the model under the restriction that per-minute prices are fixed equal to true marginal costs so that operators only compete in subscription fees. This model is solved analytically and serves as a benchmark. Based on de Bijl and Peitz (2001), section 4.4 analyzes the model in which pricing in the retail market is not restricted. It also considers price cap regulation in the retail market: namely, the regulator may wish to impose a (temporary) price cap on the incumbent's subscription fee. Section 4.5 provides a discussion of results and a discussion of related policy questions.

4.2 A Model of Facility-Based Entry

We consider two operators, an incumbent (operator 1) and an entrant (operator 2). The model is a simplified version of the model used in de Bijl and Peitz (2001). Assume that the two networks have a full-coverage network. This is a natural starting point when analyzing fixed telephony. The networks consist of a long-distance backbone, a local access network, and switches. In each period $t = 1, \ldots, T$, each operator i chooses a per-minute price p_i^t and a subscription fee m_i^t. The market shares resulting from competition and consumers' choices are denoted by $s_1^t = s_1[p_1, p_2 m_1, m_2; t]$ and $s_2^t = s_2[p_1, p_2 m_1, m_2; t]$.

4.2.1 Consumer Demand

The consumer side consists of consumers with mass n who subscribe to either one of the networks. To avoid head-to-head competition à la Bertrand, we assume that networks are horizontally differentiated. Consumers are assumed to be uniformly distributed on the [0,1]-

interval. Operator 1 is located at $l_1 = 0$, and operator 2 at $l_2 = 1$. Consumer $z \in [0,1]$ incurs a disutility $-\theta|l_i - z|$, which is linear in the distance between consumer location and the location of the operator. The parameter θ expresses the substitutability between networks: If $\theta = 0$, networks are perfect substitutes; the larger θ, the more differentiated networks are.[4]

Each consumer subscribes to exactly one operator. The consumer who is identified by its location z subscribes to operator 1 if $v_1[p_1, m_1; t] - \theta z > v_2[p_2, m_2; t] - \theta(1 - z)$, where $v_i[p_i, m_i; t]$ denotes the conditional indirect utility of a network at the ideal location z. The realized market share of operator i is equal to

$$s_i^t = \frac{1}{2} + \frac{v_i[p_i^t, m_i^t; t] - v_j[p_j, m_j; t]}{2\theta}.$$

An operator's market share increases if the operator offers a relatively larger level of net utility to consumers and decreases otherwise. One can observe that larger values of θ make it more difficult to gain market share.

Conditional indirect utility for a network at an ideal location takes the following form:

$$v_i[p_i, m_i; t] = U_i[t] - m_i + u[x[p_i]] - p_i x[p_i].$$

This indirect utility consists of a traffic-independent part and a traffic-dependent part. Clearly, net utility is decreasing in prices. We implicitly assume that net utility of each network is positive for all consumers, that is, $v_i - \theta > 0$.

First, consider the traffic-dependent part. Given a per-minute price equal to p_i, each consumer has an individual demand of $x[p_i]$ call minutes and derives utility $u[x]$ from calling x minutes.[5]

Second, consider the traffic-independent part. Here, the consumer has to pay the subscription fee m_i. A consumer derives a fixed (and possibly operator-specific and time-dependent) utility from subscribing to network i, $U_i[t]$, which is independent of the number of telephone calls that are made.[6] We postulate that the fixed utility can be written as $u_i^0(1 - q_i[t])$. The different terms are understood as follows: The first term u_i^0 is an individual effect, which are long-run fixed utilities. In our analysis we assume that networks are symmetric in the long run so that $u_1^0 = u_2^0 = u^0$. The second term $q_i[t]u_i^0$ reflects the disutility due to the (partial) lack of track record of network i, $q_i[t]$, where $1 \geq q_1[t] \geq 0$ and $\lim_{t \to \infty} q_i[t] = 0$. With respect to this track record, we postulate that there exists an asymmetry between the incumbent and the entrant: An entrant has to build up the reliability of its network and the reputation for quality. Hence, in early periods we have $q_2[t] > q_1[t]$. In particular, in our simulation we assume that the incumbent does not suffer from such an initial lack of a track record so that $q_1[t] = 0$ for all t. Depending on the reliability and reputation of the former state monopolist, this assumption can be modified.

The track record captures utility differences between operators stemming from quality differences that may exogenously vanish over time. Entrants may be quick to roll out networks to offer voice telephony and gain market share, but initially their networks may not satisfy the same quality standards as the incumbent's network.[7] The track record also captures the utility derived from availability and quality of services that are additional to basic telephony (e.g., wake-up calls, information services, voice mail) that may be added by the entrant over time. An alternative specification in which previous market share enters is provided by de Bijl and Peitz (2001) (see also de Bijl and Peitz 2002).

Example One concrete specification of demand and utility functions would be the following: $u[x] = ax - \frac{1}{2}bx^2$ $(a, b > 0)$ so that $x[p_i] = (a - p_i)/b$ and $v_i[p_i, m_i; t] = U_i[t] + \frac{1}{2}(p_i - a)^2/b - m_i$. For the purpose of illustration, utility is assumed to increase linearly with the track record of the new firm up to some period t^*. We write $q_2[t] = 1 - \min\{t - 1, (t^* - 1)\}/(t^* - 1)$. This is also the specification that will be used in the simulations.[8]

4.2.2   Costs, Traffic Volume, and Profit Functions

Following the theory on competition in telecommunications (e.g., Laffont and Tirole 2000), we distinguish among three different types of costs: fixed costs that are independent of traffic and the number of consumers served, connection-dependent but traffic-independent "fixed" costs, and traffic-dependent costs.

The first type of costs, C_i, is independent of the number of connections. Such costs may be incurred initially—for instance, the costs of building a backbone—and are possibly sunk when pricing decisions are taken.

The second type of costs is connection-dependent but traffic-independent: the per-period and per-connection fixed cost of the local access network, which will also be denoted as the fixed cost of the local loop. This cost captures, for instance, the maintenance cost of the local loop and may also include the investment cost that has to be recovered. Operator i's fixed cost of the local loop is denoted by f_i. Connection-dependent but traffic-independent costs affect the gain per consumer and therefore operators' pricing decisions.

The third type of costs are traffic-dependent. Marginal costs of telephony are close to zero, if one strictly applies the definition of marginal costs. In reality, operators typically impute fixed costs to telephony traffic, enabling them to define a reference point for prices (although these costs do not directly depend on traffic). We follow this latter understanding of costs and define "marginal costs" as the costs that a sales/marketing department attributes to traffic when making pricing decisions.[9]

Costs that are also perceived as traffic-dependent are charges for interconnection and access. These charges are typically incurred on a per-minute basis. Total traffic-dependent costs therefore include an operator's marginal cost, as defined in the previous paragraph, and charges paid to other operators for interconnection and access. Let c_{ik} denote operator i's traffic-dependent cost per minute associated with a telephone call of type k, as explained later. We will follow the convention in the literature, where it is typically assumed that the marginal cost of a call does not depend on whether the call is on-net or off-net:

$$c_{i1} - c_{i2} = c_{i3}.$$

In the case of off-net calls and incoming calls, the operator of the network where the call originates pays a per-minute terminating access fee to the operator of the network where the call terminates. Period-t terminating access prices paid to operator i are denoted by τ_i^t. Access prices are *reciprocal* in period t if $\tau_1^t = \tau_2^t$ and nonreciprocal or asymmetric otherwise. We distinguish three types of telephone calls:

• *on-net calls:* calls that originate and terminate on a single operator's network ($k = 1$) with associated costs c_{i1} for operator i;
• *off-net calls:* calls that terminate on another operator's network ($k = 2$) with associated costs $c_{i2} + \tau_j^t$ for operator i;
• *incoming calls:* calls that originate from another operator's network ($k = 3$) with associated costs $c_{i3} - \tau_i^t$ for operator i.

To derive profit functions, we have to specify consumers' calling patterns. We assume that when a consumer makes a telephone call, the

Table 4.1
Net revenues

Source	Operator 1	Operator 2
On-net traffic	$ns_1^t s_1^t x[p_1^t](p_1^t - c_{11})$	$ns_2^t s_2^t x[p_2^t](p_2^t - c_{21})$
Off-net traffic	$ns_1^t s_2^t x[p_1^t](p_1^t - c_{12} - \tau_2^t)$	$ns_2^t s_1^t x[p_2^t](p_2^t - c_{22} - \tau_1^t)$
Incoming traffic	$ns_2^t s_1^t x[p_2^t](\tau_1^t - c_{13})$	$ns_1^t s_2^t x[p_1^t](\tau_2^t - c_{23})$
Subscriptions	$ns_1^t(m_1^t - f_1)$	$ns_2^t(m_2^t - f_2)$

receiver of the call can be any other consumer with equal probability, independent of the network to which she subscribes. In the aggregate, the shares of on-net and off-net calls of an operator are equal to its and its competitor's market share, respectively.[10]

Profits are generated from different sources. The expressions for these terms of the profit function are easily expressed (see table 4.1).

Operator i's period-t profits, denoted by π_i, are the sum of net revenues from on-net traffic, profits from off-net calls, profits from incoming traffic, and profits from subscription minus fixed costs that are independent of the number of subscribers. Profit functions depend on both operators' prices, which reflects that the operators strategically interact with each other. Fixed costs not attributed to traffic or connection, although they clearly affect profits, do not influence pricing decisions.

4.2.3 Equilibrium

To conclude the description of the model, we recapitulate the structure of the game. Operators take terminating access prices τ_1^t and τ_2^t in each period as given. They simultaneously choose per-minute prices p_1^t and p_2^t, and (monthly) subscription fees m_1^t and m_2^t. Consumers observe these prices, choose where to subscribe, and make their telephone calls in period t. Operators receive profits $\pi_1[p_1, p_2, m_1, m_2; t]$ and $\pi_2[p_1, p_2, m_1, m_2; t]$ in period t.

Operators maximize period profits while taking the prices chosen by its rival firm as given. Equilibrium values of functions and variables are marked with superscript $*$. For example, in an equilibrium in period t, operator 1's per-minute price is denoted by p_1^{t*}. A Nash equilibrium in period t, which is characterized by prices $p_1^{t*}, p_2^{t*}, m_1^{t*}, m_2^{t*}$, satisfies the following conditions:

1. Each operator's prices p_i^{t*} and m_i^{t*} maximize its profits given the other operator's prices p_j^{t*} and m_j^{t*} for $i = 1, 2$, where $i \neq j$.

2. Consumers choose a network and a quantity of call minutes to maximize net utility, and the operators take this behavior into account while choosing prices.

In an equilibrium in period t, none of the operators has an incentive to deviate from its pricing strategy (p_i^{t*}, m_i^{t*}), if

$$\pi_1 \lfloor p_1^{t*}, p_2^{t*}, m_1^{t*}, m_2^{t*}; t \rfloor \geq \pi_1 \lfloor p_1, p_2^{t*}, m_1, m_2^{t*}; t \rfloor$$

and

$$\pi_2 [p_1^{t*}, p_2^{t*}, m_1^{t*}, m_2^{t*}; t] \geq \pi_2 [p_1^{t*}, p_2, m_1^{t*}, m_2; t]$$

for all admissible p_1, p_2, m_1, m_2. In our simulations we check that the solutions to the system of first-order conditions, (p_i^{t*}, m_i^{t*}), are a global maximizer of $\pi_i[\cdot, \cdot, p_j^{t*}, m_j^{t*}; t]$. For details, see de Bijl and Peitz (2001).

We consider a sequence of Nash equilibria for periods $t = 1, \ldots, T$. This sequence generates the same outcome as the subgame-perfect equilibrium of the game that encompasses all T periods as different stages.

4.2.4   Surplus and Welfare

The market outcome and the impact of regulation can be evaluated by assessing consumers surplus, profits and market share of each operator, and welfare. It is possibly important to consider not only welfare but also consumer surplus because regulation may decrease the former but increase the latter (and transfers from producers to consumers may only be achieved through regulation). A regulator wishing to ensure that consumers benefit from entry and competition, may be interested in maximizing consumer surplus under the constraint that the operators make enough profits to have incentives to invest in infrastructure and quality of service. Alternatively, it may want to maximize a weighted average of consumer surplus and profits for each firm.

Producer surplus in period t, PS^t, is equal as the sum of profits in the industry. Consumer surplus in period t, CS^t, defined as the consumers' aggregate net utility, is equal to

$$CS^t = ns_1 \lfloor p_1^t, p_2^t, m_1^t, m_2^t; t \rfloor v_1 \lfloor p_1^t, m_1^t; t \rfloor + ns_2 \lfloor p_1^t, p_2^t, m_1^t, m_2^t; t \rfloor v_2 \lfloor p_2^t, m_2^t; t \rfloor$$

$$- \frac{n\theta}{2} ((s_1[p_1^t, p_2^t, m_1^t, m_2^t; t])^2 + (s_2[p_1^t, p_2^t, m_1^t, m_2^t; t])^2).$$

The last term in the expression for consumer surplus is the disutility that consumers incur owing to the subscription to a network that does not possess ideal characteristics. The welfare level in period t, W^t, is equal to the total surplus that is realized in the market, $W^t = PS^t + CS^t$.

4.2.5 Welfare: The Costs and Benefits of Liberalization

Consider two technologically symmetric networks, that is, their cost structures are identical. In this case, we ask, Is a cost-based duopoly superior to a cost-based monopoly in terms of welfare? Note that first-best pricing involves per-minute prices equal to (true) marginal cost, that is, $p_i = c_{11}$. Since we assume that all consumers participate in the market, the level of the subscription fee is arbitrary.[11] We can consider subscription fees equal to the fixed costs of a connection, $m_i = f_i$.

In our model, a duopoly leads to the following social costs, compared to a monopoly:

- Connection-independent fixed costs, C_i^t, are duplicated.
- The entrant initially lacks a track record of quality.

In our model, a duopoly leads on the other hand to social benefits:

- The differentiated duopoly better fits a consumer population with heterogeneous tastes.

Other social benefits (that are not incorporated into the model) are those associated with competition reducing the X-inefficiency of the incumbent, that is, socially wasteful expenditures can be avoided. Such expenditures were possibly included in the profits of the incumbent. Also, mature competition creates a level-playing field, and this possibly reduces the social costs of regulation, which were not introduced into the model. Last but not least, it is often claimed that a protected monopoly leads to dynamic inefficiencies by not providing the right incentives to invest.

If fixed costs C_i^t are negligible in the long run, duopoly is welfare improving upon monopoly (at cost-based prices). This is so because in the long run the entrant will have built up a track record of quality and offers the same utility v_i as the incumbent at prices $p_1^t = p_2^t$, $m_1^t = m_2^t$. Because of the initial lack of a quality track record, the entrant's network offers lower fixed utility in early periods. Therefore, a duopoly is welfare improving upon monopoly in the short run if the better average fit owing to product differentiation overcompensates the lower utility associated with the lack of track record in the short run. Considering intertemporal welfare, if the discount factor is sufficiently close to 1 and the time horizon T sufficiently long, then a cost-based duopoly dominates a cost-based monopoly in terms of welfare for sufficiently low fixed costs C_i^f.

Even if a cost-based duopoly leads to lower welfare in our model, one can still make the case for competition by referring to unmodeled advantages of competition such as those mentioned earlier. In what follows, we take the decision to introduce competition as given.[12]

4.3   A First Analysis

The analysis in which per-minute prices are flexible is rather complex. Therefore, based on Peitz (2001), we present in this section a simple model in which per-minute retail prices are fixed at true marginal cost levels, that is, $p_i = c_1$, $i = 1, 2$. Operators are not allowed to adjust per-minute prices to perceived marginal costs. This implies that under positive access markups both operators will suffer from losses for off-net traffic whereas on-net traffic does not contribute to profits. Profit functions can be written as

$$\pi_i = ns_i s_j x[c_1](c_1 - c_2 - \tau_j) + ns_i s_j x[c_1](\tau_i - c_3) + ns_i(m_i - f_i)$$

$$= ns_i(s_2 x[c_1](\tau_i - \tau_j) + m_i - f_i).$$

By looking at the profit functions we make the following remark:

Remark 1   In the model with fixed per-minute prices, profits are neutral to the level of reciprocal access prices. This holds not only if the market is symmetric but also if it is asymmetric.

In the model with flexible per-minute prices, profit neutrality can be shown under symmetric competition but not under asymmetric competition.[13] This suggests that our simple model does abstract from an important element that arises from differences in individual demand due to different per-minute prices under asymmetric competition. Nevertheless, we will see that our simple model is quite useful for the analysis of asymmetric access price regulation.

We obtain a unique equilibrium candidate that solves the first-order conditions of profit maximization.[14] If asymmetries between networks are sufficiently small, then the solution to the first-order conditions indeed is an equilibrium. In particular, we assume that the expressions for m_i^* and s_i^* that follow are positive for both operators (under cost-based access price regulation). This means that we implicitly assume that networks are not too asymmetric. Subscription fees have equilibrium values

$$m_i^* = \frac{1}{3}(2f_i + f_j) + \theta + \frac{1}{3}(U_i - U_j) + \frac{1}{3\theta}((U_i - U_j) + (f_j - f_i))x[c_1](\tau_i - \tau_j).$$

(1)

Market shares, in equilibrium, are[15]

$$s_i^* = \frac{1}{2} + \frac{(U_i - U_j) + (f_j - f_i)}{6\theta}.$$

The market share is positive if $(U_i - U_j) + (f_j - f_i) + 3\theta > 0$. We can now make the following remark:

Remark 2   In the model with fixed per-minute prices, in an interior equilibrium, market shares are independent of access prices.

This implies that total surplus is independent of access prices. Equilibrium profits reduce to

$$\pi_i^* = \frac{n}{36\theta^2}((U_i - U_j) + (f_j - f_i) + 3\theta)^2(2\theta + (\tau_i - \tau_j)x[c_1]).$$

From these expressions we immediately obtain a number of interesting and intuitive comparative statics results.

Result 1   In the model with fixed per-minute prices

i. a higher access price of operator i leads to higher profits of operator i and lower profits of operator j, $j \neq i$;

ii. lower fixed costs of the local loop of operator i lead to higher profits of operator i and lower profits of operator j, $j \neq i$;

iii. similarly, a higher fixed utility offered by network i leads to higher profits of operator i and lower profits of operator j, $j \neq i$;

iv. if networks become more differentiated profits of both operators increase.

Our main question is what regulatory policy should be adopted such that it satisfies three objectives: a high total surplus (as a measure of welfare), a high consumer surplus (because competition is supposed to ultimately benefit consumers), and high profits of the smaller network (to stimulate entry). This proposition tells us that the profits of operator 2 are increased by setting asymmetric access prices with $\tau_2 > \tau_1$. If we see operator 2 as the entrant that offers initially a lower brand utility, then asymmetric access price regulation that favors the entrant achieves that the entrant's profits are higher than under cost-based access price regulation. This means that asymmetric access price regulation is a tool to stimulate entry.

Does the goal to stimulate entry conflict with the goal to protect consumers? As noted earlier (see Remark 2) market share is independent of access prices, which are fixed by the regulator (or arise through cooperative or noncooperative choices by the operators). This implies that total welfare is independent of access prices.[16] Changes in access prices merely lead to a redistribution of surplus between operators and consumers. Consumer surplus can then be written as total surplus minus total or industry profits. That is,

$$CS = W - n\theta$$

$$- \frac{n}{90}((f_1 - f_2) + (U_2 - U_1))((f_1 - f_2) + (U_2 - U_1) - 3x[c_1](\tau_1 - \tau_2)).$$

Note that consumer surplus depends on the difference of access prices $\mu \equiv \tau_1 - \tau_2$. Operators can be asymmetric on the cost side or the demand side. Suppose that both have the same cost structure and that the only difference between the two operators is that operator 2 is (initially) less attractive, that is, $U_1 > U_2$. We then find that

$$\frac{\partial CS}{\partial \mu} = -\frac{3nx[c_1]}{90}(U_1 - U_2) < 0.$$

Consequently, not only the entrant but also the consumers benefit from access price regulation that favors the entrant ($\tau_2 > \tau_1$).

Result 2   In the model with fixed per-minute prices, asymmetric access price regulation that favors the weaker operator leads to higher profits of this operator and to higher consumer surplus while total surplus remains constant.

We can see the unambiguous effect on consumer surplus by looking at subscription fees (using the fact that market share does not change; see Remark 2). Not only do consumers in the aggregate benefit but each individual consumer benefits from asymmetric regulation because subscription fees of both operators are lower than under reciprocal access price regulation.[17]

Summarizing, this model provides strong reasons for the regulator to use asymmetric regulation in markets in which an entrant is initially at a disadvantage. We will see in what follows that this conclusion remains valid if operators are free to set per-minute price.

4.4   New Competition in Telecommunications Markets

In this section we analyze the model of section 4.2 with the help of simulations.[18] We characterize the evolution of a telecommunications market under a certain parameter constellation (see the appendix). In contrast to the previous section, both operators are unconstrained in their choice of two-part tariffs.

4.4.1   Operators' Retail Prices

Each operator has two instruments, per-minute price and subscription fee, and can separate the building of market share in terms of subscribers from the generation of call volume for each subscriber (Laffont, Rey, and Tirole 1998, 21). Given any prices of the competitor, profit maximizing prices of an operator involve a per-minute price equal to perceived marginal costs, formally

$$p_i^{t*} = s_i^t c_{i1} + s_j^t (c_{i2} + \tau_j^t) \quad \text{in each period } t.$$

In setting its per-minute price, each operator behaves as if it maximizes the difference between consumer's surplus and costs that are traffic-dependent. In this respect, it behaves like a monopolist, which uses the subscription fee to extract consumer surplus and sets the usage price equal to marginal costs. The reason is that the gain in consumer surplus from a cut in the per-minute price below perceived marginal costs is less than the associated cost that the operator incurs, whereas a reduction in the subscription fee translates one-to-one into greater consumer surplus. Hence, in competing for market share, the subscription fee is a more effective instrument than per-minute price.

One can show that an operator that sets its per-minute price equal to perceived marginal costs makes zero profits from the total amount of on-net and off-net traffic. Consequently, the only sources of profits are

Figure 4.1
Cost-based regulation: Subscription fees

revenues from subscription and revenues from incoming traffic.[19] In equilibrium, an increase in the product differentiation parameter θ has no direct effect on per-minute prices, while it directly pushes the subscription fees upward (there are possibly also indirect effects through changes in market shares).

4.4.2   Cost-Based and Reciprocal Access Price Regulation

In our simulations the fixed utility disadvantage of the entrant decreases linearly over time up to period t^*, which is set equal to 11 (one period corresponds to two months). Subscription fees respond to this fixed utility difference. For instance, under cost-based regulation, in period 2 the fixed utility difference is equal to 45 euros and the difference in subscription fees is equal to 30 euros (period 5: 30 euros and 20 euros, respectively; period 8: 15 euros and 10 euros, respectively). The evolution of subscription fees is depicted in figure 4.1. Under cost-based regulation all variables can be expressed analytically, and it is possible to dispose of numerical methods (see section 4.3 for the analytical results with $\tau_i = c_3$).

Similar to subscription fees, also market shares evolve linearly over time until the entrant has fully built up its track record of quality. With our parameter values the entrant first gains a market share of around 8.3 percent, which is augmented by around 4.2 percent each period.

Under cost-based regulation, none of the operators obtains profits from incoming calls, and profits in equilibrium are $\pi_i^t = ns_i^t(m_i^t - f_i) - C_i^t$. Here, we look at profits gross of fixed costs C_i^t. Since the entrant's

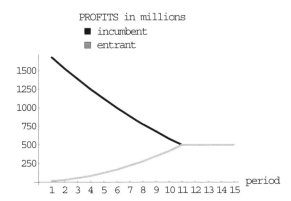

Figure 4.2
Cost-based regulation: Profits

market share and subscription fee increase linearly over time, profits are increasing and convex over time until the entrant has caught up with the incumbent. Correspondingly, the incumbent's profits are decreasing and convex over time (see figure 4.2).

As explained in section 4.2, welfare in a mature duopoly dominates welfare under monopoly for C_i^t sufficiently small because of beneficial product differentiation. In initial periods, there is a social cost to duopoly because of the lack of the entrant's track record. If those social costs are high, welfare is possibly higher under a regulatory regime, which makes it harder for the entrant to gain market share in early periods. The trade-off between the gradual buildup of a track record, which makes the entrant more attractive, and the gain in market share explains why welfare can be decreasing over time in early periods, as demonstrated in figure 4.3. As competition matures, the incumbent's profits decline, and this is only partially offset by the increase in the entrant's profits so that producer surplus is declining over time. At the same time consumers gain from more mature competition, which is reflected by the increasing trajectory of consumer surplus (see figure 4.3).

In our simulations, introducing a reciprocal access markup does not substantially change the picture in terms of the slopes of the trajectories of the variables. The only notable exception is the per-minute price that was constant under cost-based regulation. Since per-minute price equals perceived marginal costs, the entrant's per-minute price is decreasing over time as it builds up a track record of quality. The reason is that it has a small market share in early periods leading to

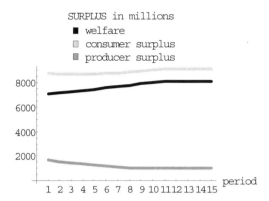

Figure 4.3
Cost-based regulation: Surplus

relatively high perceived marginal costs. These costs are significantly higher than those of the incumbent because a call originating on the incumbent's network is most likely to terminate on the incumbent's network when the incumbent's market share is large.

Under a positive reciprocal access markup, the entrant has a lower market share than under cost-based access pricing because of its higher perceived marginal costs. Whether or not the entrant is doing better under reciprocal access price regulation in a period in which it has not yet fully built up its track record cannot be said unambiguously. Our simulations give the result that aggregated over time it receives lower profits under a reciprocal access price markup than under cost-based regulation.[20] In the long run, profits are not affected by a symmetric access markup: In a symmetric market losses in profits from subscription are exactly offset by gains in profits from incoming calls when comparing a positive access markup to access price equal to the marginal cost of the local loop (the profit neutrality results in mature markets has been pointed out by Laffont, Rey, and Tirole 1998).

Clearly, a positive reciprocal access markup reduces welfare and consumers surplus in the long run because perceived marginal costs deviate from true marginal costs, giving rise to a deadweight loss.

4.4.3 Asymmetric Access Price Regulation

Asymmetric access price regulation treats entrant and incumbent differently. We consider regulation that favors the entrant in early periods

Figure 4.4
Asymmetric access price regulation: Subscription fees

of competition by fixing an access price above marginal costs for calls terminating on the entrant's network. In our simulations reported here, this access markup prevails for six periods. The incumbent and, in later periods, also the entrant, are subject to cost-based regulation. This asymmetric regulation generates positive profits from incoming calls for the entrant.

While building up its track record, the entrant gains market share so that it becomes more likely over time that a consumer who is subscribed to the incumbent's network makes an off-net call. Hence, under our asymmetric regulatory regime, the incumbent's perceived marginal costs are increasing over time as long as the entrant is allowed to charge a fixed access markup (see figure 4.4); the incumbent sets a higher per-minute price than under cost-based regulation. The more aggressive behavior of the entrant can be explained as follows: An additional consumer generates not only profits for the entrant through its subscription but also additional incoming calls, which are valuable to the entrant. It turns out that under mutual-best replies both operators price more aggressively than under reciprocal access price regulation.[21] For early periods, in which the per-minute price of the incumbent does not differ much between cost-based and asymmetric regulation (this can be seen by comparing figure 4.5 with figure 4.1).

The difference between true and perceived marginal costs is quite small initially due to the small market share of the entrant (so that the analysis of section 4.3 comes quite close to what is observed in our simulation results). Nevertheless, competition is strongly affected

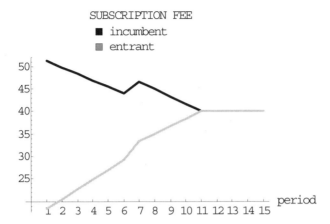

Figure 4.5
Asymmetric access prices regulation: Per-minute prices

because the entrant gains from incoming traffic. In our simulation, the evolution of market share is only slightly better for the entrant under asymmetric regulation than under cost-based regulation (they do not change in the version of section 4.3), but its profits in early periods are much larger in relative terms.

To facilitate the comparison between cost-based and asymmetric access price regulation, we present in tables 4.2 and 4.3 profits and consumer surplus for period 1 and period 6. Note that the results in the first and second columns are analytical, corresponding to cost-based regulation and asymmetric access price regulation such that the incumbent's per-minute price is fixed to true marginal costs (see section 4.3). The third column is derived from simulations. Numbers show that asymmetric access price regulation is effective in stimulating competition by increasing the entrant's profits and consumer surplus.

Trajectories of profits under asymmetric regulation are depicted in figure 4.6. Using our parameter constellation, we see that profits in period 1 are 16 instead of 14 million euros and, in period 6, they are 196 instead of 170 million euros (see tables 4.2 and 4.3). This makes asymmetric access price regulation a powerful instrument to improve the entrant's profits in early periods. Entrants whose fate depends on short-run profit evaluations of financial markets may need such an initial regulatory stimulus to become or remain active in the market.

More intense competition in early periods works in favor of consumers so that consumer surplus is higher under asymmetric regu-

Table 4.2
Profits and surplus in period 1: Cost-based versus asymmetric access price regulation

	Cost-based access prices	Asymmetric access prices with fixed per-minute prices	Asymmetric access price regulation with flexible per-minute prices
π_1^1	1680.56	1428.47	1429.04
π_2^1	13.89	15.97	15.97
CS^1	7073.61	7323.62	7323.01
W^1	8768.06	8768.06	8768.02

Table 4.3
Profits and surplus in period 6: Cost-based versus asymmetric access price regulation

	Cost-based access prices	Asymmetric access prices with fixed per-minute prices	Asymmetric access price regulation with flexible per-minute prices
π_1^6	1003.47	852.95	854.03
π_2^6	170.14	195.66	195.53
CS^6	7568.40	7693.40	7692.15
W^6	8742.01	8742.01	8741.71

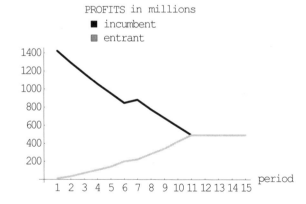

Figure 4.6
Asymmetric access price regulation: Profits

lation than under cost-based regulation. Welfare is lower for two reasons: First, a small number of consumers subscribe to the entrant's network who would have subscribed to the incumbent under cost-based regulation. Due to the initial lack of the entrant's track record, this constitutes a loss in social surplus. Second, the deviation of the incumbent's per-minute price from true marginal costs creates a dead-weight loss. Both these effects are rather negligible in our simulation. (In our analysis with fixed per-minute prices, regulation was neutral to welfare and purely redistributive.)

Comparing our analysis in this section to the one in the previous section, tables 4.2 and 4.3 suggest that the analysis in section 4.3 is a helpful approximation of the results obtained by simulation. We observe that the distortionary effect due to higher per-minute prices is small. Net utilities of consumers and market shares are hardly affected, although there is a significant effect on the incumbent's retail prices: For instance, in period 6, the incumbent's subscription fee is approximately 44 euros if per-minute price is flexible whereas it is approximately 46 euros if per-minute price is fixed at true marginal costs.

4.4.4 Price Cap Regulation

If the incumbent is subject to price cap regulation that includes a restriction on its subscription fee, the price cap is likely to be binding in early periods when the incumbent still enjoys substantial market power. In these periods the forces of competition may be insufficient from the viewpoint of the regulatory authority to guarantee "reasonable" prices for consumers. We remark that price cap regulation that achieves this goal does not need to be phased out; it automatically becomes obsolete as competition matures, that is, as competitors gain strength. So it can remain in place without inflicting any harm.[22] We consider a price cap that is only applied to retail prices; the wholesale price (that is the access price) is separately regulated.

With respect to retail prices the regulator may have different concerns. To eliminate a deadweight loss, he may force the incumbent to set its per-minute price equal to true marginal costs (see section 4.3). To avoid consumers having to pay an "excessive" subscription fee, he may separately impose a maximal retail price. Only one of these two prices may be fixed or both of them.[23]

As in de Bijl and Peitz (2001), we only consider a price cap on subscription fees (for more on price cap regulation, see de Bijl and Peitz

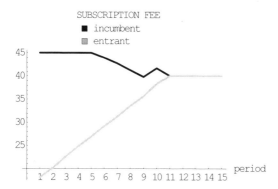

Figure 4.7
Price cap regulation: Subscription fees

2002, chaps. 3 and 4). This reflects the importance that a regulator may attach to universal service provision, which is typically embodied in a low subscription fee. For example, in the Netherlands, telecommunications authority Opta has made sure that the former incumbent KPN Telecom offers a budget subscription (among other contracts). The aim of this contract is for every customer to be connected, to be reachable, and to be able to make phone calls if needed, although the per-minute price is usually higher for budget contracts.

Consider a price cap on subscription fees together with asymmetric access price regulation. We comment on results obtained from simulations for asymmetric access price regulation in place for nine periods.[24] As argued earlier, a subscription fee is binding in those periods in which the incumbent enjoys a considerable degree of market power, as can be seen in figure 4.7. Because the incumbent is not restricted in its per-minute price, it increases the per-minute price above perceived marginal costs in those periods in which the price cap is binding for the subscription fee. As time passes, the market power of the incumbent declines; this implies that the shadow price on the price cap restriction decreases and the per-minute price decreases, ceteris paribus. This tendency of a lower per-minute price is only partially offset by an increase in perceived marginal costs (see figure 4.8).

The per-minute price is an imperfect instrument for the incumbent to make profits compared to the subscription fee. In equilibrium, both operators make lower profits than in the absence of price cap regulation because the incumbent prices more aggressively. Consumers, on the other hand, gain from price cap regulation.

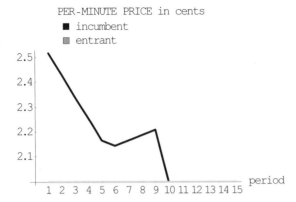

Figure 4.8
Price cap regulation: Per-minute prices

Compared to cost-based regulation, the entrant may do better than under combined price cap and asymmetric access price regulation. This is not necessarily so: A tough price cap regime may even inflict losses on the entrant so that it may refrain from entering in the first place. This makes price cap regulation a difficult policy instrument because one has to balance consumer interests with the goal of stimulating entry. Furthermore, price cap regulation such as pure subscription fee regulation can lead to strong distortions in the incumbent's pricing structure away from true marginal costs, and such pricing leads to a welfare loss.

The effect of price cap regulation on the per-minute price can be avoided if the incumbent's per-minute price is regulated separately. Under such an intrusive regulation, the regulator can fix the incumbent's per-minute price at its socially efficient level, that is, at true marginal costs. A binding price cap on the subscription fee then makes the incumbent compete more aggressively than under cost-based regulation (as well as under regulation that only fixes the subscription fee). This affects the entrant's profits negatively. A temporary access markup for the entrant generates positive profits from incoming calls, thus enabling the entrant to approach or reach profit levels that would be realized under cost-based regulation.

To summarize, when imposing separate price caps on both retail prices of the incumbent, the regulator can also ameliorate the prospects of the entrant by complementing the price cap with asymmetric access price regulation.

4.5   Discussion and Conclusion

This chapter has explored the role of regulation in an asymmetric market. First, consider wholesale price regulation. In early periods after liberalization the entrant is at a disadvantage (because of lower fixed utility). We have shown that, in early periods, asymmetric access price regulation that gives a positive access markup to the entrant and is cost-based for the incumbent is an effective instrument to increase consumer surplus and enhance profits of the entrant. An access markup for the entrant makes entry more attractive and, given entry, increases competition. Once an entrant has gained competitive strength so that, under symmetric regulation, it competes more or less on equal terms with the incumbent, asymmetric regulation should be replaced by cost-based regulation if regulation is not abolished.[25] This conclusion is consistent with the general objectives and principles on effective competition spelled out by the British regulator Oftel (see Oftel 2000, app. I).

This conclusion appears to be robust in particular with respect to the strategy space of the operators.[26] As shown by Peitz (2001) and de Bijl and Peitz (2002, chap. 6), asymmetric access price regulation has the same qualitative effects on the entrant's profits and consumers' net utilities under two-part tariffs with or without termination-based price discrimination, flat fees, and linear prices. Therefore, we formulate a regulatory pricing principle for the wholesale market.

Regulatory pricing principle for the wholesale market: In early periods after liberalization, the regulator should set asymmetric access prices such that only the entrant enjoys an access markup. This has two positive effects on competition: A potential entrant is more likely to enter and, given entry, competition is more intense. In later periods access price regulation should be cost-based. This type of wholesale price regulation is effective in protecting consumers and encouraging entry at the same time; losses in total surplus are likely to be small.

Even under such asymmetric wholesale price regulation, the incumbent may enjoy substantial market power so that the regulator may want to intervene in the retail market directly to protect consumers. A price cap on the incumbent's subscription fee serves the goal of making a connection available to all consumers at an "affordable" price. Note, however, that such regulation leads to lower profits of the entrant so that the goal to protect consumers in the short run has to be carefully weighed against the goal to encourage entry (de Bijl and Peitz

2002, chaps. 3, 4). In addition, the deadweight loss from distorted per-minute prices may be substantial.

Regulatory pricing principle for the retail market: A price cap on the incumbent's subscription fee leads to "affordable" subscriptions for all consumers. Profits of both operators suffer so that entry becomes more difficult. This type of retail price regulation is effective in protecting consumers but it may discourage entry. Losses in total surplus can be substantial.

We briefly discuss two further issues related to asymmetric regulation that have not been addressed in our analysis. These considerations are important for the application of asymmetric regulation.

In our analysis, regulatory policy did not depend on market outcomes. Owing to the initial uncertainty on the side of the regulator how the market will evolve, it seems problematic to implement a policy in practice that does not depend on realized market outcomes. On the other hand, if the replacement of asymmetric by reciprocal access price regulation depends on market outcomes, operators can strategically exploit the endogeneity of regulatory variables by taking into account the effect of their decisions on the relevant market outcomes. This may be harmful for competition. For instance, a market share–based criterion gives incentives to incumbents and entrants to behave less aggressively: The incumbent prefers a rapid replacement of asymmetric regulation, and the entrant the opposite. Both operators thus have an incentive to raise their subscription fees.

In our analysis, we also postulated that in the long run both operators are equally efficient. If some of the asymmetries between operators are time-persistent, the regulator has to worry about inefficient entry. Note that even under cost-based regulation, operators with different cost levels can both enjoy positive profits in an oligopolistic market in which price-cost margins are not competed away. Applying asymmetric instead of cost-based access price regulation and thus providing a temporary advantage for entrants, the regulator must keep in mind that this may attract less efficient entrants.

Appendix: Parameter Constellation

We spell out our parameter configuration in the following list:

Demand parameters	a	20 euro-cents
	b	0.015 euro-cents
	θ	20 euros

	u^0	50 euros
	$\alpha_1 = \alpha_2$	1
	t^*	11
	n	50,000,000
	s_1^0	1
Cost parameters	$c_{11} = c_{21}$	2 euro-cents
	$c_{12} = c_{22}$	1.5 euro-cents
	$c_{13} = c_{23}$	0.5 euro-cents
	$f_1 = f_2$	20 euros

The regulatory regimes are as follows: under cost-based regulation, the (reciprocal) access price is set equal to 0.5 euro-cents in all periods. For the reciprocal access markup, we set the access price equal to 1 in all periods. Asymmetric access price regulation is invoked for a limited number of periods and replaced afterward by cost-based regulation. We consider asymmetric access prices for six and for nine periods. In the former case we speak of short-lived asymmetric regulation, in the latter of long-lived asymmetric regulation. In the moderately asymmetric regime, the price to access the entrant's network is 1 euro-cent, whereas in the strongly asymmetric regime the price to access the entrant's network is 2 euro-cents. Under price cap regulation, we consider moderately asymmetric access prices and a price cap on the incumbent's subscription fee of 45 euros per period.

Notes

This chapter was written while Paul de Bijl was at CPB Netherlands Bureau for Eonomic Policy Analysis. Martin Peitz gratefully acknowledges financial support from the Deutsche Forschungsgemeinschaft (Heisenberg Fellowship).

1. See also Peitz (2002) and de Bijl and Peitz (2002).

2. There does not exist a consensus in the literature whether regulation should be allowed to be asymmetric or not (see Perrucci and Cimatoribus 1997).

3. This insight is also obtained in de Bijl and Peitz (2001) and Peitz (2001). In this chapter, we combine analytical and simulation work.

4. This is the Hotelling specification that has also been used in the seminal papers by Armstrong (1998) and Laffont, Rey, and Tirole (1998).

5. Since individual demand of a subscriber to operator i is defined by $x[p_i] = \arg\max_x \{u[x] - xp_i\}$, individual demand is derived by solving the first-order condition for utility maximization $u'[x] = p$.

6. Asymmetries on the demand side have been introduced by Carter and Wright (1999, 2001) and de Bijl and Peitz (2001, 2002). Note that we do not allow utility to depend on the number of received calls. On this see Jeon, Laffont, and Tirole (2001).

7. For the sake of simplicity, we did not make endogenous the decisions such as to what extent to upgrade a cable network. We focus purely on pricing decisions and see our specification as an interesting starting point because some asymmetries between networks are likely to persist in the medium term independent of the decisions of the new operators.

8. We specify demand as linear. This can be seen as the linear approximation of a nonlinear demand function. For this it would be important to have a good estimate of the slope of the demand curve in the neighborhood of the realized equilibrium.

9. This should be kept in mind when making welfare comparisons: per-minute prices equal to these marginal costs may not be welfare-maximizing because in the first-best per-minute prices are equal to true marginal costs (in what follows, we abstract from such considerations).

10. For instance, given prices and realized market shares, the total volume of call minutes that originates on network 1 is equal to $ns_1 x[p_1]$. Then a fraction s_1 of this volume, that is, $ns_1 s_1 x[p_1]$, terminates on network 1. Similarly, the traffic volume terminating on network 2 is $ns_2 s_1 x[p_1]$.

11. Clearly, for high subscription fees some consumers eventually no longer subscribe so that the assumption of full participation only makes sense for sufficiently low subscription fees.

12. Nevertheless, before the government decides to liberalize a market, it is important to ask whether competition (regulated or not) indeed improves upon a regulated monopoly.

13. In their simulations de Bijl and Peitz (2002) observe that the larger operator does not gain from an access price different from marginal costs. This is formally shown in Carter and Wright (2001). We would also like to point out that in our simple model a reciprocal access price cannot be used as a collusive device.

14. Note that "typically" ($|\tau_1 - \tau_2|$ not too large) best responses are upward-sloping and networks are strategic complements.

15. We require that the expression for m_i^* and s_i^* are positive for both operators (under cost-based access price regulation). This gives restrictions on the asymmetry between networks.

16. To see this, note that access prices above costs do not distort per-minute prices because the latter are fixed. Since market share remains constant, both costs and gross utilities are not affected by changes of the access prices.

17. We see this from equation (1): The incumbent network enjoys a fixed utility advantage so that all consumers who subscribe to this network pay less as $\tau_2 - \tau_1$ is increased. Since the sign of the fixed utility difference and that of the access price difference are reversed for the entrant, all consumers who subscribe to the entrant's network pay less as $\tau_2 - \tau_1$ is increased.

18. For analytical results, see Peitz (2001).

19. Per-minute price equal perceived marginal cost holds in the symmetric setup of Laffont, Rey, and Tirole (1998) and asymmetric setups as in this chapter or de Bijl and Peitz (2001, 2002). Note the difference from the analysis in the previous section. Nevertheless, results in the two versions coincide under cost-based access price regulation.

20. On reciprocal access price regulation in an asymmetric market, see de Bijl and Peitz (2002, chaps. 3 and 4), de Bijl and Peitz (2001), and Carter and Wright (2001).

21. This result appears to be robust in our simulations. It would be desirable to have this as a general (analytical) result, as in section 4.3. See Peitz (2001).

22. In practice, the price cap is changed every year according to a predefined rule such as RPI-X. In particular, if the productivity gain is overestimated a price cap may become binding as competition matures. In effect, it does not become obsolete.

23. The regulator may alternatively impose a joint retail price cap so as to make a connection together with a certain number of call minutes available at a certain price.

24. A more detailed analysis of simulations is found in de Bijl and Peitz (2001). Some numbers have to be rescaled to account for differences in market size.

25. Regulation is not needed in our model in the long run if in the absence of regulation, operators negotiate the reciprocal access price. In this case they choose access price equal to marginal costs in our model.

26. We conjecture that our qualitative results also hold under partial consumer participation.

References

Armstrong, M. 1998. "Network Interconnection in Telecommunications." *Economic Journal* 108: 545–564.

Armstrong, M. 2002. "The Theory of Access Pricing and Interconnection." Forthcoming in M. Cave, S. Majumdar, and I. Vogelsang, eds., *Handbook of Telecommunications Economics* 295–384. Amsterdam: North-Holland.

Carter, M., and J. Wright. 1999. "Interconnection in Network Industries." *Review of Industrial Organization* 14: 1–25.

Carter, M., and J. Wright. 2001. "Asymmetric Network Interconnection." Mimeo., University of Auckland.

de Bijl, P., and M. Peitz. 2002. *Regulation and Entry into Telecommunications Markets.* Cambridge, UK: Cambridge University Press.

de Bijl, P., and M. Peitz. 2001. "Dynamic Regulation and Competition in Telecommunications Markets—A Framework for Policy Analysis." Mimeo., CPB Netherlands Bureau for Economic Policy Analysis.

European Commission. 2000. "Europe's Liberalised Telecommunication's Market—A Guide to the Rules of the Game." European Commission staff working document.

Jeon, D.-S., J.-J. Laffont, and J. Tirole. 2001. "On the Receiver Pays Principle." Mimeo., IDEI, University of Toulouse.

Laffont, J.-J., and J. Tirole. 2000. *Competition in Telecommunications.* Cambridge, MA: MIT Press.

Laffont, J.-J., P. Rey, and J. Tirole. 1998. "Network Competition: I. Overview and Non-discriminatory Pricing." *Rand Journal of Economics* 29: 1–37.

Oftel. 2000. Oftel strategy statement. "Achieving the Best Deal for Telecoms Consumers." Available online at ⟨http://www.oftel.gov.uk/publications/about_oftel/strat100.htm⟩.

Peitz, M. 2001. "Asymmetric Access Price Regulation in Telecommunications Markets." Mimeo., University of Frankfurt.

Peitz, M. 2002. "On Access Pricing in Telecoms: Theory and European Practice." Mimeo., University of Frankfurt.

Perrucci, A., and M. Cimatoribus. 1997. "Competition, Convergence and Asymmetry in Telecommunications Regulation." *Telecommunications Policy* 21: 493–512.

5

Remarks on de Bijl and Peitz's "New Competition in Telecommunications Markets: Regulatory Pricing Principles"

Ingo Vogelsang

De Bijl and Peitz have written a clear paper that addresses three important subjects:

- The trade-off between entry competition and welfare
- The trade-off between price regulation and competition
- The effects of symmetric and asymmetric access price regulation

The analytical models and numerical simulations deal with competition between full coverage (integrated or local) network providers. The authors use a simple framework and get interesting results. In particular, asymmetric access price regulation, where the incumbent prices access at marginal costs while the entrant charges an extra markup, has beneficial effects on entry and the intensity of competition until the entrant has caught up with the incumbent. In contrast, price cap regulation on subscriptions, while benefiting consumers, can discourage entry. Thus, price cap regulation in this context could become a risky tool. How sensible are the assumptions leading to those results? How sensitive are the results to specific assumptions?

Crucial assumptions on demand are as follows:

- The perceived quality/reputation difference between incumbent and entrant depends on the passage of time only. This implies that consumer surplus per unit of sales by the entrant increases exogenously over time, so that at low interest rates the optimal policy would be to retard entry by a few years, until the quality difference has vanished. Experience dependent quality would be harder to model and would likely lead to penetration pricing.

- Consumer welfare is measured as consumer surplus. A problem of the quality/reputation assumption on welfare could be that the difference is only due to lack of information. Thus, actual subscribers of the entrant could experience the same surplus as subscribers of the incumbent. While I see no practical way to find out, this observation means that consumer surplus analysis is possibly biased against entry.

• Subscription utility is assumed to be independent of usage or the price of usage. This eliminates trade-offs between subscription and usage prices.

• The assumption of 100 percent market penetration means that net welfare effects from entry and competition can only come from cost reductions, subscriber heterogeneity, and increased usage. Moreover, truly cost-based subscription fees may vary between the extreme urban and rural areas by a ratio of 1:20 in Europe and 1:100 in the United States. It is hard to believe that penetration would stay constant along price differences that would reflect such large cost differences.

The main ingredients of costs are: fixed cost to run a network, customer-specific fixed cost, and variable costs consisting of costs for on-net calls, off-net calls, and incoming calls.

Liberalization leads to a welfare trade-off. The duplication of network-specific fixed costs and the initial quality disadvantage of the entrant are weighed against advantages from product differentiation and higher usage. Not captured are benefits from higher penetration.

The initial analytical model has fixed per-minute prices, not covering variable costs. Firms compete for consumers via subscription fees only. Thus, this is essentially a flat rate model. The result that access charges have no effect on market shares (Remark 2) seems to come from the fact that the effect of access charge changes on subscription fees is the same for both networks. The assumptions on demands are obviously such that the direct effects and cross-effects cancel each other (total demand stays put). Thus, although the access charge appears in the price formula for the subscription fees, it cancels out exactly in market shares. All other results in this model are related to this one. The question is whether this is a general property or whether it is dependent on very specific model assumptions, such as the linearity of the demand curve.

The simulation model with access price regulation only has a downstream usage price $P = MC$ as the equilibrium outcome. I wonder how general this result is and whether it depends on the utility of subscription being independent of the usage fee. The authors then concentrate on subscription fees, which converge over time, due to reduction in quality difference. Under reciprocal, cost-based access prices, welfare first declines then increases. Consumer surplus increases monotonically. Under asymmetric access price regulation the entrant's market share increases early, due to a sort of reciprocal calling effect (via symmetric calling patterns) that provides access revenues in addition to revenues from end users. So, entrants can make themselves whole from access charge revenues even if they price end users below costs. While consumer surplus and the entrant's profits are higher under asymmetric than under symmetric access regulation, the welfare differences are negligible.

In the last simulation model, price cap regulation for the incumbent's subscription fee (but not on the usage fee) improves consumer welfare but reduces incentive for entry. This comes from the perceived quality difference, which implies that the entrant has to be cheaper than the incumbent, in order to gain market share (or, in this model, wait until the quality difference goes away). The authors consider myopic decisions only. In a strategic setting, the question arises, Can low price caps prevent predation (if they are a credible commitment) and therefore help entry?

What do we know about demand and cost functions? The chapter uses a single set of cost parameters. Confidence in simulation results requires many runs with different parameter constellations to see if the results are robust. In particular, the current welfare results are extremely close. In my view, the interplay between the two types of fixed costs assumed by the authors would be interesting. Where do these two types of fixed costs appear in reality or in cost models? How do they change with the density of the network? For example, in a circular network there would be no fixed costs of connecting individual subscribers. In contrast, in a star network, there would be no common fixed costs.

In conclusion, the chapter comes up with interesting, provocative results that are worth further analysis of the underlying assumptions and parameter specifications.

6

The Interplay between Regulation and Competition: The Case of Universal Service Obligations

Steffen H. Hoernig and
Tommaso M. Valletti

6.1 Introduction

Regulators have long been aware of the social aspects of communication and have been intimately involved with the various services—telecommunications, post, broadcasting, and so forth—since their beginnings. Due to the widespread use of these services, many social dimensions must be covered by regulators. Initial "public interest" arguments meant that virtually all aspects could be regulated. For example, the 1927 Radio Act in the United States gave federal regulators the power to issue a licence to a broadcaster if they found that it was in the "public interest, convenience or necessity." The absence of any clear definition of "public interest" means that the Federal Communications Commission (FCC)—the U.S. regulator—could determine the number and identity of broadcasters, the terms and conditions of their operation, and even their broadcast content.

In this chapter we address some broader social aspects of communication regulation, as well as the competition issues that are raised by the adoption of particular policies. To give an example, the interplay between regulation and competition can be seen in the current "broadband debate." Higher bandwidth services, such as high-speed Internet service, video on demand, and interactive electronic commerce, have been deemed by many governments to be of fundamental importance to the development of their economy; see, for example, Oftel (1999). A particular concern is the provision of these services to residential customers and also to small businesses. This has highlighted the lack of competition in local telecommunications markets. In the United Kingdom, broadband services are likely, in the medium term, to be provided using enhancements (Digital Subscriber Line, or DSL) to the fixed copper loop telephone network; this sector is dominated by the incumbent British Telecom, which supplies over 85 percent of all access lines. In the United States, local access is provided both by cable and local telephone companies; the issue there is what carriage requirements to impose on entrants to the local access market. Finally, the content that can be delivered over high-bandwidth access lines has lead to regulatory initiatives such as the European Union's Action Plan on Promoting Safer Use of the Internet, adopted on January 25, 1999.

We do not attempt to cover all aspects of regulation in this chapter. Instead, we focus on the interaction between the two objectives stated by most telecoms regulators. For instance, the U.S. Telecommunications Act of 1996 directs the FCC to "promote competition and preserve and advance universal service."

6.2   Definition and Evidence

There are several reasons given for imposing universal service obligations (USOs). First, it is often thought that utilities such as electricity, water, and telecommunications services are necessities that should be readily available to all, simply on the grounds of equity. Second, this argument can be supplemented with the idea that complete access to essential services stimulates economic development and growth. Third, there may be significant positive externalities associated with a service (such as a communication network) that the market, left unregulated, would fail to incorporate, leading to insufficient coverage of the network. A USO may be required to correct for this market failure. For these and other arguments, see Cremer et al. (1998).[1]

Even if the general principles behind USOs are agreed upon, there still is the problem of putting them into practice. There are three aspects to this: (1) What exactly should be provided and to whom? (2) Who should be required to fulfil a USO? (3) Who should pay for the costs of a USO?

The exact definition of universal service is not clear. The most commonly used notion refers to achieving a "minimum quality level" of a "basic package" of services to all consumers and at "affordable prices." In the case of telecommunications, this sort of statement can be found in FCC and European Commission (EC) communications; see the FCC's CC Docket 96-45 and the EC communication COM(96) 73. Each part of this statement is open to interpretation—what is a minimum quality level, what constitutes a basic package, what prices are affordable? Hence the FCC has listed a set of services and quality levels that are included in universal service (e.g., voice-grade access to the public switched network, Touch-Tone, etc.), and detailed maximum prices that can be charged for specific services and on average across all services. This exercise is, of course, problematic. Technological progress means that the set of basic services is constantly expanding, and minimum quality levels are ambiguous (e.g., wireless services allow greater mobility, but typically have lower sound quality and completion rates).

In the past, incumbent telecom operators were responsible for USOs; indeed, in the United Kingdom, this is still the case.[2] In the United States, USOs are not restricted to incumbents, and universal service subsidies are paid to any company that accepts a commitment to service all consumers in its area. The subsidies are typically paid for by cross-subsidization: The income from more profitable markets (such as long-distance or business customers) is used to cover losses incurred by charging low prices to low-income or high-cost consumers. The alternative of financing universal service subsidies through general taxation is not generally used in telecommunications, although it is used in other markets; for example, in the United Kingdom, subsidies to winners of railroad franchises are covered from general taxes. This is despite the fact that financing from general taxation could be a cheaper (i.e., less distortionary) way to raise the required revenue.

USOs are under increasing pressure. The first source of pressure appears to be political, but actually has solid economics to back it up. A major problem with USOs is that they are blunt. A USO to cover high-cost rural areas at the same price as low-cost urban areas benefits high-income rural consumers at the expense of low-income urban consumers. More precisely, it may be inefficient to further a particular objective—higher welfare for rural residents—through distorting the prices of particular services. This point has been made formally by Atkinson and Stiglitz (1976), who show that, under certain circumstances, the best way to redistribute income is through the taxation of income, not consumption. In their model, consumers differ in their income levels (actually, in their ability levels, which affect income). Hence their result speaks most directly to the issue of subsidies to low-income consumers. It is straightforward, however, to reinterpret their model in terms of low- and high-cost consumers. One of the key conditions required for this result is that low- and high-income consumers have the same relative preferences for consumption goods (i.e., the marginal rate of substitution between consumption goods is independent of income). In this case, taxing consumption—effectively what occurs when the prices of telecommunications services are altered—in order to fund universal service is unnecessarily inefficient. A better way to redistribute income (which, after all, is what a universal service subsidy does) is to tax income. To encourage people to live in high-cost rural areas, the theorem suggests that a location-specific income tax break is better than offering a telecommunications subsidy.

Changes in the assumptions underlying the Atkinson-Stiglitz theorem will, evidently, change the result. For example, it may be that the marginal rate of substitution between consumption goods is not independent of income. Then it may be worth taxing those goods that the rich have a relative preference for and subsidizing the goods preferred (relatively) by the poor. Nevertheless, the result is important for emphasizing that USOs must be assessed carefully for their validity and not simply accepted.[3]

Abstracting now from theoretical motivations that may justify the imposition of USOs, how have they fared *in practice*? To answer this question, one needs to understand first why telephone penetration may be different in different areas. After surveying the existing empirical literature on the topic, Riordan (2002) summarizes that the major predictor of residential telephone penetration is poverty. In particular, an income redistribution that would lower the poverty rate of an area by 10 percent, while holding the median income constant, would add 2.5 percentage points to telephone penetration in the United States. Published research generally finds that the price elasticity of residential demand is very low—of the order of −0.02. This is a bit worrisome since the lack of responsiveness of demand could undermine both targeted and untargeted public programs that subsidize penetration. However, the price elasticity for low-income people is significantly higher, giving some support for universal service policies that target low-income households. There is also some (weaker) evidence that network externalities matter, justifying policies that may expand the reach of service beyond the level that would be chosen individually by people and to overcome a coordination problem when too few people connect if it is expected that too few people connect. Race also seems an important predictor in the United States. Asian populations are more likely, and black and Hispanic populations less likely, than white households to have telephones.[4]

It may be argued that network externalities should no longer be central to the debate on universal service for many "mature" services in developed countries, given that the level of penetration reached is already high. In addition, operators themselves may use pricing strategies to coordinate consumers, thus internalizing the network externality. These views are not immune to criticism. For instance, even if the marginal consumer confers a small externality, this has to be multiplied by a large number. For example, suppose that each individual gains a benefit of 1 from being able to communicate with any other individual; and suppose that there are N individuals on the network. Then the total value of the network is the number of pairings $N(N-1)$, which is close to N^2 when N is large. This square relationship between the number of members of a network and the value of the network is known as Metcalfe's law, and it still does provide a theoretical argument for universal service programs. However, it is clear that there are also limits to this kind of justification for subsidies. In particular, subsidies should be at the margin, and it is not necessary to subsidize the majority of infra-marginal customers that would be on the network without any inducement. It is perhaps fair to say that there is now a consensus that targeted programs fare better than uniform subsidies and that the latter are unlikely to improve average consumer welfare. There also seems to be room for the introduction of more optional tariffs for local services. A "menu" of contracts, designed with the needs of the poor and of the low-volume users in mind, could be designed at a low cost in order to induce more people to subscribe without having to subsidize the large majority of the population.

The FCC has recently established a program of subsidies for the highest cost wire centers in the highest cost states in the United States. The estimates obtained by the FCC for the average cost of local telephone services are used to calculate a "benchmark" that determines the eligibility of operators to receive universal service funds (subsidies are "portable"; namely, they are paid to whichever firm provides the service). The intention of the recent legislation is to move from implicit to explicit subsidies, while promoting the affordability of telephone service and access to the network. These are laudable goals but one should check the data to see whether the intentions are implemented in practice by federal and state programs. Rosston and Wimmer (2000) assess the costs and benefits of universal service programs at the state level, assuming that states provide subsidies to those areas with costs higher than the benchmark (net of federal subsidies). In order to evaluate the impact of different policies, one must have information about customers' responses to price changes, something that is completely ignored by regulations purely based on costs.

Since—as we wrote before—demand for access is typically inelastic (some people may actually be driven off the network by usage-related charges rather than access charges), they find that the current system in the United States has the unfortunate effect of requiring huge amounts of money while producing small effects on subscription rates. There are important differences among states, but the results of Rosston and Wimmer challenge the myth of affordability in a developed country by showing that the elimination of subsidies would only have a mild impact on the size of the network. If the current programs fail with respect to subscribership, their magnitude could still be justified by horizontal equity considerations. Rosston and Wimmer show how they fail in this respect too: Winners may be rich households living in rural areas, while losers in urban areas include a disproportionate percentage of poor, black, and Hispanic households. Also in this case, targeted programs are cheaper and perform better than cost-based rules that pay a subsidy to all consumers in an area, whether they need the subsidy or not. However, targeted programs themselves may still be wasteful. Some authors believe there is no need to continue either type of subsidy, since the impact on telephone penetration is negligible.[5] The main reason for keeping such programs in place—they would argue—is then to redistribute income and/or to use them for political reasons given the rents at stake.

6.3   Universal Service in the European Union

The current European Union (EU) regulatory framework requires national regulatory authorities (NRAs) to impose obligations to ensure that a defined minimum set of services of specified quality are available to all, regardless of their geographical location, and at an affordable price, where affordability must be seen in the context of the national situation. There are also obligations to provide pay phones to cover reasonable needs, and directory services. In addition, there are provisions for specific measures for disabled users and users with special needs. A member state may impose these obligations on one or more operators.

Despite the natural rhetoric in claiming that the objective is to give EU citizens a world-class communications infrastructure, delivering the best deal in terms of prices, quality, and so forth, the EU has left the actual implementation of its recommendations to Member States. Originally, the EC tried a more proactive role, suggesting the creation of some specific funds, one per Member State, that would control the use of EU structural funds for regional development projects. These projects could be targeted at those countries that were greatly in need of basic infrastructure. While these plans are indeed still a possibility, they have not been adopted for universal service provision, highlighting the lack of authority on the EU telecommunications industry. Hence the details of USOs are entirely left to NRAs. On the other hand, the EU does regulate how a Member State may design a universal service fund. Only simple public switched telephony services, which include voice, fax, and data transmission, may be funded. Providers of Internet services, value-added services, and private networks are exempted from contributing to USOs. Finally, there are two funding options. The first is to levy supplementary charges on top of regular interconnection charges, and the second is to create a universal service fund. The EC has clearly stated that it prefers the latter option, whereby the universal service cost is paid either out of the state budget, by eligible market participants, or by end users though a tax.

We cannot review here all the single national experiences. However, it is important to stress three points: (1) historically, USOs have been intertwined with the liberalization process occurring within a given country; (2) the stance that a given country decided to take with respect to USOs reflected the general national philosophy toward the importance of competition in the telecommunications industry; and (3) where USO costs have been calculated (but not necessarily funded), the best practice consisted in the calculation of net avoidable costs based on Long Run Incremental Cost (LRIC), which is good accounting practice but does not necessarily reflect economic principles. In practice, this has led most countries not to implement any funding because the universal service costs were deemed to be too small. As we argue in what follows, different reasons were behind this outcome.

To give a few examples, quite a lot of confusion arose in the early days on the links between access deficit contributions (ADCs) and USOs. This was due to different stages in the price rebalancing process accompanying liberalization. For instance, we have already mentioned that the United Kingdom decided that the costs incurred by British Telecom (BT) for USOs did not justify any payment. That was due to the small figures involved (gross costs of around £50–70m in 1999, less than 0.3 percent of telecommunications turnover). Price rebalancing in the United Kingdom started back in 1984 with the privatization of BT; hence when the discussion of USOs became central in the late 1990s, line rental rates had already been increased close to their relative costs. Since BT also received direct revenues from universal service, on top of some indirect benefits, the regulator decided that USOs did not represent an unjust burden and did not require any funding (the NRA will review this decision in 2003). Finland, which has a well-developed telecommunications infrastructure, does not even have an explicit definition of USO in its legislation.

On the other hand, in France the regulator calculated figures much higher than in the United Kingdom (FF 5,000–6,000m in 1997 and 1998—around 4% of telecommunications turnover) that did include the lack of rebalancing (hence the loss made on access by France Telecom), requiring other operators to pay a surcharge in their interconnection charge. Only in 2000 France introduced a new mechanism entirely based on a universal service fund, where all the operators must contribute according to their volumes of traffic. This case reflects a preference for a sort of protection of the incumbent operator that, according to the French view, would ensure that the country would receive essential services. On the other hand, entrants have to bear some of the costs, making USOs a potential barrier to entry.

Italy started with a tariff structure much closer to that of France than to that of the UK. Telecom Italia calculated big access deficits (decreasing from lira 5,500 billion in 1997, to 4,100 in 1998, to 3,300 in 1999) on top of USOs (lira 650 billion in 1999, 390 in 2000). However, the NRA systematically challenged the figures put forth by the incumbent, cutting them down to considerably lower levels (USOs: lira 120 billion in 1999, 114 in 2000), which then had to be funded by fixed and mobile operators, proportionally to their revenues. The Italian regulator is now considering the introduction of "pay-or-play" mechanisms where USOs may be fulfilled by various operators.

In Germany no operator a priori has USO, but they can be imposed in specific markets if it is acknowledged that they are underprovided, or if the incumbent operator Deutsche Telekom AG (DTAG) decides to change its terms or range of providing universal service. In this case, DTAG is obliged to give one year's advance notice, so that the regulator has enough time to intervene.

A particular area of concern is universal service in telecommunications for the thirteen countries that are in the process of negotiating accession to the EU. Most accession countries have implemented universal service policies because of their commitment to transpose the acquis communautaire. This may be worrying because it is not clear if universal service policies that are valid in EU (rich) countries with fully developed networks should be replicated on a similar scale in (middle- and lower-middle-income) accession countries. According to a recent study commissioned by the EC (WIK 2001), these policies would be too costly given the other pressing needs for tax revenues such as for health care, education, or pensions.

The WIK study recommends focusing instead on addressing USO problems with market-based solutions, with modest schemes being added incrementally to market outcomes. For instance, they recommend targeted schemes, tariff rebalancing, and deaveraging of tariffs. The latter, in particular, can help overcome the reluctance of operators to build networks and add subscribers in high-cost rural areas. Another problem of accession countries is that they may not even have the appropriate institutional endowment to handle the level of detail and intervention that is required to administer USO programs. EU law should then not require these countries to adopt measures that are beyond their present economic means.

6.4   USOs and Competition

A major challenge facing USOs comes from the introduction of competition. Telecommunications markets in many countries have been opened up to competition. In the United States, the breakup of AT&T in 1984 allowed competition in previously monopolized markets. In the United Kingdom, the first competitor to the previously nationalized BT was licensed in 1982; in 1991, the market was opened further and several new operators were licensed. In both cases, the idea was to use competitive forces to assist in the regulation of dominant operators. But this has consequences for the financing of USOs. USOs are supported by cross-subsidization. This cross-subsidization is sustainable while a single firm operates across the various markets, as was the case in the United States and in the United Kingdom until the early 1980s. But when a second firm is able to operate, it will choose to enter the more profitable markets (precisely the ones that generate the cross-subsidy)—a process known as cream skimming. This has three implications that we address in turn. First, the distortions in prices that the USO requires can lead to inefficient entry. Second, the subsidy required to support the USO is higher than what it would be if entry could not occur. Since financing the USO is distortionary, this means that the social cost of the USO is higher. Finally, USOs that come in the form of a uniform pricing requirement have strategic effects that need to be recognized by regulators. Notable examples of such strategic effects are coverage decisions and auctions for minimum subsidies required to supply a high-cost region.

6.4.1 Entry

The point on the possibility of inefficient entry is most clearly seen in a single market case. (The following example is taken from Armstrong (2001).) Suppose that there is a single group of consumers with inelastic unit demand for telecommunications service. The incumbent can provide this service at cost C per consumer, giving each consumer gross utility U. The price that the incumbent charges is mandated to be P per consumer; if the consumers belong to a high-cost market, then typically $P < C$. An entrant can provide the same service at cost c, giving gross utility of u; it charges a price p, where p is not restricted (since the USO is imposed only on the incumbent).

Social welfare is the sum of consumer surplus and firms' profits; so welfare when the incumbent serves the market is $(U - P) + (P - C) = U - C$, and when the entrant serves the market, it is $u - c$. Hence entry is socially desirable if and only if $u - c \geq U - C$, namely, if $C \geq c + U - u$. Given the incumbent's price, the entrant can attract consumers if its price satisfies $u - p \geq U - P$, that is, if $P - U + u \geq p$. Entry will occur whenever the maximum price that the entrant can charge covers its cost, that is, when $P - U + u \geq c$, or $P \geq c + U - u$. Comparing this with the socially optimal condition for entry, we see that whenever P does not equal C (which is typically the case when USOs are involved), entry occurs inefficiently. When $P > c + U - u > C$, entry occurs when it is socially undesirable. When $P < c + U - u < C$, entry does not occur, even though it is socially desirable.

A well-designed universal service fund could be instrumental in order to align the private with the social incentives. To see this, imagine an output tax $t = P - C$ has to be paid into an industry fund when supplying the areas in question. Then the entrant would indeed enter only when it is socially efficient. Notice that the tax corresponds to the opportunity cost of the incumbent when it loses a customer after entry has occurred. In practice, operators should pay into the fund when they enter a profitable market $(P > C)$ and receive a subsidy from the fund when they serve otherwise loss-making areas. This argument can be extended to incorporate access pricing. Armstrong (2001) shows that a variant of the Efficient Component Pricing Rule would be efficient, charging access at cost so long as an output tax calculated along the lines shown earlier is also in place. The general moral that emerges is that when there are retail distortions due to a USO, a retail instrument should be used in combination with an appropriate access charge. Use of the access charge alone both to provide the right entry incentives and to correct the retail distortion is inferior.

6.4.2 Subsidies

We now turn to the second type of interaction that USOs and competition might produce. When consumers are heterogeneous, with some being high-cost and others low-cost, a USO subsidy set without regard to competition will be "too" low. Imagine, for the sake of the argument, that there are x customers in an urban area, with unit cost equal to 1, and $(1 - x)$ customers in a rural area where it costs 2 to supply each one of them. Also imagine that at first there is only one regulated monopoly firm and that the regulator chooses a "bracketed" uniform price $1 < p < 2$ for all the customers, due to the typical requirement of average geographic price uniformity. In order not to make losses, the monopolist supplier will have to be paid a subsidy per customer equal to the difference between the average cost and the uniform price, that is, $s = (2 - x) - p$.

Consider now what happens if there is potential entry. The previous situation would not be sustainable due to cream skimming. If the potential entrant is an operator not subject to universal service requirements (and not eligible to any subsidy), it could target the customers in the urban area only. Also imagine now the incumbent is not subject anymore to a geographic averaging requirement (more on this later); however, it still has to charge at most the previous price p to all customers. Potential competition then brings the price in the urban area down to its cost, namely, 1. In equilibrium, urban customers would still be supplied by the incumbent since it would still get a subsidy s' per customer while the entrant is not eligible. It is then straightforward to calculate the subsidy that is now needed for the incumbent to break even: $s' = (2 - p)(1 - x)$. The result is that the new subsidy per customer has to be higher than before: $s' - s = x(p - 1) > 0$. The reason is simple. The "old" subsidy assumes that the operator can earn excess profits from low-cost consumers that can be used to finance service to high-cost consumers. Competition eliminates these profits, and so increases the required subsidy (see Laffont and Tirole (2000), for further elaboration on this).

6.4.2.1 Multimarket Oligopolies and Coverage

The third interesting implication arises precisely from the geographic averaging requirement that the regulator often still imposes even in a competitive environment and that we neglected earlier. The effects from these obligations have been studies by Anton, Vander Weide, and Vettas (2002), Choné, Flochel, and Perrot (2000) and Valletti, Hoernig, and Barros (2002). These authors show that a USO affects the way in which operators compete. In particular, a uniform pricing restriction creates linkages between markets, along the lines identified in Bulow, Geanakoplos, and Klemperer (1985). This makes operators less aggressive in those markets, leading to higher equilibrium prices and deadweight loss.

Following Valletti, Hoernig, and Barros (2002), we assume that there is a continuous set $[0, x^{max}]$ of a priori independent markets, ordered by the fixed cost of serving them—from the cheapest to the most expensive—but identical in terms of the population served. In a first step we assume that an incumbent firm and an entrant have decided to cover the areas $[0, x_1]$ and $[0, x_2]$, respectively, with $x_2 < x_1$. For simplicity we assume zero marginal cost and that firms compete in quantity competition with linear demand functions $P = 1 - Q$, similar to Anton, Vander Weide, and Vettas (2002), while Choné, Flochel, and Perrot (2000) and Valletti, Hoernig, and Barros (2002) treat the arguably more realistic case of price competition. Under positive marginal cost, or price competition with sufficiently differentiated goods, the results are qualitatively the same. If no uniform pricing constraint is imposed, and in the absence of other price regulation,[6] it is clear that the equilibrium in each market is determined independently, with $P^C = 1/3$, the Cournot equilibrium price, in the duopoly area $[0, x_2]$, and $P^M = 1/2$, the monopoly price, in the monopoly region $[x_2, x_1]$.

A uniform pricing constraint imposed on the incumbent makes this kind of discriminatory pricing impossible, but more important creates two opposing incentives in all markets that link them strategically: The incumbent would wish to set a high price to cash in on his captive consumers, while competing effectively in the duopoly area. This leaves the incumbent at a strategic disadvantage in the duopoly markets, benefiting the entrant.

With quantity competition, a uniform pricing constraint can be interpreted as the constraint to not charge a higher price in the monopoly markets than in the duopoly markets, which is equivalent to requiring that in these markets the incumbent sell a quantity equal to the sum of quantities in the duopoly markets. Incumbent and entrant solve as follows:

Incumbent: $max_{q_1}\ q_1(1 - q_1 - q_2)x_2 + (q_1 + q_2)(1 - q_1 - q_2)(x_1 - x_2)$

Entrant: $max_{q_2}\ q_2(1 - q_1 - q_2)x_2$

While the entrant's best response $q_2 = 1/2 - q_1/2$ is the usual Cournot best response, the incumbent's best response is $q_1 = 1/2 - (1 - x_2/2x_1)q_2$. It depends on *relative coverage* $k = x_2/x_1$, and therefore also the ensuing equilibrium will do so. The result is *price bracketing*, with the equilibrium price $P^{UP} = 1/(2 + k)$ between the Cournot and monopoly prices, $P^C < P^{UP} < P^M$. For $k = 0$ we obtain $P^{UP} = P^M$, and for $k = 1$, $P^{UP} = P^C$. A lower relative coverage k turns the incumbent's reaction function downward and leads to lower equilibrium total quantity $Q = (1 + k)/(2 + k)$ and a higher equilibrium price P^{UP}. This means that the lower prices created by competition that were supposed to be distributed everywhere through the uniform pricing constraint may hardly materialize if the relative coverage of the entrant remains small.

This effect is compounded if the incumbent is required to cover the whole country $[0, x^{max}]$, and the entrant can freely choose its coverage. Valletti, Hoernig, and Barros (2002) show that the larger the mandated coverage of the incumbent, the larger the equilibrium coverage of the entrant will be, but this increase in coverage is less than proportional: *relative* coverage decreases. This means that through the strategic effect prices will rise as mandated coverage is increased even though the competitive position of the entrant is effectively strengthened. As a result, the entrant and newly served customers are the ones who gain from a higher mandated coverage, while previous customers may lose out. The welfare of the latter decreases because they face higher prices, unless strong network effects compensate for the price increase.

If firms compete in prices instead of quantities, some additional effects may arise if the services offered are close substitutes: Valletti,

Hoernig, and Barros (2002) have shown that in this case the incumbent has a strong incentive to lower the intensity of competition with the entrant. One instrument to achieve this is (strategic) quality degradation, where the incumbent deliberately offers lower quality to some customers. If these consumers are then more likely to buy from the entrant, in this way competition is effectively restricted to a smaller set of customers, while the incumbent on the surface still offers his services to all of them. For close substitutes, the resulting rise in the equilibrium uniform price more than compensates for the loss in customers and leads to higher profits for both firms, while consumer welfare decreases.

6.4.2.2 Multimarket Oligopolies and Auctions for Subsidies

The tension between universal service and competition represents a considerable challenge for regulators. A promising line of research to resolve this tension is the use of universal service auctions, in which operators bid for a level of subsidy (competition for the market), with the market structure after the auction determined by the bids in the auction (competition in the market).

Anton, Vander Weide, and Vettas (2002) have analyzed this question in a framework of two markets. Let us call $[0, x_2]$ the (profitable) urban market, and $(x_2, x^{max}]$ the (loss-making) rural market (now $k = x_2 / x^{max}$). Starting from two firms serving only the urban market, how high will the subsidy be that is necessary to auction off the obligation to serve the rural market, in the presence of a uniform pricing constraint? In this initial situation, firms play the Cournot equilibrium, with equilibrium price $P^C = 1/3$ and profits $\pi_C = x_2/9$ (gross of fixed cost). From a nonstrategic point of view, the subsidy should be equal to the losses generated by serving the rural market, subject to the restrictions imposed on pricing in this market, that is, $s = F - \pi_r > 0$, where π_r are rural profits, and F is the fixed cost of serving the rural market, assumed to be larger than even the monopoly profits.

The strategic effect discussed earlier weakens the competitive position in the *urban* market of the firm serving both markets, resulting in lower urban profits for this firm, and higher profits for the other firm. Therefore the firm that takes on the USO must be reimbursed not only for the costs of serving the rural market, but also for the lower profits it will make in the urban market. Furthermore, the auction must solve the "free rider" problem caused by the increase in profits of the firm that continues to serve only the urban market: Each firm would like the other one to win the auction unless the subsidy is high enough. If ex post urban profits under uniform pricing are $\pi_u = x_2/(2+k)^2 > \pi_c$, and the profits of the firm serving both markets are $\pi_{ur} = x_1/(2+k)^2 - F < \pi_c$, the subsidy must be such that both firms are indifferent between winning the auction or not, $s' = \pi_u - \pi_{ur}$, which leaves them with profits $\pi_u > \pi_c$. The need to take into account the strategic effect of serving both markets under a uniform pricing constraint may thus raise the subsidy substantially, and even may leave both firms with higher profits than if they were just serving the urban market.

The mere *process* of the determination of the value of subsidies can have important strategic implications if a uniform pricing constraint is imposed. Returning to the previous model, assume that the incumbent firm has mandated coverage $[0, x^{max}]$ and makes losses in the markets with the highest fixed cost. If the subsidy required to cover these losses is calculated with respect to the price level and coverage without subsidy, and paid as a lump sum, there are no strategic effects. If on the other hand the regulator or government incur a *commitment* to cover any losses that are made in the high-cost markets, without fixing the amount *ex ante*, the result is that the incumbent will be a more aggressive competitor. In the extreme case where the subsidy completely covers all losses in the high-cost markets, these markets disappear from the incumbent's objective function, and in terms of payoffs he is in the same situation he would be in if he could freely choose his coverage. Valletti, Hoernig, and Barros (2002) have shown that when both entrant and incumbent can choose coverage, the entrant's equilibrium coverage and prices are lower. This means that the incumbent makes losses in many more markets than previously, and therefore the benefit of lower prices is contrasted with a possibly substantially higher subsidy and a smaller coverage by the entrant. This result differs from that of Anton, Vander Weide, and Vettas in that the subsidy itself has strategic effects because it effectively liberates the incumbent from the mandated coverage constraint and its strategic implications.

6.5 Conclusions

We conclude by summarizing the most important problems related to USOs:

• USOs are justified on efficiency grounds while it is debatable if they are also called for on equity grounds, since there may be better tools to achieve redistribution.

• On the efficiency side, there is a sound theoretical argument for universal service programs. These can reduce the risk that customers may not subscribe to a network since they do not take into account the benefit they confer on existing users. Even if the marginal consumer confers a small externality, this has to be multiplied by large numbers.

• However, it has to be clear that there are also limits to this kind of justification for subsidies. In particular, subsidies should be *at the margin* and it is not necessary to subsidize the majority of infra-marginal customers that would be on the network without any inducement. In this respect, targeted programs fare much better than uniform subsidies. There also seems to be room for the introduction of more optional tariffs for local services. A "menu" of contracts, designed with the needs of the poor and the low users in mind, could be designed at a low cost in order to induce more people to subscribe without having to subsidize the large majority of the population.

• There is no reason to subsidize or maintain artificially distorted tariff structures in the belief that this is the only way to increase the subscriber base. As mentioned earlier, affordability should be interpreted as affordability among an incremental group of users who are considering taking up or dropping the service.

• Regulators should play carefully with USOs since they tend to be used by market players to extract too many concessions.

• Recent research has also shown that USOs have important strategic implications and affect the way firms compete against one another.

• Countries should distinguish clearly between universal availability and universal service guarantees. The former is promoted by encouraging investments and removing entry barriers. Only the latter should be explicitly linked to possible costing and financing requirements.

• The approach should be technologically neutral, enabling wireline and wireless technologies to be used to provide services. It is important to maintain incentives for competing networks and/or technologies to provide (part of) the universal service provisions.

• There are benefits from using auctions to assign USOs since the regulator does not need to calculate net costing. There are also problems. It may be difficult to have sufficient participants bidding against the incumbent (in many cases, entrants would need to use alternative infrastructure or acquire the use of the incumbent's assets). Another reason is the asymmetry of information between the incumbents and new entrants, for example, concerning the costs and benefits of serving groups of customers.

• If an auction is not feasible for these reasons, then the regulator must calculate the net cost and then proceed to financing requirements.

• Financing these costs imposes distortions, and regulators should try to minimize losses of allocative efficiency. The least distortionary way to finance net costs is probably from the government central budgets. Alternatively, funding should be recovered within the sector, raising a tax from the broadest possible base, in order to minimize the impact of the financial burden falling on end users. The answer to this depends to a great extent on the efficiency of the tax system.

Notes

1. See also Laffont and Tirole (2000, chap. 6); Mason and Valletti (2001); and Riordan (2002) for further discussions of universal service in telecommunications.

2. In the United Kingdom, British Telecom (BT) is restricted to charging geographically uniform prices to ensure that high-cost (e.g., rural) areas are serviced. The regulator—Oftel—first decided that USO costs be funded by all operators, on the basis of indicators like revenue shares. However, the limited size of the burden subsequently convinced the regulator in 1997 that there was no need to establish a fund because USOs gave BT some benefits that outweighed the direct costs (benefits included rather cloudy concepts such as brand enhancement, ubiquity, and "life-cycle" effects, where an uneconomic customer can become a more profitable BT customer in the future). In any case, the idea of a fund has not been dismissed and may become relevant in the future.

3. The idea that it is more efficient to finance USOs from general taxation has to be assessed against the efficiency of the taxation system of the country under consideration. This may make the "old" system of financing that relies on cross-subsidies still an attractive solution in developing countries, if the social cost of public funds is high or if there is some leakage of tax revenues due, for instance, to corruption. See Gasmi, Laffont, and Sharkey (2000).

4. See also Taylor (1994).

5. There are some studies on the impact that some specific programs (Lifeline and Link-Up) have had in the United States in recent years. Such programs reduce the monthly cost of the telephone service of low-income households and subsidize the installation of a new subscription for eligible households. The evidence is mildly in favor of them as an effective way of promoting universal service. See Garbacz and Thompson (2001) and Riordan (2002) for a discussion.

6. Qualitatively similar results are obtained in the presence of a price cap.

References

Anton, J. J., J. H. Vander Weide, and N. Vettas. 2002. "Entry Auctions and Strategic Behavior under Cross-Market Price Constraints." *International Journal of Industrial Organization* 20(5): 611–629.

Armstrong, M. 2001. "Access Pricing, Bypass and Universal Service." *American Economic Review Papers and Proceedings* 91: 297–301.

Atkinson, A. B., and J. Stiglitz. 1976. "The Design of Tax Structure: Direct and Indirect Taxation." *Journal of Public Economics* 6: 55–75.

Bulow, J., J. Geanakoplos, and P. D. Klemperer. 1985. "Multimarket Oligopoly: Strategic Substitutes and Complements." *Journal of Political Economy* 93: 488–511.

Choné, P., L. Flochel, and A. Perrot. 2000. "Universal Service Obligations and Competition." *Information Economics and Policy* 12(3): 249–259.

Cremer, H., F. Gasmi, A. Grimaud, and J.-J. Laffont. 1998. "The Economics of Universal Service: Theory." Economic Development Institute Discussion Paper. The World Bank, Washington, DC.

Garbacz, C., and H. G. Thompson. 2001. "A New, Improved Telephone Demand Model." Mimeo.

Gasmi, F., J.-J. Laffont, and W. Sharkey. 2000. "Competition, Universal Service and Telecommunications Policy in Developing Countries." *Information Economics and Policy* 12(3): 221–248.

Laffont, J.-J., and J. Tirole. 2000. "Competition in Telecommunications." Cambridge, MA: The MIT Press.

Mason, R., and T. M. Valletti. 2001. "Competition in Communication Networks: Pricing and Regulation." *Oxford Review of Economic Policy* 17(3): 389–415.

Oftel. 1999. "Access to Bandwidth: Proposals for Action." Consultation document issued by the Director General of Telecommunications, London.

Riordan, M. 2002. "Universal Residential Telephone Service." In M. Cave, S. Majumdar, and I. Vogelsang, eds., *Handbook of Telecommunications Economics*, chap. 10. Amsterdam: Elsevier Science.

Rosston, G. L., and B. S. Wimmer. 2000. "The 'State' of Universal Service." *Information Economics and Policy* 12: 261–283.

Taylor, L. 1994. *Telecommunications Demand in Theory and Practice*. Dordrecht: Kluwer Academic Publisher.

Valletti, T. M., S. H. Hoernig, and P. P. Barros. 2002. "Universal Service and Entry: The Role of Uniform Pricing and Coverage Constraints." *Journal of Regulatory Economics* 21(2): 169–190.

WIK. 2001. "Universal Service in the Accession Countries." A study produced for the European Commission.

II

European Spectrum Auctions: A British Success Story and Continental Failures?

7

How (Not) to Run Auctions: The European 3G Telecom Auctions

Paul Klemperer

7.1 Introduction

The 2000–2001 European auctions of "third generation" (3G) mobile telecommunication (or UMTS) licenses were some of the largest in history.

But table 7.1 shows that although the auctions cumulatively raised over $100 billion (or over 1.5% of GDP) there was enormous variation between countries.[1] This chapter discusses why.

The blocks of spectrum sold were very similar in the different countries, and most analysts assumed a roughly constant per capita value across Western Europe. Smaller countries were said to be worth a little less, centrally located countries were worth a little more (because of the possibilities of expansion to neighbors, and cost savings from sharing fixed costs with them), and richer countries were, of course, worth more.[2] So the last two effects favour Switzerland, for example, and none of this can explain much of the discrepancies in prices.

The dates of the auctions mattered more, since market sentiment toward 3G cooled dramatically over the period of the auctions. For example, analysts' estimates of the proceeds from the Swiss auction fell from as high as 1,000 euros per-capita after the U.K. auction was held to 400–600 euros per capita in the week before the Swiss auction was due to begin—but this was still a very far cry from the actual outcome of 20, as was underlined by the enthusiasm with which the lucky winners greeted the Swiss result.

Probably the bidders' valuations of the licenses at the dates of the auctions should have implied proceeds above 300 euros per capita in all the year 2000 auctions (see section 7.5). The lower revenues in the

Reprinted from *European Economic Review* 46, no. 4–5 (2002): 829–845.

Table 7.1
Revenues from European 3G Mobile Spectrum Auctions, euros per capita

Year 2000		Year 2001	
Austria	100	Belgium	45
Germany	615	Denmark	95
Italy	240	Greece	45
Netherlands	170		
Switzerland	20		
United Kingdom	650		

year 2001 auctions can be explained by changed valuations (and Denmark should be counted a success). But much of the variation in the year 2000 outcomes is due to flawed auction designs.

7.2   What Really Matters in Auction Design?

Good auction design is really good undergraduate industrial organisation; the two issues that really matter are attracting entry and preventing collusion.[3]

An important consequence is that choosing an *ascending auction*[4] is often a mistake for an auctioneer. Ascending auctions allow bidders to use the early rounds to signal to each other how they might "collusively" divide the spoils, and, if necessary, use later rounds to punish any rivals who fail to cooperate. Ascending auctions can also deter entry into the bidding since a weaker potential bidder knows that a stronger bidder can always rebid to top any bid he makes.

By contrast, a (first-price) *sealed-bid auction*[5] provides no opportunity for either signaling or punishment to support collusion. Furthermore, entry is promoted because a weaker bidder knows he has a better chance of victory. (A stronger bidder doesn't know how much he needs to bid to win, and doesn't want to bid too much because he wants to make a good profit when he does win, so the weaker bidder might win at a price that the stronger bidder would have been willing to bid, but didn't.)

Of course, sealed-bid auctions are not perfect either. The biggest disadvantage of the sealed-bid auction is the flip side of one of its advantages—because it allows bidders with lower values to sometimes beat opponents with higher values (and so encourages entry) it is more likely to lead to inefficient outcomes than is an ascending auction.[6] So an auction's design must be tailored both to its environment and to the designer's objectives.[7] Auction design is not "one size fits all."

Klemperer (2000a) provided a detailed development of these arguments. The European 3G auctions subsequently illustrated their validity.[8]

7.3   The Year 2000 Simple Ascending Auctions: The United Kingdom, Netherlands, Italy, and Switzerland

7.3.1   The UK Auction (March–April 2000)[9]

The United Kingdom ran the world's first 3G auction. It originally planned to sell just four licenses. The problem we faced was that there were also exactly four incumbent "2G" (second generation) mobile-phone operators who had the advantages over any other bidders of existing 2G brand names and customer bases to exploit, and lower costs of building 3G networks (because of the ability to piggyback on their 2G infrastructure). We were therefore very concerned that an ascending auction might deter other firms from bidding strongly, or even from entering the auction at all. So the government planned to run a hybrid of the ascending ("English") and sealed-bid ("Dutch") auctions, what we called an "Anglo-Dutch" auction. An ascending auction would have continued until just five bidders remained, after which the five survivors would have made sealed-bids (required to be no lower than the current price level) for the four licenses.[10] The idea was that the sealed-bid stage would induce some uncertainty about which four of the five "finalists" would win, and entrants would be attracted by the knowledge that they had a chance to make it to the final stage. So the sealed-bid stage would attract entry and so also raise revenue, while the ascending stage would mean less loss of efficiency than might result from a pure sealed-bid auction. The sealed-bid stage would also make collusion harder (Klemperer 2000a, 2002a). The design performed extremely well in laboratory experiments.

However, when it became possible to sell five licenses, a straightforward ascending auction made more sense. Because no bidder was permitted to win more than one license and licenses could not be divided, there was no simple way to share the spoils, so "tacit" collusion would be hard. Even more important, the fact that at least one license had to go to a new entrant was a sufficient carrot to attract new entrants. In this respect, it was also crucial that the United Kingdom was the first in the world to auction the 3G spectrum so that it was very unclear which new entrant(s) might be successful, and this made it possible to persuade a large number to play the game (see section 7.7). Going to market first was a deliberate strategy of the U.K. auction team,[11] and the fact that planning had begun in 1997 for a 2000 auction also meant that there was time for a sustained (and very successful) marketing campaign to attract entrants.

So the problems of collusion and entry deterrence that section 7.2 emphasized were minimal in the U.K. context, and efficiency considerations pointed toward an ascending design.[12]

Therefore a version of an ascending auction was actually used and was widely judged a success; nine new entrants bid strongly against the incumbents, creating intense competition and record-breaking revenues of 39 billion euros. For a full account of the auction process, see Binmore and Klemperer (2002).

7.3.2 The Netherlands Auction (July 2000)

The Netherlands' blunder was to follow the actual British design when it had five incumbent operators and five licenses. The equal numbers of incumbents and licenses created exactly the situation in which it could be predicted that very few entrants would bother to show up to an ascending auction. Indeed Klemperer (2000a), quoted in the Dutch press prior to the auction, and Maasland (2000) did predict exactly this.

Recognizing their weak positions, the strongest potential new entrants made deals with incumbents, and Netherlands competition policy was as dysfunctional as its auction design, allowing firms such as Deutsche Telekom AG (DTAG), DoCoMo, and Hutchison, who were all strong established players in other markets than the Netherlands, to partner with the local incumbents.[13]

In the end just one weak entrant (Versatel) competed with the incumbents and stopped bidding after receiving a letter from an incumbent (Telfort) threatening legal action for damages if Versatel continued to bid.[14] Although Versatel complained to the government, the government took no action, perhaps because excluding Telfort would have ended the auction immediately, and it might have been hard to impose a meaningful fine. (Hundreds of millions or even billions of euros would have been required.) The result was that the auction raised less than 3 billion euros rather than the almost 10 billion euros the Dutch government had forecast based on the U.K. experience.[15]

A version of the Anglo-Dutch design would surely have worked better. There are reasons to believe Versatel would have bid higher in the sealed-bid stage than the price at which it quit the ascending auction. And of course the fear of this would have made the incumbents bid higher. Furthermore, the sealed-bid stage would have given weaker bidders a chance (a "hope and dream," in the words of one frustrated potential entrant), which might have attracted more bidders and discouraged the joint bidding. Most likely the incumbents would still have been the winners, but the revenues would have been much closer to the U.K. levels that the government had predicted.

Six months later the Dutch parliament began an investigation into the entire auction process.

7.3.3   The Italian Auction (October 2000)

The Italian government thought it had learned from the Netherlands fiasco. It also chose roughly the U.K. design, with the additional rule that if there were not more "serious" bidders (as tested by various pre-qualification conditions) than licenses, then the number of licenses could (and probably would) be reduced. At first glance this seemed a clever way to avoid an embarrassingly uncompetitive auction à la the Netherlands, but (as I and others argued) the plan was badly flawed. It would be "putting the cart before the horse" to withdraw a license and so create an unnecessarily concentrated mobile phone market just in order to make an auction look good. And the Netherlands auction had anyway made it clear that guaranteeing just one more bidder than license does not guarantee that an ascending auction will be competitive!

By the time of the Italian sale the situation was dramatically different from the one the United Kingdom had faced. Most important, firms had learned from the earlier auctions who were the strongest bidders, and hence the likely winners, at least in an ascending auction. So weak bidders would not show up or would bid jointly in such an auction (see section 7.7), and the number of entrants would be much lower than the thirteen who had entered the U.K. auction.[16] Furthermore, an ascending auction makes collusive or predatory behavior much easier if the number of contestants is low (Klemperer 2000a, 2002b). An ascending auction was therefore a much riskier proposition than for the United Kingdom.

In the event only six bidders entered the auction to compete for five licenses and one (Blu) then quit after less than two days of bidding and only just above the reserve price.[17] Although this price was not as absurdly low as in some other countries, it still did not seem to have been set using the information from the U.K. and German auctions. So the result was per capita revenues below 40 percent of the U.K. level, or less than 14 billion euros instead of the more than 25 billion euros that the government had estimated.

While the precise nature of the Italian disaster could not have been predicted, it was clear in advance that the design was not robust. Although the reasons why attracting entry was hard were a little different from the Netherlands, the implication was the same—a sealed-bid or Anglo-Dutch design would have performed better.[18]

7.3.4 The Swiss Auction (November–December 2000)

Switzerland again copied the U.K. design and achieved the most embarrassing result of all. The Swiss ran an ascending auction for four licenses and attracted considerable initial interest from potential bidders. But just as in Italy weaker bidders were put off by the auction form—at least one company hired bidding consultants and then gave up after learning that the ascending-bidding rules would give the company very little chance against stronger rivals. And the government permitted last-minute joint-bidding agreements—essentially officially sanctioned collusion—so the field shrank from nine bidders to just four (!) in the week before the auction was due to begin. Unfortunately the reserve price had been set ludicrously low given the information available from the preceding European 3G auctions. The government postponed the auction for a month while it tried to change the rules, but this was furiously opposed by the remaining bidders who successfully argued that it was legally obliged to stick to the original rules.[19] So the bidders had just to pay the reserve price—one-thirtieth per capita of the U.K. and German prices, and one-fiftieth of what the government had once hoped for.[20]

By contrast, in a sealed-bid (or Anglo-Dutch) design joint bidding is less attractive because if strong firms bid jointly they increase the opportunity for weaker competitors, so may simply attract other firms into the bidding. For example, Deutsche Telekom or Hutchison, who had both won licenses in Germany, Austria, the Netherlands, the United Kingdom, and elsewhere, and who had quit the Swiss auction just one week earlier, might perhaps have reentered a sealed-bid contest.[21] So strong firms would have been more likely to bid independently in a sealed-bid auction, and Switzerland might have had a much more competitive auction.

7.4   The Year 2000 "Variable-Prize" Ascending Auctions: Germany and Austria

7.4.1   The German Auction (July–August 2000)

The Germans conformed to national habits (or at least to British stereotypes of them) by choosing a more complex design: Germany auctioned twelve blocks of spectrum from which bidders could create licenses of either two or three blocks, for example, four firms could win large three-block licenses or six firms could win smaller two-block licenses. This contrasted with the previously discussed auctions in which all the licenses were of predetermined (though not always identical) sizes. As always, firms could win at most one license each. The twelve blocks were sold by a simultaneous ascending auction, much like the previously discussed auctions.

The point of the design was to let the number of winners be determined by the bidders who might have information unavailable to the government about, for example, the engineering advantages of large vs. small licenses. But such an auction's outcome is driven by bidders' profits, not by consumers' or social welfare. Klemperer (2000a, 2002a) and Jehiel and Moldovanu (2001) discuss the different distortions that can result. Since the bidding in the British auction had already revealed a lot about bidders' relative valuations of different licenses,[22] it would have been wiser to fix the number of licenses in advance.[23]

The auction also proved vulnerable to collusion and entry problems: only seven bidders participated. (The entry of weaker bidders was perhaps discouraged by the ascending design, as in other auctions after the United Kingdom's, see section 7.7.) And one bidder (MobilCom) early on made what looked like a collusive offer to another (Debitel), telling a newspaper that "should [Debitel] fail to secure a license [it could] become a 'virtual network operator' using MobilCom's network while saving on the cost of the license" (*Financial Times*, 2/8/2000, p. 28). Shares in Debitel rose 12 percent in response to the remarks which, if taken literally, would be similar to the offer of a side payment for quitting the auction. But, as in the Netherlands case, and probably for similar reasons, the government did not punish MobilCom; in particular, excluding MobilCom would have risked ending the auction almost immediately when the price level was about 3 percent of what the auction finally achieved.[24]

Although Debitel did not quit immediately, MobilCom's suggestion might have made dropping out of the auction seem less unattractive, and Debitel did stop bidding at a relatively low level—just 55 percent of the per capita revenue achieved by the U.K. auction. There were then two natural outcomes, depending on the strategies followed by the two dominant incumbents, Deutsche Telekom and Vodafone-Mannesman, each of whom had about 40 percent of the existing German mobile market. Either these dominant firms could raise the price to force the weaker firms among the remaining six to quit, which would yield high revenue for the government but a concentrated industry. Or they could lead all six remaining firms to tacitly "collude" to reduce their demands to two blocks each, thus ending the auction quickly and giving the government a lowish revenue but a more competitive industry. (A problem with the German approach of auctioning many small blocks is that it is often easy for firms to see how to collusively divide them.)

Vodafone-Mannesman ended a number of its bids with the digit "6," which, it was thought, was a signal that its preference was to end the auction quickly with six remaining bidders.[25]

Surprisingly, however, Deutsche Telekom first continued to push up the price while it was well below the levels that the weaker firms had shown themselves willing to pay in the U.K. auction, but then ended the auction before pushing any of the weaker firms out, giving up just when the price approached the level at which the weaker players had quit the U.K. auction.[26] Some observers wondered whether Deutsche Telekom's objectives were affected by the fact that it was majority owned by the German government.[27] In any case, the government ended up with both high revenues (94% of the U.K. revenues per-capita) and an unconcentrated mobile phones market!

But the fragility of the design was emphasized by the Austrian sequel.

7.4.2   The Austrian Auction (November 2000)

Austria mimicked the German design (again conforming to national habits?). Again interest in entering an ascending auction was limited, and just six firms competed for the twelve blocks available. Because the government had set a very low reserve price—just one-eighth of the per capita price that the identical German 3G auction had achieved three months earlier—there was an obvious incentive for the six firms to tacitly agree to divide up the market to obtain two lots each.[28] Any bidder who might have been inclined to compete for a third unit knew he would have to push the price up a very long way to drive out another bidder (and he would then have to pay this high price on all three units). So the bidding stopped very soon after starting at the reserve price. It is rumoured that the bidding only lasted the few rounds it did in order to create some public perception of genuine competition and reduce the risk of the government changing the rules. The final price was less than one-sixth of the per capita revenue raised in the United Kingdom and Germany, and the only reason that Austria did any better than Switzerland was that its reserve price was not quite so ridiculously low.

7.5   Bidders' Valuations of Licenses

The available evidence about firms' and the wider market's valuations of the licenses sold in the year 2000 auctions suggests revenues could probably have been in the range of 400–650 euros per capita, and certainly above 300 euros per capita, in all these countries.

The Netherlands government cancelled its July bond issue in anticipation of receiving over 600 euros per capita, while the Italian government expected around 450, and the Swiss telecom regulator predicted revenues of around 400 euros per capita just five days before the auction. Analysts' estimates were consistent with these numbers, or higher, right up to the auction in Italy and Switzerland, and until a month before the Netherlands and Austrian auctions.[29]

It is also clear that the winners of all these four "failed" auctions were delighted—some reports said "euphoric"—about the outcomes. Some non-winners also valued the licenses at higher prices than the winners paid, but were deterred by the auction designs. And when the denouement of the Swiss auction became clear and the government tried to revise the rules, a winner (Swisscom) threatened legal action to preserve the status quo.[30]

Meeks (2001) studies the jumps in Swisscom's share price when the number of bidders in the Swiss auction fell from five to four (for four licenses, thus crippling the auction), and again when the Swiss government dropped its attempt to rewrite the rules. The share-price changes are highly statistically significant and, controlling for general market movements, correspond to the market expecting that bidders would pay several hundred euros per capita less in the auction than was earlier anticipated.[31]

However, perceptions of the values of 3G licenses did fall dramatically over the course of the auctions. For example, some analysts marked down expectations of the Swiss proceeds from 1,000 euros per capita to 400–600 euros per capita between the end of the U.K. auction and the planned beginning of the Swiss auction (the last of the year 2000 auctions). License values fell even further after the Swiss auction.

In part valuations were caught up in what now seems to have been a dotcom and technology bubble. The Dow Jones European telecom stock price index fell by over one-third between the U.K. and Swiss auctions, and then fell even more precipitously by almost another 50 percent—to less than one-third its level during the U.K. auction—by the time of the Danish auction. In part there were a number of negative "shocks" about both the development of the 3G technology itself and likely consumer interest in it. And the values are highly leveraged since they reflect the difference between the (large) expected revenues and the (also large) expected costs of developing the required network infrastructures.[32] So a small reduction in expected revenues has a proportionally much larger effect on license values. Furthermore the option values of licenses are not necessarily high since the licenses come with "roll-out" investment requirements attached to them.

In 2001, valuations collapsed.[33] Typical analysts' estimates prior to all the year 2001 auctions were around one-tenth of the levels predicted the year before, or about 50 euros per capita.

7.6 The Year 2001 Auctions

7.6.1 The Belgian and Greek Auctions (March and July 2001)

Not only were valuations low by spring 2001, but Belgium and Greece seemed particularly unattractive to new entrants. In Belgium a very dominant incumbent (Belgacom's Proximus) had two-thirds of the existing mobile market and was substantially owned, and many people thought favoured, by the state. Greece is not a rich country. So probably little more could be done in these countries than set an appropriate reserve price to the incumbent operators who had established second generation customer bases and therefore still valued 3G.

Both countries held auctions for four licenses—and in each case attracted only the three incumbents, who therefore obtained licenses at the reserve prices which yielded about 45 euros per capita in each case.

It is very hard to argue plausibly that an auction design deterred much entry when a license goes unsold,[34] and there is also no obvious reason to criticise the reserve prices that these governments chose. Indeed their auctions yielded more than twice the per capita revenue of the Swiss farce, even though, as discussed, their timing was much less propitious and their markets are much less profitable.[35]

7.6.2   The Danish Auction (September 2001)

The Danes, who ran the last of the Western European auctions, were in a particularly tricky position. Not only were valuations still very low,[36] but Denmark planned to sell the same number of licenses (four) as it had incumbent operators—exactly the situation that the Netherlands had so spectacularly fumbled. But the Danish designers had in fact read Klemperer (2000a), and they took its arguments seriously. Denmark chose a sealed-bid auction to give weaker bidders a chance of winning, in the hope both of attracting new entrants and of scaring the incumbent operators into making higher bids.[37]

It was a resounding success, attracting a serious bid from a new entrant and shocking analysts with revenues of 95 euros per capita, or almost double most expectations.[38,39,40]

7.7   How Did the Sequencing Matter?

The entry and collusion problems of the later auctions were exacerbated by the very fact that they were later.

7.7.1   Learning to Play the Game

It is notable that the only successful auctions (from the seller's viewpoint) were the first of their type; there was enough time between plays of the European game for bidders to learn from the early auctions and adjust their strategies for the later ones.

The United Kingdom's successful simple ascending auction design was closely copied by the Netherlands, Italy and Switzerland, with results that, we have seen, went from bad (Netherlands and Italy) to worse (Switzerland). The U.K. sale taught firms the costs of participating in a competitive auction, and they became increasingly successful at forming joint-ventures that ensured the subsequent auctions were less competitive.[41]

We also saw that the German auction followed the U.K. and Netherlands auctions, but was a more complex ("variable-prize") ascending design. The dominant firms clearly misplayed their hands, with excellent results from the government's viewpoint. But when the Austrians copied the German design three months later, the firms had learnt to coordinate their behavior during the auction, and it was the firms that won the Austrian round.

Finally the Danes pulled off a success with a sealed-bid design. We have argued that this kind of design may prove more robust to future gaming by firms but that, of course, remains to be seen.

7.7.2   Learning Opponents' Valuations

Section 7.7.1 assumes firms need to learn because they are boundedly rational, rather than because they lack information. But firms also learn about their rivals, and this was critical to why the first auction, the United Kingdom's, had thirteen bidders while no subsequent auction had more than seven.

Firms learnt from the U.K. auction whether they had any realistic chance of victory, and companies that recognized they were clearly outgunned did not want to invest their time and effort in bidding in later auctions.[42] Certainly they did not want to bid in ascending auctions that pretty much guarantee the strongest bidders will win.

Furthermore, a bidder who learnt that others' valuations were somewhat higher than its might have figured that its best hope was to buy or lease part of a license after the auctions. In this case the bidder might have stayed out of the later auctions to keep its valuation private and so strengthen its bargaining position in the aftermarket. Again, this may be a particular problem in ascending auctions since they make losers' valuations more transparent.[43]

The elimination of some firms, and the fact that the remainder had learnt something about each other's valuations for the licenses, may both have been important factors in making bargaining between the bidders easier, facilitating the joint ventures and "collusion" that emerged in the later auctions.[44]

7.7.3 Complementarities

Markets that were auctioned later were more valuable to those who had won earlier ones that fitted well with them in a network, and an early win also allowed a firm to influence suppliers about the development of the technology in ways that would help the firm in later markets. These "real" complementarities reinforced the learning effects discussed in the previous subsection, and further discouraged losers of early auctions from entering later auctions, especially ascending ones.[45,46]

7.7.4 Budget Constraints

It is hard to believe that capital-market constraints mean many very profitable investments are foregone. However, if some bidders faced higher financing costs than others then, as above, even a slight relative weakness could have encouraged them to quit the auction process, at least as long as ascending auctions were being used. It is certainly clear that many firms were caught by surprise by the change in market sentiment towards telecoms, and some firms faced difficulties in borrowing.

The issues in this section clearly need more careful analysis; the area seems ripe for research.[47]

7.8 Conclusion

A key determinant of success of the European telecom auctions was how well their designs attracted entry and discouraged collusion (as is true for most auctions; see Klemperer 2002a). The sequencing of the auctions exacerbated the entry and collusion problems.

The organizers of most of the auctions after the United Kingdom's, and of the Netherlands and Swiss auctions in particular, failed to give enough attention to attracting entry and magnified their problems by permitting joint-bidding agreements prior to the auctions. The German and Austrian auctions demonstrated the vulnerability of ascending auctions to "collusive" behavior during the auctions, and there were also rumors of collusion in the ascending auctions in Italy, the Netherlands, and Switzerland. All these problems were aggravated by most later auctioneers' failure to use the information from the U.K. auction to set sensible reserve prices.

The auctions also showed that auction design is not "one size fits all." The ascending design that worked very well for the United Kingdom worked very badly in the Netherlands, Italy, and Switzerland because of entry problems, and this was predictable (and predicted) in advance. These other countries would clearly have done better if they had included a sealed-bid component in their auctions, as Denmark did, and as the United Kingdom would have done if entry had been a concern there.

We have emphasized the revenues generated by the different auctions because they differed so greatly. "Assigning the spectrum efficiently," interpreted roughly to mean maximizing the sum of the valuations of those awarded licenses, was most governments' main objective, but we cannot assess whether the auctions achieved this.[48] There was no obvious inefficiency, but there also seems no reason to believe that alternative designs (such as the Anglo-Dutch) would have been much less efficient, and they would have yielded higher revenues from some of the sales. Whether it would have been better to run a single grand European auction is beyond our scope.[49] But there was no appetite for a coordinated process at the time and, as we saw, the United Kingdom did well to steal a march on its rivals by going it alone and auctioning first.

Acknowledgments

I was the principal auction theorist advising the U.K. government's Radiocommunications Agency, which designed and ran the U.K. mobile phone license auction described here, but the views expressed in this chapter are mine alone. Although some observers thought some of the behaviour described in this chapter warranted regulatory investigation, I do not intend to suggest that any of it violates any applicable rules or laws. I am very grateful to the referees and to many colleagues including Bruno Bosco, Jeremy Bulow, Tim Harford, Paul Hofer, Emiel Maasland, Roland Meeks, Margaret Meyer, David Salant, Tommaso

Valletti, Mark Williams, and especially Marco Pagnozzi, for helpful advice.

Notes

1. Other major European countries used "beauty contest" administrative procedures, with generally dismal results (Klemperer 2000c; Binmore and Klemperer 2002).

2. Other issues affecting license values were population densities, regulatory regimes, and the coverage requirements imposed on the licenses.

3. See Klemperer (2000a, 2002a, 2003). By contrast, a graduate knowledge of modern auction theory is at best of lesser importance and at worst distracting from the main concerns (Klemperer 2002b).

4. An ascending auction is the kind of auction typically used to sell an art object or antique. The price starts low and competing bidders raise the price until nobody is prepared to bid any higher, and the final bidder wins the prize at the final price he bid. Mobile phone licenses are often sold in *simultaneous* ascending auctions that are much the same except that several licenses are sold at the same time with the price rising on each of them independently, and none of the licenses is finally sold until no one wishes to bid again on any of them.

5. In a first-price sealed-bid auction, every bidder makes a single "best-and-final" bid, and the winner pays the price he bid.

6. Of course it is not necessarily socially inefficient to allocate a license to a bidder with a lower value, for example, if that bidder is a new entrant who will increase competition and hence consumer and social welfare. Allowing resale is not a perfect substitute for an efficient initial allocation, because resale does not resolve all inefficiencies (Cai 1997; Myerson and Satterthwaite 1983; Cramton, Gibbons, and Klemperer 1987).

7. We assume governments auctioning spectrum licenses care both about efficiency and revenue, because of the substantial deadweight losses of raising government funds by alternative means. (Typical estimates are that deadweight losses are between 17 and 56 cents for every extra $1 raised in taxes (Ballard, Shoven, and Whalley 1985).) The United Kingdom and Switzerland, at least, were explicit that revenue mattered even though efficiency was the main objective (Binmore and Klemperer 2002; Wolfstetter 2003).

8. Klemperer (2000a) was revised as Klemperer (2002a). The papers also give applications to auctions of other commodities than spectrum.

9. I was the principal auction theorist advising the Radiocommunications Agency, which designed and ran the U.K. auction. Ken Binmore had a leading role and supervised experiments testing the proposed designs. Other academic advisors included Tilman Börgers, Jeremy Bulow, Philippe Jehiel, and Joe Swierzbinski.

10. All four winners would pay the fourth-highest sealed bid and, since the licenses were not quite identical, a final simultaneous ascending stage would follow to allocate the licenses more efficiently among the winners. See Binmore and Klemperer (2002).

11. We deliberately maintained this strategy even when the complications engendered by the Vodafone-Mannesman takeover battle led many to suggest that the U.K. auction be postponed.

12. In particular, the five licenses were of very unequal sizes. A sealed-bid component to the design might have resulted in an inefficient allocation of licenses among winners.

13. A slightly different view is that there may not initially have been a problem because one of the incumbents (Ben) was weak. But after Ben strengthened its hand by joining with Deutsche Telekom, there was definitely the same number of strong bidders as licenses, and no hope for entrants in an ascending auction. This view places more of the blame for the auction's failure on weak anti-trust policy, although the ascending design increased the incentive to joint-venture (see section 7.3.4).

14. Telfort claimed Versatel "believes that its bids will always be surpassed by bids of the other participants in the auction," so it "must be that Versatel is attempting to either raise its competitors' costs or to get access to their 2G or future 3G networks," and said it "will hold Versatel liable for all damages as a result of this" (see van Damme 2002).

15. The auction's problems were aggravated by the government's belief that it could not legally set binding minimum prices. The rules therefore specified that lots that received no bids at the beginning of the auction would have their minimum prices reduced. Since bidders were permitted to sit out some rounds of bidding, all but one did this at the start of the auction driving the minimum prices down toward zero and making the government look ridiculous. (Starting the prices at zero would have been functionally equivalent and reduced political embarrassment.) Setting a binding reserve price based on the information revealed by the U.K. auction would clearly have improved the outcome.

16. Two losers in the U.K. auction (Sonera and Telefonica) formed a joint venture and several weak bidders quit the auction process altogether. Curiously, the Italian government also eliminated two weak bidders prior to the main auction in a "beauty contest" phase.

17. Government officials claimed there had been "collusion" by which Blu entered simply to avoid invoking the rule reducing the number of licenses, thus allowing every other bidder to win a cheap license. But an investigation found no evidence. Blu was a joint venture between British Telecom and Italian-based firms whose main business was not in telecoms, and perhaps they were unable to agree terms for competing seriously.

18. Note that firms in a sealed-bid auction want their rivals to think them weak, so other bidders would probably not have gambled on Blu being genuinely weak. Even in the ascending auction they seemed surprised when Blu quit at such a low price. And, of course, in a sealed-bid contest Blu might have bid more, or other firms might have entered. The two weak bidders that the Italian government eliminated prior to the auction (note 16) might also have scared the stronger bidders into more aggressive bidding if they had been permitted to compete in a sealed-bid contest.

19. By contrast, the United Kingdom retained the right to cancel its auction in circumstances like these. This also reduced the incentive to joint venture in the United Kingdom.

20. Actually the auction yielded 2.5 percent more than the reserve price because slight differences between the licenses led to a little competition for the best license.

21. Although there were also rumours (investigated by the regulator) that Deutsche Telekom "collusively" agreed not to participate in the auction in return for subsequently being able to buy in to one of the winners.

22. The United Kingdom auctioned two large (roughly, three-block) and three small (roughly, two-block) licenses, and the bidding showed that the strongest new entrants, and probably also the two smaller incumbents, valued small licenses almost as much as

large ones, but the two larger incumbents valued large licenses considerably more than small ones, so five or six winners was probably socially correct in the United Kingdom. The correct number also depends on the likely competitiveness of the market, which the German regulator is best qualified to judge for Germany.

23. Not only were consumers' interests unrepresented in the choice of the number of winners, but the auction's complexity generated other potential problems. A bidder might have stayed in the auction in the hope of being one of five winners, but suddenly found itself one of six winners, and been quite unhappy and even tried to default. Also, the possibility that the auction would end with a bidder being the high bidder on just one block, in which case the block would be re-auctioned, created both considerable uncertainty for bidders and the possibility of an inefficient allocation, since the price in the re-auction could be very different from that in the original auction. The government was lucky that these problems did not arise.

24. The government had failed to set a meaningful reserve price.

25. According to the *Financial Times* (3/11/2000, p. 21), "One operator has privately admitted" to this kind of behaviour. A weaker player behaved similarly. It is also understood that Mannesman (successfully) signalled a desire to cooperate with Deutsche Telekom in the 1999 2G auction (Klemperer 2002a), and Mannesman may have seen the earlier auction as setting a precedent for behaviour in the 3G auction.

26. The two weakest bidders in Germany both quit the U.K. auction very close to its end. One announced in advance of the German auction that it was willing to pay the U.K. price.

27. Deutsche Telekom's behaviour reminds me of my father-in-law whom I often see join a queue but quit in frustration before the front of the line. Rational behaviour generally involves sizing up the queue first, and then either quitting quickly (cf. ending the auction quickly) or gritting one's teeth and waiting to the end (cf. waiting for another firm to quit the auction.) In fact my father-in-law's behaviour might be more rational than Deutsche Telekom's, since he might learn about the queue's behaviour. Deutsche Telekom learned nothing new after Debitel quit (except that no one else was quitting), although it might have felt pressured by the stock market response to the climbing auction prices.
   (Put more technically, the cost to Deutsche Telekom of allowing the price to rise a small bid increment, Δ, before ending the auction approximated 2Δ, while the benefit was the probability of a weaker bidder quitting in the interval Δ times the value of that outcome. So it cannot have maximized Deutsche Telekom's expected profits to end the auction when the probability of a weaker bidder quitting in the next increment was increasing—as it surely was. Grimm, Riedel, and Wolfstetter (chapter 14) argue the behaviour may have been rational, but they use a model that abstracts from this issue.)
   Given that Deutsche Telekom had pushed up the price so far, should V-M now have changed its strategy and continued pushing the price up further? Not if it retained pessimistic views about the cost of driving out a weaker firm.
   Furthermore, if V-M, only, had successfully continued to demand three blocks and driven a weaker bidder out, the rules would then have required the re-auction of a block (see note 23) with unpredictable results, and Deutsche Telekom might have ended up with three blocks at a much lower price than V-M, an outcome that V-M's management probably wished to avoid. (Grimm, Riedel, and Wolfstetter also abstract from this concern.) In any case, V-M cooperated with Deutsche Telekom in ending the auction.

28. The agreement may not have been completely tacit. The largest incumbent, Telekom Austria was reported the week before the auction as saying it "would be satisfied with

just two of the twelve blocks of frequency on offer and if the [5 other bidders] behaved similarly, 'it should be possible to get the frequencies on sensible terms' ... but that it would bid for a third block if one of its rivals did" (*Reuters*, October 31, 2000, "Austrian UMTS Auction Unlikely to Scale Peaks"). If taken literally, this could be interpreted as both offering a "collusive" deal, and threatening "punishment" if its rivals failed to accept the offer.

29. Later estimates for Austria and the Netherlands reflected these auctions' obvious design flaws.

30. Even in the United Kingdom where the high revenues took commentators by surprise, several losing bidders seem to have secured funding in advance of the auction to levels that implied revenues of 300 euros per capita (and all the losers bid at least that far), one winner claimed to have predicted the final price to within 10 percent, a second winner was said to have guessed the final price to within 20 percent, and another winner resold a fraction of its license at a profit shortly after the auction. And before the U.K. bidding had gone very high, a new entrant in Germany announced a willingness to pay up to a price that would imply proceeds of around 660 euros per head from the German auction.

Furthermore, Cable, Henley, and Holland et al. (2002) analyse share price movements around the U.K. auction and argue that the market was neither surprised by the prices paid in the United Kingdom (the evidence is from movements of the share prices of the incumbents, whose winning was not news, but whose payments were news) nor felt that the winners overpaid (the evidence comes from the share prices of entrants whose winning or losing was news).

31. The excess returns beyond general European telecom and Swiss market movements correspond to 570 euros per head at the first event and (after intermediate ups and downs) 190 euros per head at the second event. A 95 percent confidence interval is $+/-$ 320 euros per head so the first event, at least, suggests a change of at least 250 euros per head in the expected revenues from the auction hence that expected revenues from the auction had been (well) over 250 euros per head.

32. The costs of building infrastructure were estimated to be far more than was paid for licenses.

33. The collapse seems to have been gradual. The French beauty contest in late January 2001 suggested valuations were still one-third to one-half the previous summer's levels. (Two firms agreed to pay the French government a price corresponding to total proceeds of 330 euros per capita, while others probably valued licenses this highly but refused to pay so much in the hope of negotiating a lower price.)

34. Furthermore, although the Belgians just copied the U.K. design, the Greek rules made the payment terms much easier (effectively lowering the reserve price) if a fourth bidder appeared—so the government was willing to sacrifice revenue to attract an additional entrant and create a more competitive market for 3G services. And if five or more bidders had appeared, the Greek auction would have used sealed bids—making entry yet more attractive.

35. In particular, Greece's GDP per head is less than one-third of Switzerland's, and its neighbours—Albania, Macedonia, Bulgaria, Turkey—do not quite stack up against Switzerland's—Germany, France, Austria, Italy (and of course Liechtenstein)—or make it a key piece of the European puzzle.

36. In a defining moment in the 3G process, shortly before the Danish auction, a new entrant in Norway (Sonera) handed the license it had won in the previous year's beauty contest back to the government for free, completely writing off its investment. Admittedly Norway is an unattractive market and the licensees must pay annual fees, but "in spite of Sonera splashing out 4 billion Euros on licenses, most analysts now value them at zero" (*Financial Times*, August 11–12, 2001, p. 1).

37. The designers saw little point in running an Anglo-Dutch auction, since the chance of attracting many new entrants was very tiny in the Danish context, and with just one new entrant (the actual outcome) a sealed-bid auction is equivalent. The auction was a sealed-bid auction in which all bidders paid the fourth-highest bid (and only this bid was revealed), and the government precommitted to keeping the number of bidders secret in the hope of scaring better bids from the incumbents even if no new entrant actually bid.

38. Some semi-formal support for our views about the relative successes of different auctions is provided by a simple OLS regression of price per capita on the Dow Jones European telecom stock price index (a measure of market sentiment). The United Kingdom, Denmark, and Germany performed much better than the model predicted, while Austria, Switzerland, and the Netherlands were the worst performers. Italy also appears among the worst performers if population is also included in the regression (small countries are said to be worth less per capita). Otherwise including population, GDP per head, mobile usage, or Internet usage makes little difference, as do several other natural specifications.

39. In fact the entrant was one of the winners, squeezing out an incumbent. The losing incumbent will presumably pursue 3G as a virtual network operator (the Danish government mandates licensees to rent spectrum to VNOs). So the new entrant has probably increased the competitiveness of the ultimate 3G market.

40. At almost the same time as the Danish auction, Hong Kong also planned to sell four licenses. Hong Kong originally planned a design similar to Denmark's but the strong incumbents successfully lobbied to change to a simple ascending auction—and there were just four entrants for the four licenses, even though Hong Kong was thought an attractive market.

41. And while the firms became more sophisticated, the governments became less sophisticated, leaving out safeguards that were in the U.K. auction (see, e.g., note 19) and using the United Kingdom's design in inappropriate contexts; unlike the United Kingdom's auction which spent three years in planning and development, some subsequent auctions were rushed, last-minute affairs.

42. The effects in section 7.7.2 might be mitigated if firms recognised that their opponents might bid aggressively in order to persuade them not to enter subsequent auctions, although this would be a further reason for higher prices in early auctions. Pagnozzi (2002) is exploring the issues in this section.

43. With private values and straightforward bidding up to one's value, the losers' values are perfectly revealed. (Bidders who foresee this will not bid so straightforwardly—this is just another version of our point—but entering the auction may still reveal information that could be damaging later.) Managerial incentives and compensation mechanisms may also mean that resale could not easily be at a lower price than in the original auction. And tacit collusion that rewards a non-bidder with a lower resale price would also encourage non-participation (see note 21). Of course these issues are only significant when sharing a license is (privately) efficient and renting or partial resale is easy.

44. To illustrate why a tighter distribution of beliefs about opponents' valuations facilitates bargaining, imagine two firms with privately known values for a single license, independently drawn from a distribution with lower-bound zero and decreasing hazard rate. Then bargaining is "very hard" in the sense that the expected ex ante joint surplus (before knowing either firm's value) from competing in an ascending auction exceeds the joint surplus from colluding to divide the prize equally at price zero. (If bidders' values, v, are drawn independently from distribution $F(v) = 1 - e^{-\lambda v}$—i.e., constant hazard rate λ—the winner's profits from an auction equals the expected distance between the values, $1/\lambda$, which equals the expected average value.)

With increasing hazard rates, bargaining is not "very hard" in this sense. For example, with values uniformly distributed on $[0, 1]$, bidders' expected joint surplus from the auction is $\frac{1}{3}$, but is $\frac{1}{2}$ from agreeing to divide the pie at a price of zero. So successful bargaining seems more likely, at least before bidders have invested to determine their own values.

But even in the latter case, bargaining is still "hard" in the sense that a bidder who knows he has the highest-possible value expects the same private surplus ($\frac{1}{2}$) from the auction as from collusion at a price of zero. So, with even a tiny cost of negotiating, opening negotiations might be taken to be the bad signal that one's value is not very high, and—depending on the model—neither player may be willing to make the first offer. "Easy" bargaining, in this sense, requires a still tighter distribution of valuations.

45. Bikhchandani (1988), Bulow and Klemperer (2002), Bulow, Huang, and Klemperer (1999), Klemperer (1998), and Klemperer and Pagnozzi (2002) emphasize how small differences in bidders' valuations can have dramatic effects on prices achieved by ascending auctions.

46. Awareness of these effects probably encouraged more aggressive bidding in the earlier auctions, further accentuating the downward trend in prices. The effects were mitigated by budget constraints.

47. A "declining price anomaly" is often observed in the sequential auction of identical objects such as art, wine, real estate, and radio transponders (Ashenfelter 1989; Beggs and Graddy 1997; Harford 1998; Klemperer 1999, 2000b; Milgrom and Weber 2000). But the issues in sections 7.7.1 and 7.7.2 are probably more important than the explanations usually given for this. I also know of no evidence of bidders colluding by taking turns to win the auctions; most likely there were too many players with different strengths and interests. And the auction in any given country was probably too large a one-off event to be treated as a single play in a repeated game of some kind in that country.

48. See Börgers and Dustmann (2002) and Plott and Salmon (forthcoming).

49. A simultaneous auction of all the continent's spectrum might have alleviated the entry problems that some countries faced and helped companies build the particular networks of licenses that most interested them. (In the actual process, companies had to bid in early auctions without knowing what they would win later on.) On the other hand, it would have been harder to prevent collusion. An auction for *all* radiospectrum including TV and radio, and so forth might also allocate the spectrum more efficiently between different uses.

References

Ashenfelter, O. 1989. "How Auctions Work for Wine and Art." *Journal of Economic Perspectives* 3: 23–36.

Ballard, C., J. Shoven, and J. Whalley. 1985. "General Equilibrium Computations of the Marginal Welfare Costs of Taxes in the United States." *American Economic Review* 75: 128–138.

Beggs, A., and K. Graddy. 1997. "Declining Values and the Afternoon Effect: Evidence from Art Auctions." *Rand Journal of Economics* 28: 544–565.

Bikhchandani, S. 1988. "Reputation in Repeated Second-Price Auctions." *Journal of Economic Theory* 46: 97–119.

Binmore, K., and P. Klemperer. 2002. "The Biggest Auction Ever: The Sale of the British 3G Telecom Licences." *The Economic Journal* 112(478): C74–C96.

Börgers, T., and C. Dustmann. 2002. "Strange Bids: Bidding Behaviour in the United Kingdom's Third Generation Spectrum Auction." Working paper, University College London.

Bulow, J., and P. Klemperer. 2002. "Prices and the Winner's Curse." *Rand Journal of Economics* 33(1): 1–21.

Bulow, J., M. Huang, and P. Klemperer. 1999. "Toeholds and Takeovers." *Journal of Political Economy* 107: 427–454.

Cable, J., A. Henley, and K. Holland. 2002. "Pot of Gold or Winner's Curse? An Event Study of the Auctions of 3G Mobile Telephone Licences in the UK." *Fiscal Studies* 23(4): 447–462.

Cai, H.-B. 1997. "Delay in Multilateral Bargaining under Complete Information." Working paper, University of California, Los Angeles.

Cramton, P., R. Gibbons, and P. Klemperer. 1987. "Dissolving a Partnership Efficiently." *Econometrica* 55: 615–632.

Harford, T. 1998. "Sequential Auctions with Financially Constrained Bidders. M. Phil. thesis, Oxford University. Available online at ⟨http://www.timharford.com⟩.

Jehiel, P., and B. Moldovanu. 2001. "The European UMTS/IMT-2000 License Auctions." Working paper, University College London and University of Mannheim.

Klemperer, P. 1998. "Auctions with Almost Common Values." *European Economic Review* 42: 757–769.

Klemperer, P. 1999. "Auction Theory: A Guide to the Literature." *Journal of Economic Surveys* 13(3): 227–286.

Klemperer, P. 2000a. "What Really Matters in Auction Design." May 2000 version. Available online at ⟨http://www.paulklemperer.org⟩.

Klemperer, P., ed. 2000b. *The Economic Theory of Auctions.* Cheltenham, U.K.: Edward Elgar.

Klemperer, P. 2000c. "Spectrum on the Block." *Wall Street Journal*, Oct. 5, p. 8. Available online at ⟨http://www.paulklemperer.org⟩.

Klemperer, P. 2002a. "What Really Matters in Auction Design." *Journal of Economic Perspectives.* 16(1): 169–190.

Klemperer, P. 2002b. "Using and Abusing Economic Theory (2002 Alfred Marshall Lecture to the European Economic Association)." Forthcoming in *Journal of the European Eco-*

nomic Association 1 (2003). Forthcoming in *Advances in Economics and Econometrics: Theory and Applications*, ed. R. Becker and S. Hurn. Cheltenham, U.K.: Edward Elgar. Available online at ⟨http://www.paulklemperer.org⟩.

Klemperer, P. 2003. "Why Every Economist Should Learn Some Auction Theory." In *Advances in Economics and Econometrics: Invited Lectures to Eighth World Congress of the Econometric Society*, ed. M. Dewatripont, L. Hansen, and S. Turnovsky. Cambridge, U.K.: Cambridge University Press. Available online at ⟨http://www.paulklemperer.org⟩.

Klemperer, P., and M. Pagnozzi. 2002. "Advantaged Bidders and Spectrum Prices: An Empirical Analysis." Working paper, Nuffield college, Oxford University.

Maasland, E. 2000. "Veilingmiljarden Zijn een Fictie (Billions from Auctions: Wishful Thinking)." *ESB*, June 9, p. 479. Translation available online at ⟨http://www.paulklemperer.org⟩.

Meeks, R. 2001. "An Event Study of the Swiss UMTS Auction." Research Note, Nuffield College, Oxford University.

Milgrom, P., and R. Weber. 2000. "A Theory of Auctions and Competitive Bidding: II. In *The Economic Theory of Auctions*, ed. P. Klemperer, 179–194. Cheltenham, U.K.: Edward Elgar.

Myerson, R., and M. Satterthwaite. 1983. "Efficient Mechanisms for Bilateral Trade." *Journal of Economic Theory* 29: 265–281.

Pagnozzi, M. 2002. "Post-Auction Takeovers." Working paper, Oxford University.

Plott, C., and T. Salmon. Forthcoming. "The Simultaneous, Ascending Auction: Dynamics of Price Adjustment in Experiments and in the U.K. 3-G Spectrum Auction." *Journal of Economic Behavior and Organization*.

van Damme, E. 2002. "The European UMTS Auctions." *European Economic Review* 45(4–5): 846–858.

Wolfstetter, E. 2003. "The Swiss UMTS Spectrum Auction Flop: Bad Luck or Bad Design?" In *Regulation, Competition, and the Market Economy. Festschrift for C. C. v. Weizsäcker*, 281–294. Göttingen: Vandenhoeck & Ruprecht.

8

Rationalizing the UMTS Spectrum Bids: The Case of the U.K. Auction

Tilman Börgers and Christian Dustmann

8.1 Introduction

During the years 2000 and 2001 most European countries have awarded licenses to mobile telephone companies that allow these companies to use radio spectrum for the operation of third generation mobile telephone services (UMTS licenses). The methods adopted for the award of these licenses have differed widely across European countries. Some countries such as Finland and Spain have bureaucratically decided how many licenses there should be, which size in terms of available radio spectrum these licenses should be, and which companies should own them. Other countries such as Germany and Austria have used auction type procedures to determine the number and size of licenses as well as the license holders. Finally, some countries such as the United Kingdom and the Netherlands have chosen an intermediate procedure where the number and size of licenses was determined by bureaucratic methods, but the allocation of these licenses to firms was determined in an auction.

The outcomes of the licensing process have also differed widely across European countries. Finland and Spain, for example, have issued four UMTS licenses, the United Kingdom and the Netherlands have issued five UMTS licenses, and Germany and Austria have issued six such licenses. In Finland licenses were essentially given away for free. In Spain the total payments to the government by license holders per head of the population were only €12. In Austria all successful bidders together paid approximately €103 per head of the population. In the Netherlands license holders paid approximately 169 euros per head of the population to the government. But in Germany winning bidders paid €619 and in the United Kingdom they paid €642 per head of the population.[1]

The large payments in the United Kingdom and Germany have attracted much attention. The question arises whether the bids that companies made in the auctions conducted by these two countries were based on careful business plans, or whether they were the result of some form of "bidding fever." A policy reason for being interested in this question is that the purpose of these auctions, as stated by the U.K. government and German law, was to allocate spectrum efficiently.[2] How exactly efficiency is to be understood in this context is not obvious, but a necessary condition for efficiency is presumably that bidders rationally consider the value of licenses, and that these valuations are expressed consistently in their bids. If this was not the case in the United Kingdom or in Germany, then one can reasonably entertain doubts as to whether an efficient allocation was achieved.

The purpose of this chapter is to assess whether the auction bids for UMTS licenses can be interpreted as rational bids that are based on careful valuations of the licenses. We focus on the United Kingdom's UMTS auction.[3] The United Kingdom's UMTS auction was a simultaneous ascending auction.[4] Five nonidentical licenses were for sale. The auction was organized in rounds. In each round the current leading bidder for each license could not change its bid. All bidders who were not currently leading on some license had to either overbid the currently leading bid for one license or withdraw from the auction. To overbid a leading bid, one had to raise that bid by a minimum percentage. Withdrawal was irreversible. The auction closed once bidding on all licenses had stopped. The current leading bidders were then awarded the licenses and had to pay their last bids.

All bids in the United Kingdom's auction, including bids that were not the highest bids, were instantaneously published on the Internet.[5] These data form the basis for our chapter. We take as our starting point a naive theory of what it would mean to bid on the basis of rational valuations of the licenses. This is the theory of *private values* and *straightforward bidding*. According to this theory, bidders enter the auction with fixed valuations for each license and do not revise these valuations during the auction. This is the "private values" part of the theory. The "straightforward bidding" part says that firms bid in each round for the license for which the difference between the value of the license and the minimum bid that is admissible for that license is largest, provided that this difference is positive. Moreover, bidders only place minimal admissible bids. Once the minimum bid for all licenses is larger than their value, the firm withdraws.[6]

We take this naive theory as a benchmark, not as a plausible conjecture. Indeed, we find that the data refute very clearly this naive theory of bidding for the U.K. auction. The most important deviation from the theory concerns the bidders' revealed value *differences*. Under the theory of private values and straightforward bidding, the bids placed in the auction contain important information about these differences. To explain this we give a simple example. Suppose that only two licenses are for sale, A and B, and that in a certain round the smallest admissible bid for A is £10 more than the smallest admissible bid for B. Consider a bidder who chooses to bid for A. Then this bid reveals that this bidder's value of A is at least £10 larger than his value for B. Now every bidder typically has to bid many times throughout the auction, and each new bid reveals further information about the valuation differences. For example, if the same bidder bids later for B when the price difference is £12, then we have not only a lower (£10) but also an upper bound (£12) for the difference of the values of A and B. But now suppose that the same bidder bids in an even later round for B when the price difference is only £8. Then we have an inconsistency. This bidder's behavior does not seem to reveal a consistent view of what the value difference is.

The evidence against straightforward bidding with private values that we provide in this chapter shows that bidding in the United Kingdom's spectrum auction was affected by inconsistencies of exactly the type that we have just described. The inconsistencies concerned the revealed difference between the value of a "large" (in terms of spectrum) license and the value of a "small" license. Several important bidders' behavior does not reveal any consistent estimate of this value difference. In fact, for most of these bidders their estimate of the difference seems to have increased dramatically during the auction, in one case even by a factor of six.

Note that this finding does *not* necessarily imply that the companies that bid in the U.K. auction did not have careful valuations of the UMTS licenses, or that their bidding strategies were irrational. Straightforward bidding with private values is a very narrow interpretation of the general intuitive idea of "rational bidding that is based on a careful valuation of the licenses." Wider interpretations might allow, for example, for valuations that change during the auction. One possible rationale for this would be that a "common value" element was present in the auction. As a consequence companies may have learned from observing other companies' bidding behavior during the auction about the license values. The learning might have lead to a change in their valuations that to a naive observer looks like an inconsistency. Another possibility is that allocative externalities may have been present. Such externalities exist if companies' valuations of licenses depend on which other companies win a license. Companies' beliefs about the likely winners of other licenses might have changed during the auction, and this may have lead to apparent inconsistencies.

This chapter provides a more detailed assessment of the hypothesis that behavior in the U.K. auction was consistent with "rational bidding that is based on a careful valuation of licenses" provided that a sufficiently wide interpretation of this intuitive idea is adopted. Because companies' behavior in the U.K. auction differed a lot, we focus on case studies of individual companies. We select three companies that played a particularly important role in the auction, and for which we found in our earlier paper (Börgers and Dustmann 2001) inconsistencies in their evaluation of the difference between licenses. These three companies are BT3G, TIW, and NTL Mobile. BT3G and TIW both won a license in the U.K. auction. NTL Mobile was the last company to drop out of the U.K. auction.

The three companies that we have selected for this chapter were, together with Vodafone, the most persistent bidders for the two large licenses that the U.K. government put up for sale. Because Vodafone's behavior is very easily understood,[7] one can thus also say that our chapter provides a detailed analysis of the bidding races for the two large licenses. We begin by providing detailed round-by round descriptions of these companies' bidding behavior. In this context we also show that these companies' bidding is inconsistent with the theory of straightforward bidding with private values. We then discuss the extent to which alternative hypotheses can explain the available evidence. Our main finding is that there is no hypothesis for which we can provide strong evidence from our data. However, there are some hypotheses that seem plausible, and that, if true, would not necessarily leave a lot of "footprints" in our data.

An example of a hypothesis for which we might hope to find strong evidence in our data is the hypothesis that allocative externalities were present. Suppose that we maintain the myopia hypothesis implicit in the theory of straightforward bidding, and we postulate that companies bid in each round for the license that currently offers the best value, assuming that the leaders on all other licenses will not change. Then we should find that companies reveal consistent valuation differences once we condition on the current leaders on other licenses. In this chapter we offer evidence that this was not the case in the U.K. auction.

An example of a hypothesis that does not leave a lot of footprints in our data is that companies learned from other companies' bids about the true value of licenses. Which precise form such learning takes depends on a company's prior beliefs about the value of licenses, about the information available to other bidders, and about the strategies adopted by other bidders. Depending on how these beliefs are specified, relatively arbitrary belief paths can be obtained, and consequently it is difficult to tell from observed bidding behavior whether this form of learning played a role or not. We have to rely on plausibility considerations. In some cases, these considerations lead us to conclude that social learning of the type described here may well have played a role.

We cannot reach an unambiguous answer regarding the question as to whether the U.K. bids can be explained as rational bids based on careful valuations of the UMTS licenses for sale. However, the U.K. experience provides some reason for caution. Bidders' behavior in the U.K. auction remains ill understood. It is unclear whether this auction achieved its efficiency objective. For policy issues an important further question is, of course, whether better alternative allocation methods exist. Our chapter has nothing to say about this issue.

We conclude this introduction with a brief discussion of related literature. This chapter has a companion paper (Börgers and Dustmann 2001) in which, instead of conducting case studies for particular companies, we provide a more comprehensive overview of the U.K. auction.

Our argument that the U.K. bidding data raise important open questions runs counter to the interpretation of these data by other authors. Plott and Salmon (2001) have used the U.K. data to estimate different companies' license valuations, and have then determined the percentage of bids that are in accordance with these estimates and straightforward bidding. The percentages they find vary substantially from company to company, but overall they conclude that the theory of private values and straightforward bidding does well. We come to a more negative conclusion than they do because we regard the percentages of unexplained bids as more important than Plott and Salmon do. Indeed, an easy calculation shows that if the private values that Plott and Salmon estimate were correct, then some of the bids that their approach leaves unexplained would have caused losses between one and two billion Pounds, had they been successful.

Plott and Salmon also investigate the extent to which estimates based on the first 75 or 100 rounds allow an outside observer to predict the final license winner and the price they will pay. They find that these predictions are reasonably accurate. Our investigations show that any efforts to predict on the basis of the first 75 or 100 rounds not just the final winners, but also the bids placed in the intervening rounds (101–150) would lead to very inaccurate forecasts for some companies.

The U.K. auction data have also been examined by Peter Cramton in his report for the National Audit Office (Cramton 2001). Cramton writes, "Most of the bidders pursued a strategy of bidding on the license that represented the best value. Bidders thus switched from license to license as the prices changed.... The pricing dynamics were predictable, although certainly not the absolute values of prices" (50). Cramton's report does not include a detailed discussion of empirical evidence. We argue that if one adopts the interpretations of the phrase bidding for best value described in this chapter, then the evidence that bidders bid for best value is not very strong. Additional discoveries about the behavior of BT3G, made after completing the current chapter, will be reported in a revised version of our companion paper (Börgers and Dustmann 2001).

The remainder of this chapter is organized as follows. In section 8.2 we describe the background to the United Kingdom's auction and provide some summary information about the outcome of the auction.[8] To illustrate our benchmark of private values and straightforward bidding, we discuss in section 8.3 the bids made by Orange. These bids were largely in line with our benchmark hypotheses. Section 8.4 then considers in more detail the behavior of BT3G. Section 8.5 conducts a similar case study for TIW and NTL Mobile. Section 8.6 concludes.

8.2   Background

The sale of UMTS licenses in the United Kingdom was conducted by the Radiocommunications Agency. This is an agency of the UK's government. The Radiocommunications Agency sold five licenses, labeled A, B, C, D, and E. Each license entitles its owner to the use of a part of the spectrum that is identified in the license. License A consists of $15 + 15$ MHz of paired spectrum and 5 MHz of unpaired spectrum.[9] License B consists of $15 + 15$ MHz of paired spectrum. Licenses C, D, and E consist of $10 + 10$ MHz of paired spectrum and 5 MHz of unpaired spectrum. The licenses remain in force until 2021. At the time of the auction licenses could not be traded, but the government indicated that it might enable license trading during the duration of the licenses. The licenses came with an obligation to roll out a network covering at least 80 percent of the U.K. population by 2007. License A was reserved for a new entrant into the United Kingdom's mobile phone market. The incumbent four mobile telephone operators were not allowed to bid for license A. The four incumbent mobile telephone operators in the United Kingdom were, at the time of the auction, Vodafone, Cellnet (owned by British Telecom), Orange, and One2One. On 1 May 1999 their mobile telephone subscriber shares in the United Kingdom were as follows: Vodafone (37.3%), Cellnet (30.1%), Orange (17.2%), and One2One (15.4%).

The auction was organized in "rounds." In every round except the first one, each license had a "current price" and a "current price bidder." In each round the current price bidders had to remain inactive. All other bidders had three actions available to them: (1) They could make a bid for one of the licenses. This bid had to exceed the "current price" by a minimum increment that was announced by the Radiocommunications Agency before the round began. (2) They could ask for a "waiver," that is, do nothing. Each bidder could ask for a total of three waivers only in the auction. (3) They could withdraw from the auction. Withdrawal was final: A bidder who withdrew could not reenter the auction.

The highest bid for each license became the "current price" in the next round, and the bidder who placed that bid became the "current price bidder" in the next round. If no bid was placed on a license, then the "current price" and the "current price bidder" remained unchanged. If several bidders placed identical highest bids on a license, then the "current price bidder" was randomly selected from these bidders. The auction ended when the last bidder who was not "current price bidder" for some license had withdrawn. Each "current price bidder" was then awarded its license at the "current price."

The minimum bids for the five licenses in the first round were as follows: A (£125 million) B (£107.1 million), and C, D, and E (£89.3 million). In the first round all bidders had to be active and choose one of the three actions described earlier. In later rounds the minimum increment was $x\%$ of the current price, where x was initially 5 and was later chosen by the Radiocommunications Agency.

Interested bidders had to pay an initial deposit of £50 million. A bidder who wished to increase his bid to £400 million had to pay

Table 8.1
Withdrawals

Company	Withdrew in round
NTL Mobile	150
Telefonica	133
Worldcom	121
One.Tel	101
Epsilon	98
Spectrumco	97
3G UK	95
Crescent	94

an additional deposit of £50 million. Winning bidders could choose between either paying immediately or deferring part of the payment, where an interest rate would then be applied.

All four incumbents entered the auction. Cellnet participated in the auction as BT3G. In addition, nine outsiders joined the auction: NTL Mobile, 3G UK, Worldcom, TIW, Telefonica, Spectrumco, Crescent, One.Tel, and Epsilon. The government agreed to regard these companies as independent bidders. Orange was owned by Mannesmann who, in turn, had just been taken over by Vodafone, but Vodafone gave an undertaking to the government to dispose of Orange after the auction and to take measures that ensured the independence of Orange's bidding in the auction.

The auction opened on March 6, 2000, and closed on April 27, 2000. The number of rounds was 150. The typical number of rounds per day was five. The minimum increments by which a bidder had to overbid the previously highest bid was initially 5 percent but was lowered in several steps to 1.5 percent.

The first company withdrew in round 94. All withdrawal decisions are listed in table 8.1. The final winners of the auction, and the winning bids, are listed in table 8.2.

All companies that won licenses opted to pay for these licenses immediately although the government had offered an option of deferred payment. By September 2000 all licenses had been issued.

Table 8.1 shows that the first five bidders to withdraw from the auction did so in quick succession. The withdrawals began in round 94 and ended in round 101. It therefore seems natural to call rounds 1–101 "phase 1" of the auction. After Telefonica withdrew from the

Table 8.2
Winners

Licence	Company	Winning bid
A	TIW	£4,384.7 million
B	Vodafone	£5,964.0 million
C	BT3G	£4,030.1 million
D	One2One	£4,003.6 million
E	Orange	£4,095.0 million

auction in round 133, it was clear that the auction would end once one additional bidder withdrew. Therefore, these rounds constituted the "hot phase" of the auction, and we call them "phase 3." We call the intermediate rounds, namely, rounds 102–133, "phase 2" of the auction. In phase 2 the number of bidders was first eight and then seven. It appears natural to divide phase 2 further into phases 2a and 2b, where phase 2a consists of rounds 102–121 in which the number of bidders was eight, and phase 2b, rounds 122–133, when the number of bidders was seven. For simplicity, we mostly treat phase 2 as just one phase. However, where this provides additional information, we also employ the distinction between phases 2a and 2b.[10]

Next we indicate how the prices of the licenses developed during these three phases. Here, and in the following, we mean by the "price" of a license in any particular round the minimum bid that is needed to overbid the currently leading bidder in that round. Thus the price of a license in a round equals the bid made by the currently leading bidder plus the minimum increment.[11] In figure 8.1 we show the prices of licenses A and B as well as the price of the most expensive and the price of the cheapest of licenses C, D, and E in every round. The figures show that the speed at which the prices of licenses A and B rose during the auction accelerated in phase 2 and slowed down significantly in phase 3.

8.3 Straightforward Bidding with Private Values: The Case of Orange

Our focus in this chapter is on documenting and explaining deviations from straightforward bidding and private values. To begin with, however, we give the example of a company whose behavior is largely in line with these hypotheses. We do this, first, to clarify how the data can

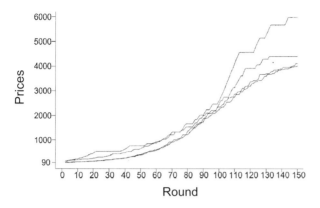

Figure 8.1
License prices in million pounds. Top line: license B; next line: license A; next line: maximum of the prices of C, D, and E; bottom line: minimum of the prices of C, D, and E.

confirm these hypotheses, and, second, to indicate that not *all*, but only *some* firms' bidding behavior deviates from the hypotheses.

The bidder whose behavior we consider in this section is Orange, one of the four incumbents in the mobile telephone market in the United Kingdom. Orange won license E. Although Orange's behavior was roughly as predicted by private values and straightforward bidding, it did not satisfy these hypotheses exactly. The most prominent deviation was that Orange typically did not bid the minimum admissible bid. Bids that exceed the minimum admissible bid are called "jump bids." Orange frequently placed such jump bids. However, the size of its jumps never exceeded 5 percent of the admissible minimum bid. On average, they bid 2.06 percent over the minimum admissible bid. These are relatively small jump bids. We discuss possible rationales for jump bids in Börgers and Dustmann (2001). For example, jump bids might have been placed with the aim of avoiding ties, which occurred quite frequently in the auction. As indicated in Börgers and Dustmann (2001), the existence of jump bids does not seem to be a very significant deviation from our hypotheses, and therefore we do not focus on jump bids.

Orange only placed bids for licenses B and E. License A was, of course, not available to Orange. That Orange never bid for licenses C and D is somewhat surprising but can easily be rationalized within the private value paradigm by assuming that Orange assigned value zero to these licenses. We therefore now focus on licenses B and E.

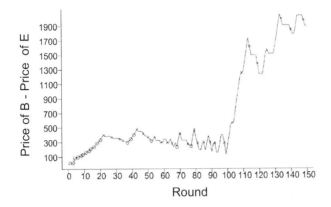

Figure 8.2
Orange's bids for large and small licenses. Bids for small licenses: x, bids for large licenses: o.

Because Orange stayed in the auction until the end, its bidding behavior does not identify the value that it attached to licenses B and E. Orange may well have attached values to these licenses that by far exceeded the final bids for these licenses. We can, however, under the private value and straightforward bidding hypothesis make inferences from Orange's bidding behavior regarding the *difference* between its value for B and its value for E. To see this denote by v_B Orange's value for license B and by v_E their value for license E. Also, denote by p_B the price of license B and by p_E the price of license E. Straightforward bidding means that Orange bids for license B if and only if

$$v_B - p_B \geq v_E - p_E \quad \Leftrightarrow \quad p_B - p_E \leq v_B - v_E$$

Thus, whenever we observe Orange bid for B in some round, we can deduce that the value difference $v_B - v_E$ is at least as large as the price difference $p_B - p_E$ in that period. Similarly, whenever we observe Orange bid for E in some round, we can deduce an upper bound for the value difference.

In figure 8.2 we show how the price difference $p_B - p_E$ (in million Pounds) evolved during the 150 rounds of the auction. We have marked each period in which Orange bid for B with a circle and each period in which Orange bid for E with a cross. Under straightforward bidding with private values, a horizontal line through figure 8.2 that intersects the vertical axis at $v_B - v_E$ will separate the circles from the crosses. Indeed, under the private value and straightforward bidding hypothesis all circles will be below that line, and all crosses will be above it. This follows from the previous inequality. Now, of course, we do not know $v_B - v_E$. But we can test in the graph in figure 8.2 whether bidding behavior is compatible with our hypothesis by checking whether there exists some horizontal line through figure 8.2 with the property that all circles are below it and all crosses are above it.

It is easy to see that we can separate circles from crosses in figure 8.2 by drawing a horizontal line that intersects the vertical axis at roughly £270 million. This leaves a few circles above the horizontal line, that is, a few bids for license B are made although the price difference is larger than this estimate of the value difference. However, the difference between the price difference and the value difference is never very large, at least not in relative terms. In what follows, we find much larger deviations from our benchmark hypothesis. Orange is one of the companies that comes closest to satisfying our benchmark hypothesis.

8.4   Bidding for License B

We now turn to our case studies. We begin by considering the two main companies that bid for license B. All companies were allowed to bid for this license. However, from round 78 onward only two companies, Vodafone and BT3G, bid for license B. We focus on these two companies. Vodafone and BT3G were at the time of the auction the two largest incumbents in the U.K. mobile phone market. If they wanted to acquire a large third generation license, they had to win license B.

Vodafone's behavior is easy to describe. They bid only for license B. Moreover they always bid the minimum admissible bid for license B, with two exceptions. In round 123 Vodafone placed a jump bid that exceeded the minimum bid by about 1.1 percent. In round 143 Vodafone placed a jump bid that exceeded the minimum bid by about 1.3 percent.[12] The latter bid was Vodafone's final bid in the auction. It clinched license B for Vodafone. Note that both jump bids were relatively small; for example, they were smaller than the next minimum bid increment. Apart from these two jump bids, Vodafone's behavior is easily explained by the private value and straightforward bidding hypothesis. They might have had a very high value of B, far beyond the price finally achieved in the auction, and a very low value for all other licenses.

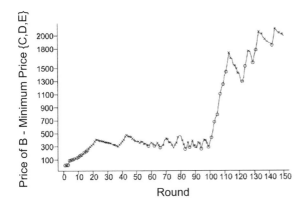

Figure 8.3
BT3G's bids for large and small licenses. Bids for small licenses: x; bids for large
licenses: o.

Unlike Vodafone, BT3G placed bids on small and large licenses.
When bidding for a small license BT3G always only bid for the
cheapest of all small licenses. All bids by BT3G were exactly equal to
the lowest admissible bid. These aspects of BT3G's behavior are thus
easily compatible with our hypotheses.

What is less clear is how BT3G chose whether to bid for a large or
a small license. We construct in figure 8.3 a graph for BT3G that is
analogous to figure 8.2 for Orange. Because BT3G always bid for the
cheapest of licenses C, D, and E, we assume that BT3G was indifferent
among the three small licenses, and therefore display in figure 8.2 the
difference (in million pounds) between the price of license B and the
lowest of the prices of licenses C, D, and E. As before we mark bids for
a large license by circles and bids for a small license by crosses. It
is clear from figure 8.3 that there is no horizontal line through the
graph that would even approximately separate circles from crosses.
Thus, there is no consistently revealed valuation of the advantage of
having a large rather than a small license.

8.4.1 BT3G's Bids in Phase 1

To understand better what happened we consider separately BT3G's
behavior in the three phases of the auction that we defined at the end of
section 8.2. Consider first phase 1. BT3G began by bidding for license B
but abandoned bids for B in round 17. In round 16, in which BT3G was

still bidding for B, the price difference between B and the small licenses was £247.3 million, whereas in round 17, when BT3G bid for a small license, it was £277.2. Thus, under the hypothesis of private values and straightforward bidding, we would conclude after round 17 that BT3G's estimate of the value difference was between £247.3 million and £277.2 million. Until and including round 56, BT3G never bid again for license B. This is consistent with the estimate just provided because throughout this period one had to pay more than £277.2 million extra to obtain license B rather than a small license.

However, in round 57, BT3G suddenly bid for license B although the price difference was now £306.7 million. BT3G then switched frequently between bidding for B and bidding for a small license. If one neglects the earlier bids, and one focuses on the bids from round 57 until the end of phase 1, then BT3G's bids revealed that their estimate of the extra value provided by license B in comparison to the smaller licenses was between £310.1 million and £319.3 million. Thus BT3G's estimate of the extra value seems to have been revised upward, but possibly only by as little as 12 percent.

8.4.2 BT3G's Bids in Phase 3

Before we turn to phase 2, we briefly consider phase 3. In this phase BT3G placed only six bids, and of these only one was for license B. The bid for license B occurred when the difference in price between license B and the small licenses was lowest in phase 3. If we thus consider bidding in phase 3 in isolation, then this was entirely compatible with the private values and straightforward bidding hypothesis. BT3G's bid in round 137 revealed that their estimate of the difference in value between a large and a small license was not more than £1,945.1 million, and their bid in round 142 revealed that the estimate was not less than £1,854.6 million.[13]

8.4.3 BT3G's Bids in Phase 2

It is now important to consider in detail what happened in the intermittent phase 2. Figure 8.3 shows that BT3G raised in three "waves" the amount that it was willing to bid extra to obtain a large rather than a small license. The first such wave began in round 101, the round in which One.Tel withdrew. In that round BT3G placed a bid on license B, although the price difference was now £440.8 million, and thus above their previous threshold of £319.3 million. BT3G kept bidding for B until and including round 111, in which the price difference had reached £1,445.5 million. This is the end of the first wave. BT3G switched back to a small license and bid for a small license even in round 119, although the price difference had now dropped back to £1,428.3 million. The second and third waves of BT3G's bidding for license B in phase 2 both consisted only of two bids each. In the second wave (rounds 122 and 124) BT3G was willing to bid for license B until the price difference had reached £1,530.8 million, and in the third wave (rounds 129 and 131) BT3G was willing to bid for license B until the price difference had reached £1,781.5 million.

8.4.4   The Main Questions

The most important deviation of BT3G's behavior from our benchmark hypothesis is the apparent rise in BT3G's evaluation of the difference between a big and a small license at the beginning of phase 2 of the auction. A second puzzle concerns why in phase 2 BT3G occasionally did not bid for license B although the price difference had fallen below a level at which BT3G had placed bids for license B before. We now discuss alternatives to our benchmark hypothesis that can explain some of this behavior.

8.4.5   What Caused BT3G to Bid for Large or Small Licenses?

8.4.5.1   Bidding in Early Rounds Is Arbitrary

The simplest explanation of the rise in BT3G's evaluation of the difference between a big and a small license is that bidding in the early rounds was arbitrary, as the number of active bidders exceeded the number of available licenses significantly, and therefore the probability of the auction ending soon was so low that bids weren't really significant. We point out, however, that our data show that BT3G's bidding behavior in these rounds is remarkably consistent. This suggests that BT3G's behavior was not arbitrary. Of course, it may have been guided by considerations other than myopic surplus maximization. We discuss this possibility later.

8.4.5.2   Budget Constraints

It seems plausible that companies that participated in the U.K. auction faced budget constraints. The government had offered successful bidders two options for paying for their licenses: either instantaneous payment after the end of the auction, or deferred payment where 50 percent had to be paid instantaneously and the remaining 50 percent plus interest had to be paid over the next five years.[14] Companies seem to have regarded the option of deferred payment as obviously too costly (National Audit Office 2001, 31). It then seems plausible that the bidders arranged their funding before or during the auction. Apparent changes in bidding strategies during the auction may have been due to changes in companies' financial situation.

In the case of BT3G, the willingness to bid more aggressively for license B from round 101 onward might be because BT3G had arranged additional finance at that time. It had perhaps become clear that more money was needed than had been initially raised. If finance was arranged in round numbers, then it might be relevant that up to round 94 the largest bid by BT3G had been £2,339.9 million (in round 94). In round 99 BT3G made its first bid that was above £2,500 million. Thus, up to that point £2,500 million might have been the budget constraint. This argument does not explain BT3G's frequent switching between large and small licenses at the later stages of the auction, but a more complicated financial history might account for that too.

There is another way in which budget constraints might have affected BT3G's bidding. If the bidders in the auction were subject to budget constraints, then each bidder may have had an incentive to drive up the prices that other bidders had to pay, either to weaken these other bidders in subsequent European spectrum auctions, or to make it harder for them to finance the investments needed to offer attractive third generation services in the United Kingdom. Thus the primary aim of the bids that BT3G made for license B in phases 2 and 3 of the auction may have been to raise the price that Vodafone had to pay for license B. It may not actually have been BT3G's purpose to win that license themselves. Such a strategy is rational only if BT3G is sufficiently convinced that every bid that it places on license B will be overbid. BT3G might have become convinced of this because, as explained earlier, Vodafone's strategy from the beginning of the auction had been to bid only for license B and to overbid every bid placed on that license. As Cramton (2001, 50) writes, one can interpret Vodafone's behavior as an expression of "its resolve in winning the B license." This exposed Vodafone to the risk that other companies such as BT3G would place bids on license B solely to raise the price that Vodafone had to pay. On the other hand, nobody could ever be completely sure that Vodafone would behave in the future as it had done in the past. The bids placed in the later phases of the auction were very large. BT3G always ran the risk that Vodafone abandoned license B, in which case BT3G would most likely be stuck with its bid. This speaks against this theory. We also note that this argument does not explain BT3G's frequent switching between license B and small licenses.

8.4.5.3   Social Learning

Companies might have learned from other companies' bidding behavior about the true value of the licenses for which they were bidding. Since Milgrom and Weber's seminal paper (1982), this effect has received much attention in the auction literature.[15]

In the current auction it seems plausible that some such social learning has taken place. But a priori one would expect this effect to be of minor quantitative importance. Social learning is an important quantitative effect only if some bidders hold private information that is potentially of large commercial significance to other bidders. At the time of the auction there was large uncertainty about the economic value of third generation mobile telephone technology, but this uncertainty seems to persist until today. It does not seem plausible that at the time of the auction any one bidder had highly significant private information.

We now turn to the data. A first potential source of information to British Telecom about the added value of holding a large license were other bidders' bids placed for license B. As we mentioned earlier, from round 78 onward Vodafone was the only other company that bid for license B. It is conceivable that Vodafone's strategy of not bidding for a small license, and its willingness to counter every bid by BT3G for license B, lead BT3G to revise its estimates of the value difference upward.

BT3G might also have learned about the value difference between a large and a small license from observing bidding on the other large license A. However, as we argue in section 8.5, it seems that the acceleration in the price of license A in phase 2 followed that for license B rather than the other way round. Thus, we believe that it is more likely that bidders for license A learned from the bidding for license B than that the bidders for license B learned from the bidding for license A.

BT3G might also have learned about the value difference between a large and a small license by observing bids placed on the smaller licenses. For example, the bids placed by NTL Mobile that we discuss later suggested that NTL Mobile's estimate of the value difference between a large and a small license gradually increased in phase 1 of the auction. Observing this effect might have led BT3G to revise its own estimate.

The precise quantitative form in which a bidder could learn in the auction from other bidders' behavior will depend on this bidder's prior beliefs as well as this bidder's beliefs about other bidders' behavior. It seems hard to find a specification of these beliefs that would explain the suddenness of the change in BT3G's behavior at the end of round 100 and the size of this change, or that would explain the apparent occasional downward shifts in beliefs in phase 2. We have not explored this issue any further, but the hypothesis seems extremely speculative.

There is another way in which social learning might contribute to an explanation of BT3G's bids. BT3G might have tried to manipulate other companies' learning behavior. In particular, it might have tried to conceal initially its estimate of the value difference between a large and a small license. One indication that this might have been the case is the fact that the estimate of the value difference between a large and a small license revealed by BT3G's early bids in phase 1 of the auction was very close to that revealed by the other incumbent who bid on large as well as small licenses in that phase, namely, Orange. Orange's bidding, though not entirely consistent, suggested that its estimate of the value difference was around £270 million. BT3G might have deliberately tried not to deviate from this too much. In the language of game theory, BT3G might have tried to play a "pooling strategy," concealing its true information from the market by behaving like a competitor.

The question arises, What could BT3G gain by such a strategy? The purpose might have been to induce other bidders to drop out of the auction. Once that was achieved in round 101, BT3G might have felt ready to place much higher bids. Thus it appears conceivable that a pooling rationale explains BT3G's strategy. A question then is why other companies did not adopt the same strategy as BT3G. In particular, Vodafone seems to have seen an advantage in exactly the opposite strategy: stating publicly a strong interest in license B, and never moving away from it. Perhaps Vodafone's managers held different subjective beliefs about the situation.

8.4.5.4 Allocative Externalities
Companies' valuation of a license may depend on which other bidders will win a license. If this is the case one speaks of "allocative external-

ities." The potential importance of allocative externalities for license auctions has been emphasized by Jehiel and Moldovanu (2000, 2001). In the case of the U.K. auction, one might speculate that BT3G's apparent changes in their valuation of license B in comparison to a small license might have been driven by BT3G's expectations of who else would win a license. We investigate now evidence that might show whether this was indeed the case. A problem we face is that the number of ways in which BT3G's valuation of license B in comparison to a small license might have depended on who else wins a license is very large. We focus here on two hypotheses that seem to us particularly plausible a priori.

The first is that BT3G's incentive to acquire a large rather than a small license might have been affected by how likely it appeared that TIW was going to win license A, as it eventually did. One reason for this might have been that TIW was backed by the financially very strong Hutchison Whampoa group, a former owner of Orange, and BT3G might have been aware of this. BT3G might have viewed TIW as a particularly formidable competitor in the U.K. market.

To evaluate whether this hypothesis contributes to the explanation of our bidding data, we ask whether BT3G revealed a consistent estimate of the value difference between license B and the small licenses if one conditions on whether TIW is the current leader on A. This assumes that BT3G took the current leadership on license A as an indication of who might win license A. The assumption is in line with the myopia assumed in straightforward bidding, but obviously it can be criticized. We see no more plausible alternative to this assumption, though.

It turns out that conditioning on whether TIW is current leader on A does not eliminate the inconsistencies in BT3G's bids. To show this we begin with table 8.3, which shows the number of bids placed by BT3G on license B and on the small licenses as a function of the event that TIW was the current leader for license A. The data shown are for all rounds. We show in parentheses the data for rounds 101–150 only.

The first fact to note is that BT3G placed significant numbers of bids on small licenses in phase 1 of the auction, both when TIW was current leader on A and when TIW was not current leader on A. As a consequence, BT3G's bidding in phase 1 of the auction revealed an upper boundary for both conditional value differences that were certainly not larger than the highest price difference in phase 1. Next observe that BT3G placed significant numbers of bids on license B in phase 2, both

Table 8.3
BT3G's bids conditional on the leading bidder for licences A (data in brackets concern rounds 101–150 only)

	TIW is current leader on A	TIW is not current leader on A	Total
BT3G bids for B	7 (4)	26 (7)	33 (11)
BT3G bids for C, D or E	11 (10)	63 (2)	74 (12)
Total	18 (14)	89 (9)	107 (23)

when TIW was the current leader on A, and when TIW was not the current leader on A. Thus, we obtain lower boundaries for the conditional value differences that are certainly much larger than the upper boundaries in phase 1 (compare figure 8.3). Thus, the inconsistencies between phase 1 and phases 2 and 3 do not disappear if one conditions on whether TIW is the current leader on A.

One might still hope that the proposed externality concerning the winner of license A could provide an explanation of BT3G's behavior in phases 2 and 3 only, neglecting phase 1. However, this is not the case. Considering first periods in which TIW was leading on A, we note that the last bid of the first "wave" of bidding for B fell into a period in which TIW was leading on A. All of the immediately following bids for a small license except the first one were also made when TIW was leading on A. As figure 8.3 indicates, this implies that there is no conditional estimate of the value difference that could rationalize BT3G's bids. Next, considering periods in which companies other than TIW were leading on A, we note that in round 113 BT3G bid for a small license, thus providing us with an upper boundary for the conditional value difference of £1,733.6 million, but in round 131 BT3G bid for license B, thus providing us with a lower boundary for the conditional value difference of £1,71.5 million. Thus, there is again no consistent conditional value difference.

The second possibility that we have investigated is that the anticipated number of other incumbents acquiring a license might have been a factor. BT3G began bidding aggressively for license B when four bidders had left the auction and a fifth had asked for a waiver round. At that stage it seemed more likely that more incumbents would hold licenses, and for some reason this might have triggered an increase in the extra value that BT3G attached to a large license in comparison to a

Table 8.4
BT3G's bids conditional on the number of leading incumbents (data in brackets concern rounds 101–150 only)

	0 incumbents leading on B, C, D, or E	1 incumbent leading on B, C, D, or E	2 incumbents leading on B, C, D, or E	3 incumbents leading on B, C, D, or E	Total
Bids for B	14 (0)	10 (4)	9 (7)	0 (0)	3 (11)
Bids for C, D, or E	0 (0)	36 (2)	34 (6)	4 (4)	74 (12)
Total	14 (0)	46 (6)	43 (13)	4 (4)	107 (23)

small license. The beginning of the second "wave" of BT3G's bids for B followed similarly immediately after Worldcom withdrew in round 121. However, the beginning of the third "wave" is not associated with any withdrawal, and instead the end of the third "wave" coincides with Telefonica's withdrawal from the auction in round 133.

An alternative way of looking at this issue is to regard the current number of incumbents who are leading bidders on a license as a predictor of the number of incumbents who will ultimately win a license, and to ask whether conditional on this predictor BT3G revealed consistent estimates of the value differences. Table 8.4 shows the frequency of bids by BT3G on license B as a function of the number of incumbents leading on a license. We have made one correction in this table, though. We have not counted an incumbent as leading bidder on a license if the bid that BT3G was about to place displaced that leading bidder. Suppose, for example, that incumbents were leading on B, C, and E and that BT3G was about to bid for B. Then we counted this as a bid for B with two (not three) incumbents leading on other licenses, because BT3G knew that it would displace the leader on B from his position. As in table 8.3, information that relates only to rounds 101–150 is indicated in parentheses.

Table 8.4 indicates that trivially there will be conditional value differences that rationalize BT3G's bids if we condition on the event that zero incumbents are leading on B, C, D, and E. In this event BT3G never bid for B. Table 8.4 also seems to indicate that we can obtain a conditional value difference for the case that 3 incumbents are leading on B, C, D, and E. In this case BT3G never bid for B. For the intermediate cases an argument similar to the one we used earlier in the context of table 8.3 suggests that there is no conditional value difference that

Table 8.5
BT and Vodafone share prices in £s

	Share price before round 1 (3 March)	Share price before round 99 (4 April)	Share price after round 150 (27 April)
British Telekom	1169.98	995.91 (−16%)	1016.44 (−13%)
Vodafone	369.5	321.5 (−13%)	279.25 (−24%)

rationalizes bids across phases 1, 2, and 3. We could consider phases 2 and 3 in isolation, but a simple analysis shows that this does not affect the conclusion.

8.4.5.5 Shareholders' Opinion

Bidders in the auction are likely to have monitored carefully the views of their shareholders. These views might have expressed themselves in share prices. Managers might, for example, have found that the share price responded very negatively to particular bids, and might have avoided such bids in the future. Table 8.5 shows British Telecom's, and, for comparison purposes, also Vodafone's share prices at the London Stock Exchange on three crucial dates: on the last trading day before the auction began, on the last trading day before phase 2 of the auction began, and on the last day of the auction. In parentheses we indicate the change in comparison to the share price on the last trading day before the auction began.[16] The table indicates that British Telecom's share price seemed to suffer more than that of Vodafone at the end of phase 1 of the auction. When the auction was over, British Telecom's share price had recaptured some of its losses whereas Vodafone's share price had gone down further.

One might argue that the stock market signaled to BT3G that its bidding in phase 1 was too conservative, and BT3G's more aggressive bidding in phases 2 and 3 might have led to the recovery in its share prices. A cross-company comparison for phases 2 and 3 suggests the reverse effect, though. The more aggressive bidder, Vodafone, suffered losses, whereas the less aggressive bidder, British Telecom, gained.

Table 8.5 hides large volatility in share prices. In figure 8.4 we show the ratio of BT3G's and Vodafone's share price at the London Stock Exchange. The purpose of considering this ratio is to keep track of the relative stock market success of the two companies. We have normalized the ratio to equal 1 on the last trading day before the auction (3

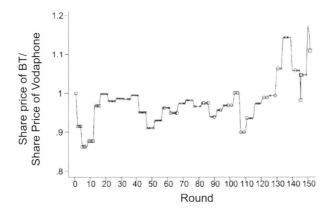

Figure 8.4
Ratio of British Telecom and Vodafone's share prices. BT3G's bids for small licenses: x;
BT3G's bids for large licenses: o; days on which the London Stock Exchange traded but
the auction didn't take place: □.

March 2000). For each round we indicate the value of the share price
ratio on the preceding trading day.

Figure 8.4 confirms that British Telecom did worse than Vodafone in
phase 1, and the figure hints at the effect that bids for small licenses led
to downward movements in the ratio whereas bids for large licenses
led to upward movements. However, BT3G's more aggressive bidding
for B in phase 2 initially lead to a dramatic fall in the share price ratio,
and if BT3G had kept track of this one might have expected the company to abandon this strategy earlier than it actually did. A consideration of phases 2 and 3 overall does not reveal any predictable effect of
bids for B on the share price ratio.

8.4.5.6   Management Disagreements

Shifts in a company's bidding strategy may also be due to changing
power structures in that company's management. Thus BT3G's more
aggressive bidding for a large license from period 101 onward may be
due to the fact that a different group in its management won control of
the bidding strategy. An indicator that there was a potential for disagreement is that Sir Christopher Bland, when becoming new chair-
man of British Telecom in April 2001, commented that in his opinion
the company "should never have bid for a third-generation telephone
license" (Hirst 2001). *The Independent on Sunday* added: "However, he
is not critical of BT's board for bidding for a license: 'Hindsight is a

wonderful thing.'" It is, however, hard to conceive of an ongoing power struggle that would induce BT3G to switch back and forth between small and large licenses as they did in the auction.

8.4.6 Summary

We find little direct evidence for any of the hypotheses we consider. However, the most plausible speculations seem to be that BT3G's initial reluctance to bid for license B was due to either budget constraints or a deliberate strategy to conceal its true valuation of license B. Management disagreements also may have affected behavior throughout the auction.

8.5 Bidding for License A

The leading bidders for license A were TIW and NTL Mobile. Both bidders participated in the auction until its end. TIW ultimately won license A, and it was NTL Mobile's decision to withdraw from the auction in round 150 that triggered the end of the auction. We conclude that these two companies were the leading contenders for license A because after round 108 there was only one bid from another bidder for license A—namely, the bid by Worldcom in round 116. In round 108 the price of license A had reached £3,000 million. At the end of the auction it was £4,384.7 million. Thus, there was a significant price increase, and it was largely due to these two contenders' bids.

The bidding competition between TIW and NTL Mobile for license A took place in phase 2 of the auction. It was settled by the end of phase 2 in round 133. At that stage TIW was the leading bidder for license A, and its position was not challenged any further in phase 3. Note, however, that NTL Mobile made some bids for small licenses in phase 3.

As outsiders to the U.K. mobile telephone market, TIW and NTL Mobile were allowed to bid for licenses A and B when bidding for a large license. However, license A was somewhat larger than license B, and it was also for most of the auction cheaper than license B. There were only fifteen rounds in which license A was more expensive than license B. The last such round was round 76. The largest difference in price was £77.6 million, which is less than 2 percent of the final price of license A. All this seems to suggest that almost always A was the better deal than B. We do indeed find that NTL Mobile never bid for license B. TIW is one of the few outsiders who did place bids on license B. However, all bids by TIW for license B occurred very early in the auction. From round 14 onward, TIW did not bid for license B again.

If we neglect TIW's early bids for B, we can simplify the argument and assume that TIW and NTL Mobile faced a choice between bidding for the large license A and bidding for one of the smaller licenses C, D, or E. When choosing among licenses C, D, or E, both companies did not necessarily choose the cheapest of these licenses. This suggests that they might have had preferences over these apparently very similar licenses. In our companion paper (Börgers and Dustmann 2001), we use a random utility model to estimate the value differences. Our estimates suggested that NTL Mobile ranked licenses in alphabetical order, or C, D, and E, whereas TIW ranked them in reverse alphabetical order, or E, D, and C. However, none of the estimated value differences was significantly different from zero. Moreover, since the prices of licenses C, D, and E stayed very close together, as can be seen in figure 8.1, this is not a major issue. To simplify our arguments, we work with the assumption that TIW and NTL Mobile were indifferent among licenses C, D, and E.

Both TIW and NTL Mobile deviated from the rules of straightforward bidding and did not always bid the minimum bid. If we ignore for TIW its somewhat erratic bids in rounds 1–13, then we find that 30 percent of TIW's bids were jump bids. For NTL Mobile the percentage of jump bids is 32 percent. The average size of TIW's jump bids after round 13 was 2.1 percent above the required minimum bid, and the average size of NTL Mobile's jump bids was 1.96 percent above the minimum bid. As before, we argue that the jump bids are relatively small, and a minor deviation from our hypotheses.

The final and most important step of our analysis is to consider how TIW and NTL Mobile chose whether to bid for a large or a small license. Figures 8.5 and 8.6 describe these choices. The figures are analogous to figures 8.2 and 8.3, which referred to Orange and BT3G. The figures indicate that neither of the two companies placed their bids in accordance with the hypothesis of straightforward bidding under private values. As was the case with BT3G, we regard these deviations from the straightforward bidding hypothesis as the most important deviations and therefore focus on them in this section.

We begin our discussion with TIW. Recall that TIW was leading bidder on license A at the end of phase 2 and was not further

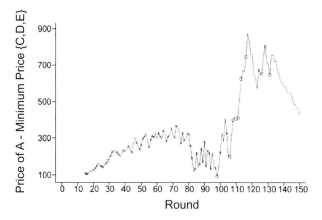

Figure 8.5
TIW's bids for large and small licenses. Bids for small licenses: x, bids for large licenses: o.

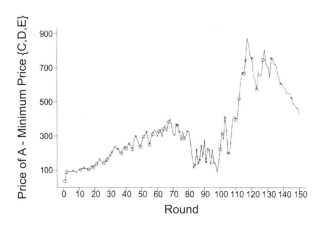

Figure 8.6
NTL Mobile's bids for large and small licenses. Bids for small licenses: x, bids for large licenses: o.

challenged in that position in phase 3. Therefore we can restrict attention to phases 1 and 2.

8.5.1   TIW's Bids in Phase 1

Note that figure 8.5 ignores rounds 1–13 because in these rounds TIW placed bids on license B that are hard to explain, as we discussed earlier. In the subsequent rounds of phase 1, TIW made only two further bids for license A. One was in round 29 when the price difference was £176.2 million. The second was in round 98 when the price difference was £92.8 million. The bid in round 29 is puzzling because in later rounds the price difference was much lower, yet TIW did not bid for license A. The second bid is easier to understand because it was made when the price difference was lower than it had been in any round since round 9. Thus we treat the bid in round 29 as an outlier and deduce that TIW's revealed extra value attached to license A in comparison to a small license was between £92.8 million (the price difference in round 98) and £107.7 million (the price difference in round 14).

8.5.2   TIW's Bids in Phase 2

TIW's first bid in phase 2 was a bid for license D in round 104. This bid was entirely consistent with its behavior in phase 1. However, in round 106 the company suddenly started to bid for license A again. At this stage the price difference between A and the small licenses was £200.2 million, a difference that in phase 1 it would have regarded as prohibitive. TIW continued with four further bids for license A. The last of these bids, in round 116, was at a price difference of £745.4 million. As in the case of BT3G, we find that in the early rounds of phase 2 there was apparently a sudden and dramatic revision upward in TIW's estimate of the extra value of a large license.

TIW's four further bids in the auction are somewhat surprising because they suggest a downward revision of the estimate of the difference. In round 124, when the price difference had dropped to £674.7 million, TIW refused to bid for A and instead bid for E. In round 126, when the price difference was £653.2 million, TIW returned to license A. Thus it seemed that its estimated value difference was now between £653.2 million and £674.7 million. The final two bids by TIW were compatible with this estimated value difference. This value difference thus rationalizes all bids by TIW in phase 2b of the auction.

8.5.3   NTL Mobile's Bids in Phase 1

NTL Mobile in phase 1 gradually moved its revealed estimate of the extra value of holding large license A upward. For example, in round 1 NTL Mobile bid for license A when the price difference was only £35.7 million. In round 2 it was willing to bid again for license A although now the price difference had gone up to £89.2 million. This second bid was the highest bid in its round, and NTL Mobile entered rounds 3, 4, and 5 as the leading bidder for license A. In round 5 it was over-bid by another bidder. In round 6, when the price difference between license A and the small licenses had reached £96.8 million, NTL Mobile decided not to bid for A again, but to switch to C. At this stage it seemed that NTL Mobile's estimate of the added value of a large license in comparison to a small license had been pinned down quite precisely. However, shortly afterward, in round 11, when the price dif-ference was £103.7 million, NTL Mobile bid again for A. In round 13 when the price difference had gone up to £114.2 million, NTL Mobile abandoned A again. At that stage NTL Mobile's evaluations seemed to have been narrowed down again, except that in round 19, when the price difference was £116.6 million, NTL Mobile returned to license A. This pattern continued until round 68 when NTL Mobile bid for license A at a price difference of £402.4 million.

There was then a break in NTL Mobile's behavior. For the rest of phase 1 of the auction, NTL Mobile bid only one more time for license A although the price difference between license A and the smaller licenses fell considerably. NTL Mobile was not even willing to bid for license A in round 83 when the price difference had fallen back to £118.8 million. The one bid that it did make for license A is hard to explain. It was made at a price difference of £287.5 million in round 77.

8.5.4   NTL Mobile's Bids in Phase 2

Phase 2 of the auction began in NTL Mobile's case really in 100. At that stage four firms had withdrawn, and One.Tel had asked for a "waiver." These waivers had turned out to be advance indicators of the withdrawal of a bidder. In phase 2 NTL Mobile began to bid much more aggressively for license A. We can distinguish three "waves," although the first and third wave are relatively short. NTL Mobile began bidding for license A at a price difference of £222.5 million in round 100. It abandoned license A though in round 103 when the price difference went up to £411.6 million and wasn't even willing to bid for A in round 105 when the price difference had fallen to £200.2 million. In round 110 a second "wave" started, and NTL Mobile returned to license A at a price difference of £396.9 million and was willing to bid for license A even at much higher price differences. In fact, the next seven bids of NTL Mobile can all be rationalized by postulating a value difference between £666.1 million and £673.1 million. NTL Mobile concluded phase 2 with a surprising bid for license A in round 127 when the price difference had gone up to £749.2 million.[17]

8.5.5 NTL Mobile's Bids in Phase 3

NTL Mobile did not bid for license A at all in phase 3 but instead bid three times for a small license. This is surprising because TIW entered this phase as the leading bidder for license A and was not challenged any further in that position. As a consequence the price difference between license A and the small licenses dropped in phase 3 and was only £381.1 million at the end of the auction. Despite this drop in the price difference, NTL Mobile did not return to bidding for A.

8.5.6 The Main Questions

As in the case of BT3G in the previous section, the most important question is, What led TIW and NTL Mobile to bid so much more aggressively for a large license after the end of phase 1? In the case of NTL Mobile we have, however, additional interesting questions: What caused the gradual increase in NTL Mobile's estimate of the value difference in the early part of phase 1? What caused NTL Mobile to abandon bidding for license A in the late part of phase 1? Why did NTL Mobile not bid for license A in phase 3? We now investigate whether the ideas introduced in the previous section can answer these four questions.

8.5.7 TIW's and NTL Mobile's Bids: Some Explanations

8.5.7.1 Bidding in Early Rounds Is Arbitrary
The break between phase 1 and later phases is explained most easily by arguing that bids in phase 1 were placed in arbitrary ways because it was unlikely that the auction would close soon. As indicated earlier,

we do indeed find that TIW's bids in rounds 1–13 are hard to rationalize, and those bids might be regarded as arbitrary. TIW's choices in rounds 14–100 do not seem arbitrary, however. Indeed, TIW systematically avoided bidding for A.

Unlike TIW, NTL Mobile made bids for license A throughout the first one hundred periods. Its behavior does not appear to be arbitrary, but it seems to reveal a gradually increasing value difference between license A and the small licenses.

To dismiss early bids for A as arbitrary one would, moreover, have to argue that the fact that many bidders were still left in the auction implied that bids for license A were almost certain to be overbid by some other bidder. However, for license A, unlike for license B, there was no bidder who was clearly determined to win the license. Thus, any bid that was placed on license A seemed to run the risk of being the last bid for that license.

8.5.7.2   Budget Constraints

Could budget constraints explain TIW's decision to place so few bids for license A in the first phase of the auction? We argue that this is not a plausible explanation. The highest bid that TIW placed in the first phase was £2,339.1 million for license D in round 100. In all rounds up to round 98, a budget of this size would have permitted TIW also to bid for license A.

The impact of budget constraints appears to be more interesting in the case of NTL Mobile. NTL Mobile twice ceased to bid for license A in a somewhat unexpected manner. The first instance followed round 77 in which NTL Mobile became leading bidder for license A. When NTL Mobile was overbid by Worldcom in round 79,[18] NTL Mobile refused to counter. The minimum admissible bid for license A in round 79 was £1,601.9 million. NTL Mobile bid instead for the smaller license D at £1,343.5 million. It then continued bidding for the smaller license for a while, even though the price difference between a large and a small license had by then fallen. One might think that this was due to budget constraints. However, already in round 86 NTL Mobile was able to bid £1637.2 million for license D that was more than had been necessary for license A in round 79. Thus, we believe that it is unlikely that NTL Mobile's abandonment of license A in phase 1 was due to budget constraints.

NTL Mobile's last bid for license A was in round 127 when it bid £4,277.7 million. This bid was overbid by TIW in round 131. NTL Mobile did not bid again for license A, nor did any other bidder. To overbid TIW, NTL Mobile would have had to bid £4,494.4 million. NTL Mobile instead bid for smaller licenses, with its highest subsequent bid being £3,970.5 million. Thus it may well have been that NTL Mobile had a budget constraint of, say, £4,300 million, and that this was the reason it did not continue to bid for A. Thus, we conclude that budget constraints may provide a plausible explanation for NTL Mobile's second, although not for its first, abandonment of license A.

As explained in the previous section, the existence of budget constraints introduces an additional bidding motive into auctions: Bidders might place bids to raise the price which their competitors have to pay, with the intention of weakening the competitors in future interactions. One might speculate in this way that NTL Mobile placed its last bids for license A without serious intention of buying license A, but instead to raise the price that TIW had to pay. The owners of NTL Mobile, NTL, and France Telecom might have anticipated that one of them would acquire a license through a takeover, as France Telecom indeed did, and that therefore they had an incentive to financially weaken a potential competitor, TIW. If this strategy was pursued it was very risky, because bids for A always seemed to run the risk of being the last bid for A, and therefore could not be placed spuriously. We therefore do not attach much weight to this hypothesis.

8.5.7.3 Social Learning
TIW and NTL Mobile were both outsiders to the U.K. mobile telephone market. This suggests that more established firms might have had better information about the chances of third generation technology in the United Kingdom, and that TIW and NTL Mobile tried to deduce other firms' information from these firms' bidding behavior. We begin by considering whether this hypothesis can help explain the apparent sudden increase in phase 2 of both companies' estimates of the additional value of a large license in comparison to a small one. In this context it seems interesting that bidding for A lagged a bit behind bidding for B. For example, the unexpectedly high bids for license B that we have identified in the previous section were placed from round 101 onward. We find that unexpectedly high bids for license A began to be placed from round 106 onward. Bidding on license B ceased for a while between rounds 113 and round 121. Similarly, no new bid was made for license A between rounds 117 and 122. Bidding for license B ceased again between rounds 126 and 128. Similarly, bidding for A stopped between 128 and 130. Thus, one might speculate that the outsiders who bid for license A learned from the insider bids placed on

license B that the difference in value between a large and a small license was larger than they had originally thought. It is surprising, however, that outsiders were ready to revise their initial beliefs so quickly and to such a large extent.

As in the case of BT3G, we might also speculate that TIW tried to "hide" its true valuation of a large license in the early rounds of the auction and that its purpose was to manipulate the learning of other firms. However, this speculation is hard to reconcile with the fact that TIW placed some aggressive jump bids for licenses A and B in the very first rounds of the auction.

Social learning might be an explanation for the apparent rise in NTL Mobile's estimate of the value difference in the first 68 rounds of the auction. NTL Mobile might have observed other companies' willingness to bid for a large license, and it might have revised its own estimate of the value difference in the light of what it observed. However, it is hard to see why this effect abruptly stopped after round 68.

8.5.7.4 Allocative Externalities

TIW and NTL Mobile's valuation of the difference between a large and a small license may have been a function of which other companies seemed likely to win a license. We begin by examining whether TIW's willingness to bid for license A rather than a small license was a function of which company was the current leading bidder for the other large license, license B. Table 8.6 shows the number of TIW's bids for license A and small licenses depending on whether Vodafone, BT3G, or some other company was the current leading bidder for B. We ignore rounds 1–13 for the reasons explained earlier.

We interpret table 8.6 in conjunction with figure 8.5. Consider first the event that Vodafone is the current leader on B. The fact that conditional on this event TIW placed bids both on license A and on small

Table 8.6
TIW's bids conditional on the leading bidder for B (data in brackets concern rounds 106–150 only)

	Vodafone is current leader on B	BT3G is current leader on B	Other current leader on B	Total
TIW bids for A	7 (5)	2 (2)	0 (0)	9 (7)
TIW bids for C, D, or E	42 (2)	6 (0)	4 (0)	52 (2)
Total	49 (7)	8 (2)	4 (0)	61 (9)

licenses, both in the first 105 rounds and also in the subsequent rounds, immediately implies that there is no value difference that could rationalize TIW's bids across the different phases of the auction. The same conclusion can easily be obtained by inspection of table 8.6 and figure 8.5 for the event that BT3G was current leader on B. In the event that a company other than Vodafone or BT3G is current leader on B, we observe bids by TIW only in the first 105 rounds of the auction, not later. Therefore, this case is not relevant to our discussion here.

We have also investigated whether conditioning on the total number of incumbents leading on any license might allow us to find value differences that rationalize TIW's bids. However, as in the case of BT3G, this is not the case. We omit the details. Our conclusion is that there is no evidence that TIW's bids were affected by allocative externalities.

We next turn to the question of whether allocative externalities might have affected NTL Mobile's bids. The potential externalities that we discuss are again, first, whether the current leader on license B might affect whether NTL Mobile bids for a large or a small license, and, second, whether the total number of incumbents leading on any license might affect NTL Mobile's decision. If our primary interest is in explaining the escalation in bids for a large license from round 100 onward, then the picture is similar to the picture in the case of TIW. We find no evidence that externalities can contribute to an explanation of NTL Mobile's choices. We omit the details.

This leaves the question of whether allocative externalities might contribute to an explanation of NTL Mobile's behavior if we restrict attention to either phase 1 or to phases 2 and 3. We do not have any positive results to report concerning phase 1. As regards phases 2 and 3, one might argue that in phase 3 it had become clear that Vodafone was the most likely winner of license B and that the number of incumbents holding a license would most likely be 4. Perhaps NTL Mobile abandoned bids for license A in phase 3 because it judged the added advantage of a large license over a small license to be relatively small in an environment with this sort of competition. To explain the data, however, the size of this effect must be larger than seems intuitively plausible.

8.5.7.5 Shareholders' Opinion

We consider first whether TIW's bidding in the auction might have been influenced by trading in their shares. We focus on trading of TIW at New York's NASDAQ stock exchange where TIW is traded as

Table 8.7
TIW's share price (in U.S. dollars)

	Share price before round 1 (3 March)	Share price before round 106 (5 April)	Share price after round 116 (12 April)	Share price after round 150 (27 April)
TIW for B	239.688	176.25 (−26%)	141.25 (−41%)	146.875 (−39%)
NASDAQ Telekom Index	1178.5	946.44 (−20%)	867.9 (−26%)	792.17 (−33%)

TIWI. Table 8.7 indicates TIW's share price at four important moments: before the auction, at the end of the phase in which TIW had not shown strong interest in a large license (i.e., on the last trading day before round 106), after round 116 in which TIW bid for license A and the difference between license A's price and the small licenses' price was maximum among all rounds in which TIW bid for A, and at the end of the auction. To have a standard of comparison, we also list NASDAQ's telecommunications index for these dates. TIW is one of the companies included in this index.[19]

One might argue that the fact that TIW's shares lost more than the telecommunications index in the first phase of the auction triggered a change in TIW's bidding strategy. However, as in the case of BT3G, we find that the evidence for this is very weak. The difference between the performance of TIW's shares and the telecommunications index does not appear to be dramatic. On the other hand, TIW's aggressive bidding for license A between round 106 and 116 accompanied a very steep decline in TIW's share price. Yet, even after this period TIW placed bids for license A. Thus, we conclude that there is no strong evidence in favor of the claim that TIW's bidding behavior was influenced by the performance of its share price.

We now consider NTL Mobile. This company was jointly owned by NTL and by France Telecom. The joint ownership makes it less likely that we can find direct relationships between bids and share prices. Nevertheless we briefly consider the share prices of the companies involved. We indicate in table 8.8 the share prices of NTL as traded on New York's Stock Exchange (NYSE) and of France Telecom as traded at the Paris Bourse (now part of the Euronext stock exchange). We indicate these prices before and after the auction and also for three other important dates: after round 68 when NTL Mobile abandoned bidding for license A for a while, before round 100 when NTL Mobile

Table 8.8
NTL's and France Telecom's share prices (in U.S. dollars and euros)

	Share price before round 1 (3 March)	Share price after round 68 (27 March)	Share price before round 100 (4 April)	Share price after round 127 (14 April)	Share price after round 150 (27 April)
NTL	96.06	101 (+5%)	85.56 (−11%)	72.25 (−25%)	75.88 (−22%)
France Telecom	215.5	195.5 (−10%)	162.1 (−25%)	155.0 (−28%)	163.0 (−24%)

resumed bidding for license A, and again at the end of round 127 when NTL Mobile abandoned bidding for license A a second time.[20]

The stock exchange's response to NTL Mobile's initial bidding strategy does not seem to have been particularly negative. Indeed, NTL's initial performance is the best among all companies considered in this chapter in the comparable period. Thus, we cannot argue that NTL Mobile's initial change of strategy would have been triggered by negative share price developments. Abandoning the large license seems to have been accompanied by a much larger and sharper fall in share prices. So, we cannot rule out that NTL Mobile resumed bidding for license A in response to the large drop in the share prices of its constituent companies. The more aggressive bidding for license A was accompanied by a large drop in NTL's shares, but by a very modest reduction in France Telecom's shares. It is hard to see in this any explanation of the fact that NTL Mobile abandoned bidding for license A at the end of phase 2. We conclude that share price movements might contribute to an explanation of why NTL Mobile resumed bidding for license A in round 100, but they do not help us understand better the other aspects of NTL Mobile's behavior.

8.5.7.6   Management Disagreements

Unlike in the case of British Telecom, we have no direct evidence of the possibility of disagreements among the managers considered in this section. However, the fact that NTL Mobile had two owners, NTL and France Telecom, may be a significant factor. One reason why these owners' interests might not have been completely aligned may be that they had different plans for the period after the auction. France Telecom may already have anticipated during the auction that it might take over a company owning a U.K. license rather than buying one itself, whereas NTL may not have had any such plans. A company that was considering buying a successful bidder later may have not wanted to reveal its evaluation of a license in the auction, unlike a company that was not considering such a move. The precise way in which such disagreements might have affected bidding is, however, unclear.

8.5.8   Summary

As in the previous section, we find little direct evidence for any of the hypotheses we consider. However, plausible speculations are that social learning might explain the gradual rise in NTL Mobile's bids for license A in the first periods of the auction and the sudden rise in TIW and NTL Mobile's bids for license A in phase 2 of the auction. Budget constraints might provide an explanation for NTL Mobile's abandonment of license A in phase 3. We have not found any plausible explanation for why NTL Mobile ceased to bid for license A in phase 1 after round 68.

8.6 Conclusion

This chapter, together with its companion paper (Börgers and Dustmann 2001), provides a relatively complete analysis of the bids placed in the United Kingdom's spectrum auction. Our purpose in conducting this analysis was to establish whether the bids placed during the United Kingdom's auction can be explained as rational bids for carefully derived valuations of the licenses, or whether the bids placed in this auction can only be interpreted as the result of "bidding fever." We conclude from the data that it is certainly not trivial to rationalize the bidding behavior that has been observed. Where the data could provide hard evidence for some rationalizations, they refuse to do so. However, there are plausibility considerations that cannot be directly confirmed or rejected by the data, and that rationalize some of the bids which we have seen. Further evidence in similar auctions is needed if a better understanding of bidder behavior in license auctions is to be achieved. A well-founded judgment about the reliability of license auctions in achieving efficient allocations can be formed only once our understanding of bidder behavior has improved.

Notes

A companion paper (Börgers and Dustmann 2001) gives a more comprehensive overview of the UMTS auction in the United Kingdom. A revised version of Börgers and Dustmann (2001) will also report additional insights into bidders' behavior that we found after completing this chapter. The authors are grateful to Paul Klemperer, Pedro Rey, and Klaus Schmidt for comments. This chapter was written while Tilman Börgers was visiting the Center for Economic Studies in Munich and Christian Dustmann was visiting the Center for Labor Economics in Berkeley, CA. Both authors thank their respective host institutions for generous hospitality. Tilman Börgers's research was also supported by the Economic and Social Research Council (ESRC) through the Center for Economic Learning and Social Evolution (ELSE). Tilman Börgers was a member of a group of economists who advised the United Kingdom's Radiocommunications Agency on the design of the auction that is discussed in this chapter. This chapter is based on publicly available information only. No use was made of confidential information acquired while advising the Radiocommunications Agency. All opinions expressed in this chapter are those of the authors alone.

1. The information about the number of licenses and the payments made was obtained from the following Web sites: ⟨www.itu.int⟩ (Finland and Spain), ⟨www.tkc.at⟩ (Austria), ⟨www.regtp.de⟩ (Germany), ⟨www.spectrumauctions.gov.uk⟩ (UK), and ⟨www.wapworld.nl⟩ (Netherlands). Currency rates were obtained from ⟨www.oanda.com⟩, and population statistics from ⟨www.oecd.org⟩. Detailed further information about European UMTS auctions is available online at ⟨www.econ.ucl.ac.uk/auction/⟩.

2. In the United Kingdom, Telecommunications Minister Barbara Roche emphasized efficiency as the main goal of the auction in a statement to the House of Commons on 18 May 1998. In Germany, §44 of the Telekommunikationsgesetz—namely, the law that governs spectrum allocation—states that efficiency and absence of technical interference are the main goals of spectrum allocation.

3. An analysis of Germany's auction is for two reasons harder: first, the auction rules in Germany were more complicated than in the United Kingdom, and, second, unlike the United Kingdom, Germany did not publish all of the bids made in the auction, but only some.

4. The following account of the rules of the U.K. auction is very brief, and leaves out many important details. A more complete account of the rules of the auction is in section 8.2.

5. At the time at which this chapter was written, this information was publicly available online at ⟨http://www.spectrumauctions.gov.uk/auction/auction_index.htm⟩.

6. This theory of bidding in simultaneous ascending auctions is studied in one of the fundamental theoretical papers on simultaneous ascending auctions (Milgrom 2000). If bidders hold private values, then straightforward bidding is rational (see appendix 1 of Börgers and Dustmann 2001) and it implies efficiency of the outcome of the auction (see appendix 2 of Börgers and Dustmann 2001).

7. See our comments in section 8.4.

8. This section reviews some material that we originally presented in Börgers and Dustmann (2001). For a detailed account of the discussions that preceded the U.K. auction and of the role of academic economists in these discussions, see Binmore and Klemperer (2002).

9. Paired spectrum allows more efficient use of the spectrum than unpaired spectrum.

10. We are grateful to Paul Klemperer for suggesting the distinction between phases 2a and 2b.

11. Notice that our use of the expression "price" of a license differs somewhat from the Radiocommunications Agency's use of the expression "current price," which was explained earlier in this section.

12. Cramton (2001, 50) writes that "Vodafone often would use jump bids (bids above the minimum bid) to express its resolve in winning the B license." But the claim that jump bids occurred *often* is an error.

13. A value difference in this interval also rationalizes BT3G's six bids in phase 2b except the bid for license C in round 126 when the price difference was only £1,762.6 million.

14. Special rules applied to Vodafone and Orange because of the connection created between these two companies by Vodafone's successful takeover of Mannesmann, which owned Orange.

15. In this chapter we use the phrase "social learning" rather than the more conventional terminology of "common" or "affiliated values" in order to emphasize that what matters is really the informational effect that one firm can learn from another firm's private information by observing its actions.

16. The source for the share price information in table 8.5 and figure 8.4 is Datastream.

17. Considering phases 2a and 2b separately does not add much insight into NTL Mobile's behavior. In phase 2b the company placed only two bids. Both were for A. One of them was compatible with the earlier revealed price difference, and the second one was the one in round 127 to which we refer in the main text.

18. We focus on this point at round 77 rather than at round 68, which we emphasized earlier, because for the question of whether a budget constraint was effective only the very last bid for A in phase 1 matters.

19. The source for the information in table 8.7 is ⟨www.nasdaq.com⟩. We indicate daily closing prices.

20. The source for NTL's share price is Datastream. The source for France Telecom's share price is ⟨www.euronext.com⟩. We indicate daily closing prices.

References

Binmore, K., and P. Klemperer. 2002. "The Biggest Auction Ever: the Sale of the British 3G Telecom Licenses." *Economic Journal* 112(478): C74–C96.

Börgers, T., and C. Dustmann. 2001. "Strange Bids: Bidding Behaviour in the United Kingdom's Third Generation Spectrum Auction." Mimeo., Centre for Economic Learning and Social Evolution, University College London, September.

Cramton, P. 2001. "Lessons Learned from the UK 3G Spectrum Auction." Report for the National Audit Office, reproduced in National Audit Office (2001), 47–55.

Hirst, C. 2001. "Bland: BT Wrong to Bid for 3G." *The Independent on Sunday*, 29 April, p. 1.

Jehiel, P., and B. Moldovanu. 2000. "License Auctions and Market Structure." Mimeo., Centre for Economic Learning and Social Evolution, University College London and Universität Mannheim, July.

Jehiel, P., and B. Moldovanu. 2001. "The European UMTS/IMT-2000 License Auctions." Mimeo., Centre for Economic Learning and Social Evolution, University College London and Universität Mannheim, January.

Milgrom, P. 2000. "Putting Auction Theory to Work: The Simultaneous, Ascending Auction." *Journal of Political Economy* 108(2): 245–272.

Milgrom, P., and R. Weber. 1982. "A Theory of Auctions and Competitive Bidding." *Econometrica* 50: 1089–1122.

National Audit Office. 2001. "The Auction of Radio Spectrum for the Third Generation of Mobile Telephones." London: The Stationery Office.

Plott, C., and T. Salmon. 2001. "The Simultaneous, Ascending Auction: Dynamics of Price Adjustment in Experiments and in the Field." Mimeo., California Institute of Technology and Florida State University, July. Forthcoming in *Journal of Economic Behaviour and Organization*.

9 Efficiency of the British UMTS Auction: A Comment on Börgers and Dustmann

Klaus M. Schmidt

Auction theorists have developed very sophisticated tools to analyze optimal bidding behavior under various informational assumptions and for different auction rules. They have invented several new auction formats with interesting and desirable properties, and they played an important role in designing the auction formats of various large spectrum auctions in the United States and in Europe. Thus, it is often claimed that auction theory is the most spectacular success story of the application of game theory in economics. However, while some (but not all) recent spectrum auctions are generally believed to have been "very successful," it is not clear whether auction theory does accurately describe the actual bidding behavior of the involved players.

Börgers and Dustmann's chapter is one of the very few attempts to take seriously the data generated by a spectrum auction. Using the data on the actual bids in the British UMTS auction, the authors ask whether the observed bidding behavior is consistent with two assumptions, namely that bidders have *private values* and that they use *straightforward bidding* as a bidding strategy. Of course, if the observed behavior was inconsistent with these two assumptions, this would not falsify auction theory. It is conceivable that bidders do not have private values. Even if they do, straightforward bidding is not a dominant strategy and there may be many other equilibria in this game. However, if the observed behavior were consistent with private values and straightforward bidding, then the employed bidding strategies would form an equilibrium that achieves the efficient allocation. Thus, in this case the frequently made claim that the outcome of the British UMTS auction was efficient would be on much safer grounds.

Unfortunately, however, the data are not consistent with private values and straightforward bidding. The authors show that the behavior of several bidders—in particular, that of BT3G, TIW and NTL

Mobile—cannot be reconciled with these assumptions. From this, Börgers and Dustmann conclude in chapter 8 that, as a consequence, they are cautious regarding the success of the auction in achieving an efficient allocation of licenses.

There are several possible reasons why the outcome of the auction may have been inefficient.[1] Some of these reasons have little to do with the rules of the auction but are related to the (imperfect) environment in which the auction has been conducted:

• It could have been inefficient to divide the spectrum in this particular way. However, the decision on the division of the spectrum was taken at a political or perhaps technical level, and there is nothing that the auction itself could have done about it. This is why Börgers and Dustmann are right to take the form of the licenses as given.

• It may have been the case that the involved companies had incorrect or inconsistent valuations for the licenses, for example, because of bounded rationality or because of principal-agent problems or collective decision-making problems within the firms. This argument is very plausible, but it is not clear whether the auction format could or should be used to solve these internal problems of the involved companies.

• It is possible that some bidders were forced to quit the auction before the price reached their valuation because of credit constraints. This is true, but, again, the question arises whether the auction format could and should be used to correct market failures of other markets. If credit constraints are a problem, it seems preferable for the government to deal directly with this problem, say, by offering loans at a reasonable interest rate to all participating bidders, but it should not tamper with the rules of the auction.

It is more interesting to ask whether the rules of the auction themselves could have induced an inefficient allocation. In principle, this cannot be ruled out, but a closer look at the data shows that this is rather unlikely:

• It could have been the case that some bidders had private information about future market demand for 3G telecommunication services or that there was some other common value component present. However, Börgers and Dustmann argue in chapter 8 that "it does not seem plausible that at the time of the auction any one bidder had highly significant private information" (135) and that if such an effect was present, then it is likely to be of minor quantitative importance. In Börgers and Dustmann (2002) the authors point out: "At the time of the U.K. auction there had been long public discussions about the future potential of the UMTS technology, and about possible customers' demand for UMTS products. Clearly, these discussions had left a huge amount of uncertainty. However, it seems well possible that all relevant information had already reached the public domain, and that no firm had important insider information, except for information that concerned only its own situation, with no immediate relevance for other firms. If that is correct, then the private value assumption may well be a valid approximation" (14).

• Allocative externalities could have caused an inefficient allocation. However, Börgers and Dustmann (chapter 8) argue convincingly that allocative externalities did not leave any obvious footprints in the data and are unlikely to have played a significant role.

• The outcome would be inefficient if one bidding firm dropped out of the auction, even though it had a valuation for at least one of the licenses that was larger than the final price of that license (and larger than the valuation of the successful bidder for this license). If the firm is not credit constrained, this can happen only if it uses a strictly dominated strategy, namely, to drop out even though there was still a chance to obtain one of the licenses at a price lower than its reservation value. This dominance argument is easy to understand, and it seems unlikely that any firm used such a strictly dominated strategy.

• The outcome would be inefficient if one firm got stuck with one type of license and had to buy it, even though its incremental valuation for some other license was larger than the price difference to this other license. To see this, consider the following example in which there are just the two licenses B and C: (1) BT3G has valuations (150, 100) for these licenses and placed a bit of 95 on license C; and (2) Vodafone has valuations (140, 92) and placed a bit of 135 on license B. Suppose that the bidding stops at this point. Note that in this case it would be more efficient if BT3G owned license B and Vodafone owned license C.

In fact, BT3G would like to make a bid of 136 on license B, but it cannot do so because it has to stick to license C until there is another bidder who takes over this license.

Is it likely that this has happened? Consider first the bidding for license B. In Phase 3 BT3G placed six bids, only one of which was for license B. After BT3G was outbid by Vodafone on license B, it made three other bids for the smaller licenses. So it was not stuck with a small license in the very end, but it could have chosen at least three times to outbid Vodafone on license B. If BT3C did not do so, then this seems to be a strong indication that they did not want to do so because it would not have paid off.

A similar argument can be made for license A: TIW placed the winning bid on license A in round 133. Because this bid was not challenged thereafter, TIW could not switch to any of the licenses C to E, which may have given rise to an inefficiency. However, the price for license A remained constant after period 133 while the prices for licenses C to E continued to rise. Therefore, it seems difficult to imagine that TIW would have wanted to switch to a smaller licence after period 133.

To conclude, I think that the writing of Börgers and Dustmann is very interesting and important in better understanding the actual bidding behavior in real auctions with high stakes. However, I am less skeptical than the authors about the efficiency of the allocation of licenses. Even if the outcome were inefficient, this would not seem to be due to the rules of the auction that was employed in the United Kingdom but rather to the environment in which the auction had to be conducted.

Notes

I would like to thank Tilman Börgers and participants at the CESifo conference on Spectrum Auctions and Competition in Telecommunication in Munich on November 22–23, 2001, for helpful comments.

1. Börgers and Dustmann (2002) define efficiency as follows: "We use the term efficiency here in the following sense: licenses are allocated to maximize the sum of the valuations of licence holders, subject to the constraint that each bidder can hold only one license" (6).

Reference

Börgers, T., and C. Dustmann. 2002. "Strange Bids: Bidding Behaviour in the United Kingdom's Third Generation Spectrum Auction." Mimeo., University College London.

10 Some Observations on the British 3G Telecom Auction: Comments on Börgers and Dustmann

Paul Klemperer

I offer an explanation for some of the bidding in the year 2000 British 3G telecom auction and observe that Börgers and Dustmann's (chapter 8) results are consistent with the outcome having been efficient.

10.1 Introduction

Börgers and Dustmann (chapter 8) is a very valuable and insightful chapter that is full of useful detail about the actual bidding in the U.K. 3G auction and will become a key reference for anyone studying it.

As discussed in Klemperer (2002a; chapter 15) and Binmore and Klemperer (2002), the U.K. auction was one of the most successful of the western European 3G auctions. Indeed in terms of revenue raised per capita it was the most successful of all the auctions, and it is therefore appropriate to examine, as Börgers and Dustmann do in chapter 8, whether the auction's outcome was also as efficient as is often claimed. Furthermore, Börgers and Dustmann draw attention to many previously unnoted features of the bidding in the U.K. auction that do not fit well with standard theory and that may have important implications for future auctions.

I have learned a lot from Börgers and Dustmann's analysis. In what follows, I discuss just two issues of which my interpretation is slightly different.

10.2 Efficiency of the U.K. Auction

Börgers and Dustmann's analysis makes clear that an ascending auction like that of the United Kingdom runs the risk of an at least slightly inefficient outcome arising in some circumstances. However, it also seems clear that the actual outcome of the U.K. auction was efficient, or very close to efficient, in the sense of maximizing the sum of the valuations of the licence holders.

Klaus Schmidt's (chapter 9) excellent comment explains that the evidence from the bidding in the auction itself suggests that the U.K. auction was probably efficient. Evidence subsequent to the auction supports the same claim. It seems clear after the fact—and especially after the other European auctions—that the four incumbents had the highest valuations,[1] so they were efficient winners. And there is no evidence that any losing entrant had a value for a license that exceeded TIW-Hutchison's. Finally, the evidence subsequent to the auction, as well as from within it (including the interpretation of the bidding offered later), suggests Vodafone had a higher incremental value for a large license than did any other incumbent, and therefore that the allocation of licenses among winners was also correct. In short, all the available evidence suggests that the U.K. auction's outcome was efficient in the sense claimed.[2]

10.3 British Telecom's Bidding Behavior

Börgers and Dustmann also suggest that some of the behavior they document is very hard to rationalize, but I conjecture that doing sufficient research on the environment in which the auction took place will yield good explanations, as I illustrate by examining the main "puzzle"—British Telecom's (BT's) bidding.[3]

BT's bidding was such that the prices bid for the large (2×15 MHz) B and small (2×10 MHz) C, D, and E licences differed by roughly a constant in the early stages of the auction (phase 1 of the auction in Börgers and Dustmann's terminology), and then switched to differing by roughly a fixed proportion (50 percent of the price level of the small licenses) in the later stages of the auction (phases 2 and 3 in Börgers and Dustmann's terminology).[4] This pattern seems unusual, but reviewing analysts' reports suggests a clue: Some analysts assumed the value of the large license must be 1.5 times the value of a small license (reflecting an assumption that 1.5 times the amount of spectrum would allow offering 1.5 times the service[5]), while several other analysts insisted the large license was worth a fixed sum more than a small one (reflecting the additional costs—base stations, etc.—required to run the same service with a smaller licence), and it was clearly well understood in the industry that different bidders might make different choices between these two different valuation models.

Of course, if one or more bidders valued the large licence at 1.5 times the value of the small license, this cannot on its own explain the price difference being a fixed proportion of the value of the small license. For example, if BT's private valuations for small and large licences were £4 billion and £6 billion, respectively, while Vodafone's were £6 billion and £9 billion, respectively, and other bidders were closer to indifferent between small and large licences, then with "straightforward bidding" (in Börgers and Dustmann's terminology) the absolute value of the price difference would quickly move to equal £2 billion (since whenever the price difference was less than £2 billion, both BT and Vodafone would regard the large license as the best deal, and so would bid on it).[6]

However, it seems plausible that BT intrinsically valued a large license more than a smaller license by a fixed value that was considerably below 50 percent of the final price of a small license. BT may also have become very confident that Vodafone valued a large licence at 50 percent more than a small license. (Apart from any information from outside the auction, Vodafone never placed a bid on any license other than the large license in the auction.) Furthermore, BT may have wished to make Vodafone pay as much as possible for its license[7] for at least two reasons. First, this would reduce Vodafone's budget and so make Vodafone a weaker competitor in subsequent auctions (the British auction was the first of nine western European 3G auctions, and was also followed by others elsewhere in the world). And second, making Vodafone pay more would make "the market" think Vodafone had not done better than BT had in the auction. There is anecdotal evidence that BT was very concerned both about the stock market's perceptions of its performance and about the wider market's view of its position relative to Vodafone. Allowing Vodafone to win the larger license at a lower per-MHz price than BT was paying might suggest that BT's managers got a bad deal. Or it might suggest that BT was not able to make effective use of a larger license in the way that Vodafone could, and hence that BT thought it was in a weak market position, while Vodafone was clearly "number one."[8] So bidding up the large license's price to 50 percent more than the current small license price may have seemed a reasonable risk to take, even given the small chance of ending up winning the large license at hundreds of millions of pounds more than BT valued it at.[9]

Of course, even a small risk of winning the large license might seem to have a significant expected cost. But it was also possible that if BT did end up winning the large license, it might have been able to resell part of it at little or no loss, given that the auction prices would then have established a clear price per MHz. (The possibilities for resale were unclear, but Hutchison did in effect resell a fraction of the licence it won, very shortly after the auction, to KPN and DoCoMo at almost exactly the price per MHz that BT and Vodafone paid in the auction.[10]) And, anyway, observers might not think BT's managers had made a bad decision, even if BT did end up winning (and keeping) the large license for 50 percent more than the price of a small license.[11]

This theory, of course, leaves an important question unanswered. Why did BT not push up the price of the large license in the early stages of the auction? One reason is that much of the bidding in the early stages of the contest, when it was clear that there was no realistic chance of the auction ending very quickly (Börgers and Dustmann's phase 1) does not seem to have been very serious.[12] In fact, some bids were probably slightly frivolous or designed to attract media attention. For example, One2One raised its bid by slightly more than the minimum required in round 76 to bid £1,212,100,000![13] And BT did start pushing up the price difference between the large and small licences in round 99 when there were still nine bidders left (so 4 more dropouts were still required to end the auction), and did not then stop pushing up the price difference until round 112 when the large license was more than 50 percent (and more than £1.5 billion) more expensive than the small licenses.

A more serious reason why BT did not push up the price difference earlier is that BT may not have wanted to influence other bidders too early to think that license values were very high (since these other bidders might need time to adjust their views and get extra money approved by their boards, etc.). For example, if BT's valuation for a small license was £5 billion, it might have been confident that Vodafone's value exceeded £4 billion for a small license, and therefore that Vodafone would pay at least £2 billion more for a large license. But pushing the price difference up to £2 billion immediately would have sent a very clear signal about what the ultimate prices might be at a time at which the auction prices for the smaller licences were still very low, and this could only have been damaging to BT's interests.

A final possible reason why BT did not push up the price difference early on is that BT may not have become confident that Vodafone's valuation of the large license was 1.5 times its valuation of the small license until later in the auction.

Most likely BT thought that the early bidding was probably not very important but that its best strategy was to roughly mimic what straightforward bidding would have been if it had had low valuations and a correspondingly low difference in valuations. Certainly this is consistent with the evidence.[14]

So it seems possible to give a reasonable explanation for BT's bidding. Of course, this may not be the only possible explanation.[15] However, the moral is that understanding bidding in auctions often requires knowing a lot of real-world detail about the players and the context in which they are operating. Facts from outside the bidding itself—in this case, knowing the differing valuation models that different analysts used—may be the key to explaining behavior. In understanding auctions, as well as in designing them, "the devil is in the details."[16]

Notes

I was the principal auction theorist advising the U.K. government's Radiocommunications Agency, which designed and ran the U.K. mobile phone license auction discussed here, but the views expressed in this chapter are mine alone. I do not intend to suggest that any of the behavior discussed here violates any applicable rules or laws. I am very grateful to Tilman Börgers for useful comments, and to Marco Pagnozzi for our collaboration in the study of the 3G auctions and for his helpful suggestions about this chapter.

1. See van Damme (2002) and Fortis Bank (2000) for evidence and discussion of these value differences. (Indirect evidence is also provided by the fact that only one out of the thirty incumbent bidders in the eight western European ascending auctions failed to win a license—and even this single failure was attributed to collusion or organizational strife within the bidder, rather than to the incumbent having a low value; see Klemperer 2002a).

2. Cable, Henley, and Holland (2002) use stock market data to argue that "there is no evidence that the outcome of the auction was anything but efficient" (11).

3. However, Börgers and Dustmann are to be congratulated on having already explained so much; they also looked at evidence from outside the auction to explain behavior within it.

4. That BT's behavior in the later stages of the auction can be described in this way was observed independently, by Börgers and Dustmann and myself, after the November 2001 CESifo conference in Munich. The details are reported in Börgers and Dustmann's companion paper (Börgers and Dustmann 2002).

5. The technology might actually allow offering slightly more than 1.5 times the service, hence the value ratio might be slightly more than 1.5.

6. And even if, as I will argue, some of the early bidding was non-serious, the price difference would move to the fixed amount, £2 billion, as soon as the bidding became serious.

7. After the auction BT claimed it had deliberately pushed up the price that Vodafone had paid, and this was reported in the press (see Cane and Owen 2000). (At the time, this claim was pooh-poohed by auction theorists as implausible, since it was hard to reconcile with the evidence without realizing that BT and Vodafone might both have had different valuation models and also have had a reasonably clear idea of the other's valuation model.)

8. Klemperer (chapter 15) discusses the importance of bidders' concerns about relative performance in the German auction.

9. If BT was correct in its assessment that Vodafone's valuation of a large licence was (at least) 50 percent more than that for a small license, the (only) risk that BT faced was that Vodafone would quit the auction altogether. But this outcome was completely implausible, since it would imply that Vodafone's valuation for a small license was below that of Orange and One2One (which were both weaker incumbents), and at least one new entrant. The real risk would have been that BT had misjudged Vodafone's valuation difference between the licenses, and BT perhaps knew this risk was small.

10. The U.K. government now seems likely to make resale relatively easy, but this was unclear at the time of the auction, and actual resale of part of a license may in any case be unattractive since bringing a new competitor into the industry makes the remaining spectrum less valuable. Bringing new partners into a joint venture as Hutchison did therefore seems the most relevant form of resale.

11. Of course, the arguments here are in effect postulating that there may have been important common value elements to valuations. Note that with common value elements it is plausible that the large license might be worth a fixed amount (say £500 million–£1 billion) more than a small license at low prices, but a constant fraction (say 150 percent) of the small license at large prices.

12. Four bidders have informally confirmed this.

13. Additional 1's and 2's were ruled out, because all bids were required to be multiples of £100,000.

14. Although Vodafone only bid on the large license, it is very plausible that Vodafone was following a similar strategy, but mimicking a bidder with slightly less low valuations.

15. For example, there may have been much stronger common value components to valuations than usually assumed.

16. See Klemperer (2002a,b,c) for more discussion of the importance of understanding the wider context, and of apparently small details, in auction design.

References

Binmore, K., and P. Klemperer. 2002. "The Biggest Auction Ever: The Sale of the British 3G Telecom Licences." *Economic Journal* 112(478): C74–C96. Available online at ⟨http://www.paulklemperer.org⟩.

Börgers, T., and C. Dustmann. 2002. "Strange Bids: Bidding Behaviour in the United Kingdom's Third Generation Spectrum Auction." Working paper, University College London.

Cable, J., A. Henley, and K. Holland. 2002. "Pot of Gold or Winner's Curse? An Event Study of the Auctions of 3G Mobile Telephone Licences in the U.K." *Fiscal Studies* 23(4): 447–462.

Cane, A., and D. Owen. 2000. "The U.K. Cellular Phone Auction." *Financial Times, London*, 28 April, p. 23.

Fortis Bank. 2000. "The UMTS-Report." Brussels.

Klemperer, P. 2002a. "How (Not) to Run Auctions: The European 3G Telecom Auctions." *European Economic Review* 46(4–5): 829–845.

Klemperer, P. 2002b. "Using and Abusing Economic Theory (2002 Alfred Marshall Lecture to the European Economic Association)." Forthcoming in *Journal of the European Economic Organization* 1 (2003). Forthcoming in *Advances in Economics and Econometrics: Theory and Applications*, ed. R. Becker and S. Hurn. Cheltenham, U.K.: Edward Elgar. Available online at ⟨http://www.paulklemperer.org⟩.

Klemperer, P. 2002c. "What Really Matters In Auction Design." *Journal of Economic Perspectives* 16(1): 169–189.

van Damme, E. 2002. "The European UMTS Auctions." *European Economic Review* 45(4–5): 846–858.

11

The British UMTS Auction: A Response to Klemperer and Schmidt

Tilman Börgers and Christian Dustmann

We are very grateful for Paul Klemperer's and Klaus Schmidt's insightful comments. Klemperer (chapter 10) and Schmidt (chapter 9) both discuss the ex post efficiency of the outcome of the U.K. auction. Klemperer also comments on possible explanations of BT3G's bidding behavior. We begin with the latter point because the focus of chapter 8 is on bidders' behavior. Assessing the ex post efficiency of the U.K. auction was not our main purpose.

Klemperer suggests that BT3G's bids for license B were not really meant to win license B, but that their purpose was to drive up the price that Vodafone had to pay. According to Klemperer's hypothesis, BT3G thought that it did not run any risk of getting stuck with license B provided that it bid for license B if B's price was not more than 50 percent higher than the price of the smaller licenses. However, at a larger percentage difference in prices, there was, according to Klemperer's hypothesis, a risk that Vodafone would switch to bidding for a small license.

Although this theory has the merit of explaining the data, the strategy that BT3G pursued according to this theory is surprisingly risky. How could BT3G be sure that its assessment of Vodafone's strategy was correct? Throughout the auction Vodafone only bid for license B. Therefore, there was no evidence from the auction to support the belief in a 50 percent threshold. In the early stages of the auction, Vodafone was actually willing to bid for license B even at price ratios far larger than 1.5.[1] BT3G might have held hard information from inside Vodafone. But overall we feel that the risk that Vodafone would switch to a small license, or quit the auction, must have appeared substantial to BT3G. It would be surprising if a bidder such as BT3G were willing to take on such a risk. Klemperer's explanation of BT3G's behavior is a very interesting speculation, but, to us, not compelling. Of course, it may be true nonetheless.

Klemperer emphasizes the importance of information from outside the auction for the study of bidding in the auction, and we agree. There is a methodological difference between Klemperer's comment and our chapter, though. Chapter 8 deliberately relies on publicly available information only. By contrast, Klemperer cites industry sources and analysts without always documenting these quotes.

Turning to the ex post efficiency of the auction outcome, we note first that the strategy that Klemperer hypothesizes potentially undermines the ex post efficiency of ascending auctions. A bidder who drives up prices without any intention of winning might win nonetheless, namely when his beliefs about others' willingness to pay are incorrect. Such a bidder may thus inefficiently win licenses. This does not seem to have happened in the U.K. auction, but it might easily happen elsewhere.

Klaus Schmidt's argument in favor of the ex post efficiency of the U.K. auction assumes implicitly that each bidder's final decisions in the auction were rational decisions based on well-specified valuations of the licenses. Our chapter casts doubt on the assumption that bidding behavior over the whole duration of the auction was rational behavior driven by valuations. We therefore believe that there are also reasonable doubts that the final decisions can be rationalized in this way.[2]

Notes

1. BT3G might not have regarded this as a falsification of its hypothesis about Vodafone because in the early rounds of the auction license prices were perhaps known to be below bidders' actual values, as Klemperer suggests.

2. Note also that Klemperer's hypothesis regarding BT3G's strategy, if correct, contradicts Schmidt's assumption, although, as mentioned earlier, this does not seem to have caused any inefficiency in this particular auction.

III

The Behavioral Approach
to Auctions: Further
Insights from Experimental
Economics?

12

The Behavioral Approach to the Strategic Analysis of Spectrum Auctions: The Case of the German DCS-1800 Auction

Klaus Abbink, Bernd
Irlenbusch, Bettina
Rockenbach, Abdolkarim
Sadrieh, and Reinhard Selten

12.1 Introduction

Radio frequencies are a scarce resource. While sales numbers of mobile handsets have rocketed in the last few years, the spectrum to carry the traffic naturally cannot grow at the same pace. Future data-intensive technologies will put an additional strain on the limited resource. Thus, the only way out is to use the existing radio spectrum most efficiently. To this aim, auctioning off spectrum has become a common device. The idea is that those operators who can make the best economic use of the frequencies will value them highest and win the auction; thus the spectrum is allocated in a way that maximizes economic efficiency.

However, in order to allocate the spectrum to the most efficient operator in the best-suited way, the auction must be carefully designed, and the bidders need to be well prepared to be able to make best use of their available budget. Designs for spectrum auctions are often relatively complex. The money at stake is huge, which makes the implementation of a suitable bidding strategy a challenge for every bidder involved in an auction. During their preparation for a spectrum auction, participants often seek advice from academic scholars, in particular game theorists.[1] This chapter reports a case study from the Digital Cellular System on the 1800 MHz Frequency Band (DCS1800) auction held in September 1999 in Germany. In this auction, 2×10.4 MHz of spectrum in the 1800 MHz range were put up for sale among the four operators active in the German GSM market. The spectrum was earmarked as extension of the spectrum endowment for the licensed mobile telecommunications operators. New entrants were not admitted to the auction, since the spectrum was not considered sufficient to set up a new network.

One of the bidders in the auction approached us to provide strategic advice in preparation for the event. We suggested a behavioral approach rather than merely a game theoretical one. This approach is based on empirical evidence gathered in controlled experiments with student subjects as well as on the managers' own experience in training sessions.[2] The lessons learned from the experiments are complemented by theoretical strategic considerations, all of it to be integrated into the design of a bidding strategy.[3] This chapter describes the steps on the way to the implementation of a bidding strategy.

12.2 Background

At the time the auction was prepared, Germany had four nationwide GSM networks with a very asymmetric distribution of market shares. The two companies, which had already started operation in the early 1990s, were T-Mobil (today T-Mobile Deutschland) and Mannesmann Mobilfunk (MMO, today Vodafone). They were of similar size with about 7 million subscribers each at that time. Both operated only in the 900 MHz (D) frequency band. The two other GSM network operators that were active in the 1800 MHz (E) band started later (1996 and 1998). E-Plus had a subscriber basis of 3.5 million customers, while Viag Interkom (after rebranding, known today as mmO$_2$) had only 300,000 subscribers by that time. The market was booming with annual customer growth rates of 50–100 percent.

The spectrum endowment between the two groups of operators was distributed exactly opposite to the size of the subscriber basis. Both D band operators were endowed with 2 × 12.5 MHz each, while each of the E band networks could use 2 × 22.5 MHz allocated to them with their original license.[4] Increasing traffic and rising subscriber numbers made capacity constraints a concern for the D band operators.

The capacity of a mobile telecommunications network is not proportionally related to its spectrum endowment. The spectrum only defines the capacity within a given cell. Thus, capacity of the network can in principle also be increased by installing smaller cells. Capacity and cell size are not perfect substitutes. On the one hand, a small cell network still has capacity limitations if traffic is heavily concentrated within single cells. On the other hand, smaller cells allow enhanced coverage within buildings, which is a quality advantage independent from the capacity effect. However, in general there is still ample room for maneuvering to take one or the other action to increase the network's capacity.

Though urgent need for capacity extension on the side of the E band operators seemed implausible, the government decided to admit all four operators for participation in the auction. Some managers of the E network operators argued that since the new spectrum was in the E band, it should be awarded to them because of the technical homogeneity. In fact, integrating the E band frequencies in an existing D band network requires substantial investment. Furthermore, only customers having a dual band handset would benefit from the additional capacity. By that time, dual band handsets were not yet ubiquitous, though it could be expected that this would not take very long. All operators pursued a policy to subsidize the sales of handsets generously conditioned on two-year contract commitments. As a result, few customers used handsets older than two years, and most new handsets were dual band devices.

The government decided to award the spectrum to the winners in the auction for the entire term of their respective licenses. With respect to the sales prices, it did not account for the differences in the term of the licenses between the operators. All licenses had originally been granted for twenty years, but since the E band operators had started later, they had more years left. The D band operators' licenses expire in 2009, while those of E-plus band operators terminate in 2012, and Viag Interkom can even operate until 2016 on its current license.

12.3   The Auction Design

The auction design was developed with the advice of the Wissenschaftliches Institut für Kommunikationsforschung (wik). It is a variant of the simultaneous ascending auction used in the United States in earlier FCC auctions. In this type of auction, all packages of spectrum are sold in the same auction. The bids are increased in bidding rounds, where the bidders can bid on all lots simultaneously. The auction ends when no new bids are submitted.[5]

The detailed rules were communicated to the bidders relatively early. The Regulierungsbehörde für Post und Telekommunikation (RegTP) decided to fragment the 2×10.4 MHz into nine blocks of 2×1 MHz and one slightly larger block of 2×1.4 MHz. These lots were abstract; namely, a lot in the auction was not attributed to a particular frequency in the band. Rather, the spectrum was allocated to the auction winners after the auction in a technically efficient manner.

The lots 1–9 were blocks of 2×1 MHz; lot 10 was the 2×1.4 MHz block. In the first round, all bidders could place bids on any lots, with no limitations on the number of lots being bid for. The minimum bid was DM 1m[6] for each of the lots 1–9, and DM 1.4m for the larger block. There were no upper limits for a particular round.[7] A bidder submitted all his bids simultaneously. After all first round bids were collected, the highest bidders were made (preliminary) holders of the respective lots. If more than one bidder had submitted the highest bid, the one that had been submitted first determined the holder.

In the following round, all bidders could overbid the current prices, where the minimal increment was set by the auctioneer. The increment was 10 percent at the outset of the auction, but it could be decreased to 5 percent or 2 percent at the discretion of the auctioneer. All subsequent rounds were held in the same manner.

In all rounds following the first, the number of lots a bidder was eligible to bid for was limited by its active bids. The number of active bids is defined as the number of lots the bidder holds, plus the number of bids placed on other lots. The number of active bids could not be higher than it had been in the round before. Thus, if a bidder once decided not to go for all ten lots anymore, the surrendered bidding rights could not be regained later on.

After each round the following feedback was given: For each lot, the current holder of the lot, and the current price were revealed. The single bids were not made public. The number of active bids of other bidders was not announced either.

The auction ended either when no new bids were submitted, or when the auctioneer announced the end. The end of the auction could be announced at the auctioneer's discretion before any round following round 20 with a two-round lag (i.e., the auction ended two rounds after the announcement.). The holders after the last round were the winners of the items.

12.4   The Bidders' Goals, Scenarios, and the Payoff Function

At the heart of the behavioral approach are the experiments with students and company executives. For these, it is essential to reflect the goals of the involved bidders appropriately. All bidders face a task with great uncertainty, because both the bidding behavior and the goals of the other bidders are unknown. Further, even evaluating the value of spectrum for the own company is a nontrivial task, because the value is affected by very different considerations. Information needed to assess the spectrum value is often held in different departments of the company, since engineering, financial, and marketing expertise is needed to develop the company's goals in the auction.

Before setting up the experimental design, we held extensive interviews with senior managers from all over the company. Our interview partners included engineers, marketing managers, financial managers, strategic business planners and others. All interviews with the experts were held separately in order to avoid *groupthink* effects, the phenomenon that group members (esp. members of an organization) tend to harmonize their originally diverse beliefs within their group (for a review and further literature, see Esser 1998). A within group aggregation of the information that could have led to *groupthink* had to be avoided. This ensured that the full range of information on spectrum valuation that was available within the organization was actually conveyed to us. We collected the information bit by bit and used simple rules to aggregate it. Specifically, we examined the distributions of valuations and the distributions of probabilities that were reported for all possible states. We dropped all states that were only mentioned in a single interview. For all other states, we derived estimates from the distributions. Finally, using the analysis of the interviews, we could identify several factors that seemed essential for the spectrum's valuation of the four GSM operators.

The distributions of valuations that emerged from the interviews were used to define the bidders' valuation ranges used in the experiments. Furthermore, certain goals that were frequently mentioned in the interviews were also implemented in the experimental payoffs. Hence, the experimental payoff scheme was designed in a way to induce monetary incentives that were strictly correlated to the bidders' goals as derived from the interviews. Pursuing the defined goals was perfectly incentive compatible for the subjects in the experiments, because they received real monetary payoffs that depended on the extent to which they achieved the aims of the bidders they represented.

The payoff tables we used in the experiments are depicted in the appendix. Notice that each bidder can be in one of two possible *scenarios*: *expansive* or *conservative*. These scenarios reflect the uncertainty present before the auction. They differ not only with respect to the budget—expansive bidders would be expected to have a far higher budget than conservative ones—but also with respect to the goals they pursue in the auction.

Expansive operators aim at purchasing all or at least most of the spectrum. Their valuation for the spectrum is superadditive, namely, the additional value of an additional MHz increases with the quantity of spectrum. This can be the case, for example, if an operator plans to introduce a radically new technology for which a large frequency band is needed, but which cannot be covered within the original spectrum the operator already has.

The valuation function of conservative bidders, on the other hand, is subadditive; that is, the marginal value of spectrum decreases. This is the case if a bidder needs the spectrum to secure that the existing or expected services could be offered in high quality. For this goal, it is not necessary to purchase all spectrum, extending the frequency band by about 2×5 MHz would be sufficient to satisfy this goal. Purchases exceeding 2×5 MHz would still induce positive marginal value, but far less than the first 2×5 MHz.

The payoff tables also include additional goals. The bidders A and B, who represent the D band operators, need a minimum requirement of 2×2.4 MHz in order to integrate the new frequencies into their networks. Thus, the value of less than 2×2.4 MHz is zero.[8] Further, bidders A and B are concerned about their frequency endowment relative to their main competitor. The possibility of rivalistic behavior (a positive value of increasing the competitors' prices without buying spectrum) is reflected in the bonus that bidders C and D receive.

With four bidders and two scenarios for each bidder, we obtain $2^4 = 16$ combinations of scenarios. Realizing all of them in the experiments is generally not possible within the given resources, and it would have convoluted the analysis. Therefore, the most interesting scenarios had to be selected. We decided to omit combinations with both E operators in the expansive scenario, which appeared especially unlikely. This left eight experimental conditions to be implemented.

In most theory-driven auction experiments, the items are given a "value" and the payoff the subject gets is determined as the value minus the price paid. In the present environment, however, such a presentation seemed inappropriate, because some subjects (especially when they were in the conservative scenarios) would have much worse opportunities to earn money than others. Further, the non-linearity of the valuation functions would have made it tedious to compute the actual payoff consequences from the auction outcome and the money spent. To tackle both problems, we designed payoff tables for each bidder in each of the altogether eight scenarios. They contained money payoffs that had the number of MHz purchased and the percentage of the budget spent as dimensions (notice that the budget was a random draw from a given range even within a scenario). Further, bonus payoffs were provided for the additional goals that should be pursued in some scenarios (buying not less than the major rival, or inflating the competitors' prices). Hence, the payoff scheme chosen for the experiment did not correspond to a traditional simple valuation setup as typically used in auction experiments. The multiplicity of bidder's goals and the nonlinearities in valuations that had emerged as stable structural elements in our extensive interviews made this departure from traditional experimentation necessary.

12.5   The Experiment with Student Subjects

In the experimental sessions with students, student subjects recruited on the university campus played the role of the bidders. The auction is held as a "replicate" of the real auction, using essentially the same rules. Naturally, some modifications are necessary, since the real spectrum auction was scheduled for several days, while in the experimental session a number of consecutive auctions is played within a few hours. To speed up the auction process, the decision time was shortened and the minimum bid was set higher in relation to the bidders' budgets than it was expected to be in the real auction. Further, the minimum bidding increment was set to 20 percent.

The experiments were computerized with software developed using RatImage (Abbink and Sadrieh 1995). The subjects filled in an on-screen form in which they typed in their bids for the ten items, then pressed a button to submit all bids simultaneously. The decisions are transmitted to a control terminal, whose software makes all necessary calculations and sends the feedback to the subject terminals. Once the session is started, the auction is conducted fully automatically. Compared to experiments run by hand, computerized experiments allow a much speedier conduct of the experiment.

In most cases spectrum auctions are relatively complex. Therefore, a sufficient number of subsequent auctions should be played within a session, in order to enable subjects to get acquainted with the mechanism and to adapt their behavior to the strategic environment. The duration of the experiment is the limiting factor in this respect. In this case, we could conduct five consecutive auctions in the three hours scheduled for each session.[9]

The subjects were given detailed instructions at the outset of an experimental session (see the appendix). Written handouts explained the rules of the auction and the scenarios. No reference was made to the spectrum auction scenario underlying the experiment. The subjects simply set out for "lots" and were called "bidder A" to "bidder D." The set of possible scenario combinations was common knowledge, but each subject knew only the scenario its own "bidder" was in and not the scenarios of the other three "bidders."

Four groups played in parallel in each session. Each of the four groups played five consecutive auctions in the course of the session. We decided to drop the first of the five auctions played by each group, the one in which subjects were very inexperienced, from our data analysis. The eight scenarios under consideration were distributed over the sessions and the consecutive auctions in the following manner. Each scenario combination was envisaged to be played eight times in eight different markets, but no combination was played more than once by the same subjects. This was done to gather eight independent observations for each scenario combination. Further, care was taken that each scenario combination was played second, third, fourth, and fifth of the consecutive auctions the same number of times (the combination for the first auction could be chosen arbitrarily, since this was not used for the data analysis). Therefore, we ensured that all scenario combinations were played under the same circumstances, and that the results from single scenario combinations were not biased because of predominantly inexperienced subjects in one combination.[10] Four experimental sessions with a total of sixty-four subjects were conducted. When the experiment was conducted, it turned out that many groups played slightly faster than expected. In these cases, we ran an additional (sixth) auction, using a different scenario the respective group had not played before. As a result, we could gather between 10 and 12 observations for each scenario.

12.6   Experiments within the Company

In parallel to the experimental sessions with student subjects, we conducted experiments with executives from the company. Experimental sessions with company managers cannot be conducted with the same methodological rigor as can the laboratory sessions with students. The number of observations that can be gathered is naturally very limited, since the number of high-level managers who can arrange to find the time for participation in the experiment is very small. Therefore, only a handful of auctions could be played, all in the same scenario.

Nevertheless, these staff experiments are very important, for several reasons. First, these experiments already serve as training sessions, since the managers in charge of the preparation for the auction are participants in the experiment. Second, they are reassuring in terms of the validity of the results gathered in the student sessions. As in earlier studies (e.g., Dyer, Kagel, and Levin 1989), the comparison of students' to professionals' behavior in our experiment revealed no substantial differences.

The experiments were conducted in the headquarters of the company. Telecommunications operators are usually not equipped with experimental laboratories, but nevertheless comparable controlled conditions could be installed. The software was installed on computers in the managers' offices, which were interconnected via the local network. The managers typically played in teams. A further difference to the student sessions was that subjects were not paid according to their success. This seemed unnecessary because the managers' professional involvement ensured a high degree of intrinsic motivation.

In general, the same setup and the same presentation as in the experiments with students were used. Only in details had changes been made. These involve the scaling of the budget constraints and the sequence in which the bidders appear on the screen. For the student sessions these details had been rearranged in order to prevent possible inference on critical information.[11]

12.7   Experimental Results

The experimental data collected in the student and the staff sessions were analyzed in order to learn lessons for the company's bidding strategy. Figure 12.1 shows the average price per MHz in each of the eight scenario combinations.[12] Figure 12.2 shows the allocation of MHz to the four bidders in the auction, disaggregated over the single auctions played within the scenario combinations. The notation for the scenario combination is as follows: Sorted by bidders, from A to D, the name contains a "0" for a conservative bidder and a "1" for an

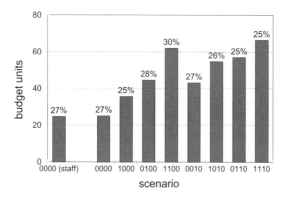

Figure 12.1
Average per MHz price (*Note:* The labels indicate average prices as percentage of the average budgets in the corresponding scenarios.)

expansive bidder. In the scenario combination 1100, for example, bidders A and B are expansive, while bidders C and D are conservative.

The analysis of the data revealed the following stylized facts.

1. Both in the student sessions and in the staff sessions the bidding was very competitive. Subjects went for all ten units in the beginning and typically reduced their bidding rights only when the budget limit forced them to do so. This generated fairly high per-MHz prices that on average were greater than one-fourth of bidders' budgets. As can easily be seen in figure 12.1, the more expansive bidders are involved in a scenario combination, the higher is the average price per unit. Particularly when the D band operators are in their expansive scenarios, prices increase dramatically. Comparing the scenario combinations 0000, 1000, and 1100, one observes that the price per MHz increases by about 50 percent in each step. Since this roughly coincides with the increase in the total budget available to the four contestants, on average the fraction of the budget spent on one MHz ranged between 25 and 30 percent in all scenarios.

2. Attempts to raise the competitors' prices, which at first sight seemed to be easy due to the fragmented packaging, were generally unsuccessful. They typically led to unwanted purchases of single units. This can be seen in figure 12.2. In the scenario combinations in which the E band operators have such a motivation (the scenarios xx10), they tend to purchase positive quantities.

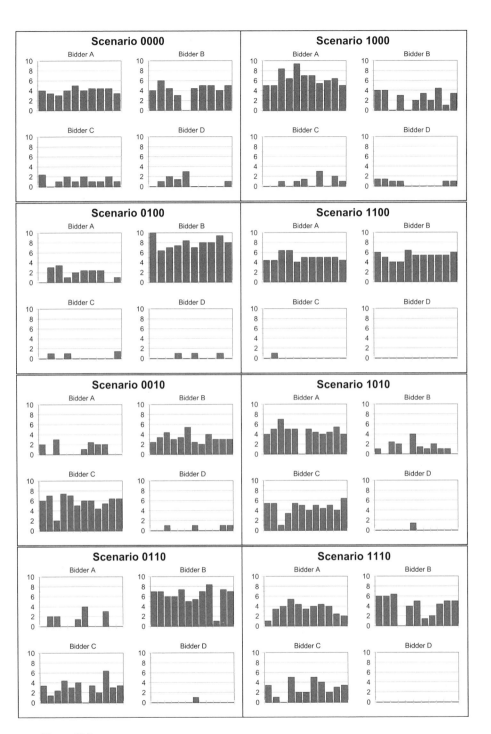

Figure 12.2
Allocation of spectrum (*Note:* Each bar depicts the number of units bought by a bidder in a session of a scenario.)

3. When two or three expansive bidders are in the market, the bidder with the third highest budget has the most difficult task. Typically, these scenario combinations lead to all buyers purchasing relatively few items. Scenario combination 1110 in figure 12.2 shows the outcome for the case with three expansive bidders; the figure for scenario combinations 0110, 1100, and 1010 depict the cases with two expansive bidders.

4. Expansive bidders attempting to buy all or most of the frequencies face a significant exposure problem. They typically fail, but often they do not manage to quit in time, and then finish with relatively few items, which are largely useless to them. One of the D band operators and one of the E band operators were assumed to pursue such a goal in their expansive scenarios. However, very rarely does an expansive bidder manage to purchase all spectrum (even if he is the only expansive bidder). In the presence of two or more expansive bidders, it appears very difficult to obtain substantially more than half of all available spectrum.

12.8   Training Sessions

In the further process of the auction preparation, another set of training sessions should be held, supplementing the experimental sessions within the company described in section 12.7. This is important because at that stage of the process, reflections on the bidding strategy are still at a very early stage. After the experiments have been analysed and a bidding strategy has been developed, it is important for the bidding strategy to be tested, revised, and fine-tuned. This process should be performed on the basis of one's own training experience.

In the training sessions, the actual bidding team should play together, taking the role of the own company in the auction. The other roles should be played by other company members, preferably not by the advisors or the managers immediately responsible for the preparation of the auction. This is because the bidding team should face a situation in which it is uncertain about the behavior of the other players, and the behavior of the other bidders is not "streamlined" with respect to the own company's bidding strategy.

The training sessions revealed that it would be very useful to be informed about the other bidders' bidding eligibility during the bidding process. The auction design did not provide any feedback on this, since only the highest bids were publicized. Thus, it was generally not possible to know the exact current bidding eligibility of other bidders during the auction. However, the design allowed for some inference to be drawn during the course of the auction.

12.9   Bidding Eligibility Software

In the beginning of the auction, every bidder has a bidding eligibility of ten units, which can later only decrease once the bidder's number of active bids has fallen. It is straightforward to see that if the holder and the current price of an item remain unchanged in a given bidding round, then all other bidders have not actively bid for that item. Thus the number of active bids of all other bidders cannot be greater than ten minus the number of items with unchanged price and holder.

However, even if all items change holder and price in a given bidding round, some inference can be drawn from the bidding eligibility of other bidders. This is due to the tie-breaking rule applied in the auction. If two bidders submit the same bids for an item (this is likely if bidders increase the current price only by the minimum increment), then the bidder who submitted the bid first becomes the temporary holder of the item. If we observe that the prices of different items have increased only by the minimum increment, but different items have different holders, then we can infer that the bidding eligibility of at least one of the bidders is less than maximum. Suppose, for example, we observe that in one bidding round all items' current prices have increased by the minimum increment, but bidder A is holder of five lots, and bidder B is standing high on the remaining five items. Then we can infer that either bidder A or bidder B is down to a bidding eligibility of five items (plus the number of items this bidder has held in the previous round), because otherwise the faster of the two would have become holder of the remaining units as well. We do not know who of the two bidders has a reduced bidding eligibility at that stage. However, in a later round this question may be resolved. Suppose, for example, that a few rounds later bidder A shows up as the holder of six or more units. At that point, we then know that bidder B had been faster than bidder A in that earlier round but had bid for only five units. Since a bidder's number of active bids cannot increase, we then know that bidder B's eligibility cannot be greater than five anymore.

Inferring other bidders' maximum bidding eligibility requires tracking the complete auction history of the auction, since sometimes information from many rounds before may be required to extract the maximum possible information. Further, many possible constellations must be considered. Therefore, we developed a software tool that calculated and displayed minimum and maximum possible bidding eligibility in every round, based on the history of the auction.

12.10   The Bidding Strategy

After the training sessions have been held, the bidding strategy can be finalized. It is essential that the bidding strategy is as much as possible a *strategy* in the game-theoretic sense, a plan that prescribes moves for *every* situation that can possibly come up in the game. "Cold" decisions are preferable to "hot" decisions; there should be as little need as possible for spontaneous unprepared actions during the auction. Decision time in the auction is often very limited; choices made in the heat of the moment may not be well thought out.

From the lessons learned in the experiment, we developed a bidding strategy recommendation. The bidding strategy consists of the entry bid, bid levels at which bidding eligibility is to be given up, and a final decision about when to quit the auction. The experimental data was used to check the robustness of the strategy, namely, to assess the variance of its profitability when played against experimentally observed types of bidding behavior. In particular, the observed behavior of the experienced subjects provided valuable information on the set of possible and probable types of bidding behavior. A main requirement was that the recommended strategy should lead to a minimum aspired payoff without being vulnerable to predatory behavior of others. The performance of the recommended strategy in this respect was not only assessed empirically in the training sessions, but was also subject to a rough theoretical evaluation. Due to the complexity of the environment, the theoretical evaluation had to be restricted to the examination of some of the strategic implications of bidding behavior, instead of pursuing a full-fledged game equilibrium. Confidentiality requirements do not allow us to reveal details about the company's bidding strategy or budget decisions.

12.11   Summary

The design of a spectrum auction is important for both the government as the seller and the bidders as the potential buyers. While the seller must customize the design according to its specific goals (efficiency, competition, or revenue), the buyers typically face the challenge of tailoring their bidding strategy for a given auction design to the company's goals. Both tasks require a careful strategic analysis of the various alternatives. Behavioral regularities induced by the design of an auction must be taken into account.

The behavioral approach can be applied to both the design of an auction and the implementation of a bidding strategy. This chapter reports a case study in which we assisted a bidder in the German DCS1800 auction in its preparation for bidding. We describe the various steps on this path: First, information that may be scattered in the company must be collected and aggregated. From the relevant influential factors, likely scenarios are worked out. These scenarios are the basis for creating the experimental environment for experimental sessions with student subjects. Accompanying sessions are held with company managers, which also serve as first training sessions for the decision makers in the company. The lessons learned from the data analysis and from the managers' experiences are integrated into the implementation of a bidding strategy, complemented by theoretical considerations. Finally, training sessions are held to apply the bidding strategy in trial auctions.

12.12   Epilogue: The Auction Outcome

The DCS-1800 auction was held in September 1999 in RegTP premises in Mainz. Though it was scheduled for up to three days, the auction eventually lasted only ninety minutes and was finished after three bidding rounds. In the first bidding round, MMO submitted the highest bids for all ten items. MMO held lots 1–5 with a current bid of DM 36.36m, lots 6–9 with DM 40m, and lot 10—the 2×1.4 MHz block—with DM 56m. Notice that lots 1–9 are perfectly homogeneous, but MMO submitted differentiated bids. After the second round, T-Mobil held lots 1–4 for DM 40.01m and lot 5 for DM 40m; MMO was still holder of the second five lots. Notice that the latter implies that T-Mobil had not attempted to overbid MMO on lots 6–10. E-plus and Viag Interkom had quit the auction. In the final third round, no new bids were submitted, and the auction ended with a total revenue of DM 416.04m.

The auction results allow various interpretations. Without claiming to have the "right" story, we give one possible account of the observed auction outcomes that seems closely related to our experimental results. First, the observed bidding behavior suggests that both T-Mobil and MMO had been in the conservative scenario, that is, had falling marginal valuations for the new spectrum. Both MMO's first round bid and T-Mobil's response clearly indicate that both companies were not aiming to outbid their competitors on all ten blocks. Second, the MMO bid indicated some sort of a priority for having the lots 6–10 rather than the lots 1–5. T-Mobil's second bid showed that T-Mobil was satisfied to acquire the relatively cheaper lots 1–5. In this way, the lots were quickly distributed with little conflict. Note that the low frequency of bids from the extramarginal bidders may indicate that the price at which the lots were bought was relatively high compared to the willingness-to-pay of the extramarginal bidders. Notice also that no communication between the companies' managers is necessary to achieve this type of allocation.[13] Third, the entry bid of MMO was well above the minimal bidding requirement, possibly to make sure that the bids would be visible. Another plausible reason for a high jump bid is that the rules provided two ways the auction could end, as described in section 12.3. It could either end because no new bids are submitted, or by announcement by the auctioneer. The latter was possible after twenty rounds. It is conceivable that the high jump bid attempted to avoid the end of the auction through a final sealed-bid stage.

Appendix

The Instructions for the Auction Experiment

Lots and Bidders

• In this auction you can bid for 10 different lots: **lot 1, lot 2, . . . , lot 10**.

• Each lot is characterized by a *capacity*. Lot 1 to lot 9 have a capacity of 1,000 and lot 10 has a capacity of 1400.

• There are 4 **bidders** in this auction: A, B, C, and D. The bidders differ in their aims they pursue in the auction and in their budget they are allowed to spend.

Rounds

• The auction is organized in consecutive rounds in which bidders can make their bids.

- Each rounds lasts for at least 5 minutes.
- A round ends if either
    all bidders have submitted their bids
  or   the time limit is over.

Valid Bids

- In the first round of the auction the **minimal bid** is fixed for each lot. In all other rounds the minimal bid is x percent higher than the highest bid for this lot in the previous round. The percentage x chosen from the range 2 to 20 by the auctioneer and is announced in the beginning of each round. In the first round the value of x is 20.
- It is not possible to withdraw a submitted bid.
- In each round each bidder has to take care that his budget is higher than the sum of his new bids added to the bids for those lots, for which he is the current holder.

Highest Bids

- At the end of one round for each lot the bidder is determined who has submitted the highest bid for that lot. This bidder is called the holder of the highest bid for that lot.
- If more than one bidder has submitted the highest bid for the same lot, the bidder, who submitted his bid first, becomes the holder of that lot.

Active Bids

- In the first round each bidder is allowed to bid for all 10 lots.
- In the following rounds the number of active bids of one bidder is not allowed to exceed the number of his active bids in the previous round.
- A bidder has an active bid on a certain lot, if either in the beginning of the current round he is its holder or he submits a bid for that lot in this round.

Information in Each Round

- Each bidder is provided with the following information concerning the **previous round**:

the highest bid for each lot

the holder of the highest bid for each lot

those lots for which *you* are the holder are displayed in red colour.

· Each bidder is provided with the following information concerning the **current round**:

the minimal bid for each lot.

End of the Auction

· The current round is the last round of the auction (i.e., the auction ends) if either

the auctioneer determines an early end of the auction,

or none of the bidders submits a new bid in the current round.

· The bidder who is the holder of a lot in the last round wins this lot.

An Early End of the Auction

· After 20 rounds the auctioneer is able to reduce the auction to two further rounds.

Number of Auctions

· We try to complete 5 auctions.

Aims and Budgets of Bidders

· For each bidder there are two possible scenarios: 0 and 1. Before an auction the scenario for the current auction for each bidder is randomly and independently determined with an equal probability for each scenario. A bidder is only informed about his own scenario.

· Each scenario contains a budget range, from which the budget is randomly and independently determined while all possible values could occur with the same probability.

· The scenarios differ in their budget ranges and in the aims of the bidders.

| Bidder A | Scenario 0 and Scenario 1 | | | | | | | | | | | | | | | | | | |
MHz bought	1000	1400	2000	2400	3000	3400	4000	4400	5000	5400	6000	6400	7000	7400	8000	8400	9000	9400	10000
10%	-100	-100	-100	400	700	900	1200	1400	1700	1740	1800	1840	1900	1940	2000	2040	2100	2140	2240
20%	-200	-200	-200	300	600	800	1100	1300	1600	1640	1700	1740	1800	1840	1900	1940	2000	2040	2140
30%	-300	-300	-300	200	500	700	1000	1200	1500	1540	1600	1640	1700	1740	1800	1840	1900	1940	2040
40%	-400	-400	-400	100	400	600	900	1100	1400	1440	1500	1540	1600	1640	1700	1740	1800	1840	1940
50%	-500	-500	-500	0	300	500	800	1000	1300	1340	1400	1440	1500	1540	1600	1640	1700	1740	1840
60%	-600	-600	-600	-100	200	400	700	900	1200	1240	1300	1340	1400	1440	1500	1540	1600	1640	1740
70%	-700	-700	-700	-200	100	300	600	800	1100	1140	1200	1240	1300	1340	1400	1440	1500	1540	1640
80%	-800	-800	-800	-300	0	200	500	700	1000	1040	1100	1140	1200	1240	1300	1340	1400	1440	1540
90%	-900	-900	-900	-400	-100	100	400	600	900	940	1000	1040	1100	1140	1200	1240	1300	1340	1440
100%	-1000	-1000	-1000	-500	-200	0	300	500	800	840	900	940	1000	1040	1100	1140	1200	1240	1340

fraction of budget spent

Bidder A receives a bonus of 500, if he does not purchase more than 1600 units less than Bidder B.

Bidder B — Scenario 0

fraction of budget spent \ MHz bought	1000	1400	2000	2400	3000	3400	4000	4400	5000	5400	6000	6400	7000	7400	8000	8400	9000	9400	10000
10%	−100	−100	−100	400	700	900	1200	1400	1700	1740	1800	1840	1900	1940	2000	2040	2100	2140	2240
20%	−200	−200	−200	300	600	800	1100	1300	1600	1640	1700	1740	1800	1840	1900	1940	2000	2040	2140
30%	−300	−300	−300	200	500	700	1000	1200	1500	1540	1600	1640	1700	1740	1800	1840	1900	1940	2040
40%	−400	−400	−400	100	400	600	900	1100	1400	1440	1500	1540	1600	1640	1700	1740	1800	1840	1940
50%	−500	−500	−500	0	300	500	800	1000	1300	1340	1400	1440	1500	1540	1600	1640	1700	1740	1840
60%	−600	−600	−600	−100	200	400	700	900	1200	1240	1300	1340	1400	1440	1500	1540	1600	1640	1740
70%	−700	−700	−700	−200	100	300	600	800	1100	1140	1200	1240	1300	1340	1400	1440	1500	1540	1640
80%	−800	−800	−800	−300	0	200	500	700	1000	1040	1100	1140	1200	1240	1300	1340	1400	1440	1540
90%	−900	−900	−900	−400	−100	100	400	600	900	940	1000	1040	1100	1140	1200	1240	1300	1340	1440
100%	−1000	−1000	−1000	−500	−200	0	300	500	800	840	900	940	1000	1040	1100	1140	1200	1240	1340

Bidder B — Scenario 1

fraction of budget spent \ MHz bought	1000	1400	2000	2400	3000	3400	4000	4400	5000	5400	6000	6400	7000	7400	8000	8400	9000	9400	10000
10%	−100	−100	−100	260	350	410	500	560	920	1160	1520	1760	2120	2360	2720	2960	3320	3560	4160
20%	−200	−200	−200	160	250	310	400	460	820	1060	1420	1660	2020	2260	2620	2860	3220	3460	4060
30%	−300	−300	−300	60	150	210	300	360	720	960	1320	1560	1920	2160	2520	2760	3120	3360	3960
40%	−400	−400	−400	−40	50	110	200	260	620	860	1220	1460	1820	2060	2420	2660	3020	3260	3860
50%	−500	−500	−500	−140	−50	10	100	160	520	760	1120	1360	1720	1960	2320	2560	2920	3160	3760
60%	−600	−600	−600	−240	−150	−90	0	60	420	660	1020	1260	1620	1860	2220	2460	2820	3060	3660
70%	−700	−700	−700	−340	−250	−190	−100	−40	320	560	920	1160	1520	1760	2120	2360	2720	2960	3560
80%	−800	−800	−800	−440	−350	−290	−200	−140	220	460	820	1060	1420	1660	2020	2260	2620	2860	3460
90%	−900	−900	−900	−540	−450	−390	−300	−240	120	360	720	960	1320	1560	1920	2160	2520	2760	3360
100%	−1000	−1000	−1000	−640	−550	−490	−400	−340	20	260	620	860	1220	1460	1820	2060	2420	2660	3260

Bidder B receives a bonus of 500, if he purchases at least as many units as Bidder A.

Bidder C — Scenario 0

MHz bought	1000	1400	2000	2400	3000	3400	4000	4400	5000	5400	6000	6400	7000	7400	8000	8400	9000	9400	10000
10%	−100	−60	0	40	100	140	200	240	700	780	900	980	1100	1180	1300	1380	1500	1580	1780
20%	−200	−160	−100	−60	0	40	100	140	600	680	800	880	1000	1080	1200	1280	1400	1480	1680
30%	−300	−260	−200	−160	−100	−60	0	40	500	580	700	780	900	980	1100	1180	1300	1380	1580
40%	−400	−360	−300	−260	−200	−160	−100	−60	400	480	600	680	800	880	1000	1080	1200	1280	1480
50%	−500	−460	−400	−360	−300	−260	−200	−160	300	380	500	580	700	780	900	980	1100	1180	1380
60%	−600	−560	−500	−460	−400	−360	−300	−260	200	280	400	480	600	680	800	880	1000	1080	1280
70%	−700	−660	−600	−560	−500	−460	−400	−360	100	180	300	380	500	580	700	780	900	980	1180
80%	−800	−760	−700	−660	−600	−560	−500	−460	0	80	200	280	400	480	600	680	800	880	1080
90%	−900	−860	−800	−760	−700	−660	−600	−560	−100	−20	100	180	300	380	500	580	700	780	980
100%	−1000	−960	−900	−860	−800	−760	−700	−660	−200	−120	0	80	200	280	400	480	600	680	880

(fraction of budget spent)

In Scenario 0 bidder C receives a bonus of 20% of the total turnover of the other bidders.

Bidder C — Scenario 1

MHz bought	1000	1400	2000	2400	3000	3400	4000	4400	5000	5400	6000	6400	7000	7400	8000	8400	9000	9400	10000
10%	−100	−60	0	40	100	140	200	240	940	1140	1440	1640	1940	2140	2440	2640	2940	3140	3640
20%	−200	−160	−100	−60	0	40	100	140	840	1040	1340	1540	1840	2040	2340	2540	2840	3040	3540
30%	−300	−260	−200	−160	−100	−60	0	40	740	940	1240	1440	1740	1940	2240	2440	2740	2940	3440
40%	−400	−360	−300	−260	−200	−160	−100	−60	640	840	1140	1340	1640	1840	2140	2340	2640	2840	3340
50%	−500	−460	−400	−360	−300	−260	−200	−160	540	740	1040	1240	1540	1740	2040	2240	2540	2740	3240
60%	−600	−560	−500	−460	−400	−360	−300	−260	440	640	940	1140	1440	1640	1940	2140	2440	2640	3140
70%	−700	−660	−600	−560	−500	−460	−400	−360	340	540	840	1040	1340	1540	1840	2040	2340	2540	3040
80%	−800	−760	−700	−660	−600	−560	−500	−460	240	440	740	940	1240	1440	1740	1940	2240	2440	2940
90%	−900	−860	−800	−760	−700	−660	−600	−560	140	340	640	840	1140	1340	1640	1840	2140	2340	2840
100%	−1000	−960	−900	−860	−800	−760	−700	−660	40	240	540	740	1040	1240	1540	1740	2040	2240	2740

(fraction of budget spent)

Bidder D

Scenario 0

fraction of budget spent	MHz bought																		
	1000	1400	2000	2400	3000	3400	4000	4400	5000	5400	6000	6400	7000	7400	8000	8400	9000	9400	10000
10%	-100	-60	0	40	100	140	200	240	300	340	400	440	500	540	600	640	700	740	840
20%	-200	-160	-100	-60	0	40	100	140	200	240	300	340	400	440	500	540	600	640	740
30%	-300	-260	-200	-160	-100	-60	0	40	100	140	200	240	300	340	400	440	500	540	640
40%	-400	-360	-300	-260	-200	-160	-100	-60	0	40	100	140	200	240	300	340	400	440	540
50%	-500	-460	-400	-360	-300	-260	-200	-160	-100	-60	0	40	100	140	200	240	300	340	440
60%	-600	-560	-500	-460	-400	-360	-300	-260	-200	-160	-100	-60	0	40	100	140	200	240	340
70%	-700	-660	-600	-560	-500	-460	-400	-360	-300	-260	-200	-160	-100	-60	0	40	100	140	240
80%	-800	-760	-700	-660	-600	-560	-500	-460	-400	-360	-300	-260	-200	-160	-100	-60	0	40	140
90%	-900	-860	-800	-760	-700	-660	-600	-560	-500	-460	-400	-360	-300	-260	-200	-160	-100	-60	40
100%	-1000	-960	-900	-860	-800	-760	-700	-660	-600	-560	-500	-460	-400	-360	-300	-260	-200	-160	-60

In Scenario 0 bidder D receives a bonus of 20% of the total turnover of the other bidders.

Bidder D

Scenario 1

fraction of budget spent	MHz bought																		
	1000	1400	2000	2400	3000	3400	4000	4400	5000	5400	6000	6400	7000	7400	8000	8400	9000	9400	10000
10%	-100	-60	0	40	100	140	200	240	940	1140	1440	1640	1940	2140	2440	2640	2940	3140	3640
20%	-200	-160	-100	-60	0	40	100	140	840	1040	1340	1540	1840	2040	2340	2540	2840	3040	3540
30%	-300	-260	-200	-160	-100	-60	0	40	740	940	1240	1440	1740	1940	2240	2440	2740	2940	3440
40%	-400	-360	-300	-260	-200	-160	-100	-60	640	840	1140	1340	1640	1840	2140	2340	2640	2840	3340
50%	-500	-460	-400	-360	-300	-260	-200	-160	540	740	1040	1240	1540	1740	2040	2240	2540	2740	3240
60%	-600	-560	-500	-460	-400	-360	-300	-260	440	640	940	1140	1440	1640	1940	2140	2440	2640	3140
70%	-700	-660	-600	-560	-500	-460	-400	-360	340	540	840	1040	1340	1540	1840	2040	2340	2540	3040
80%	-800	-760	-700	-660	-600	-560	-500	-460	240	440	740	940	1240	1440	1740	1940	2240	2440	2940
90%	-900	-860	-800	-760	-700	-660	-600	-560	140	340	640	840	1140	1340	1640	1840	2140	2340	2840
100%	-1000	-960	-900	-860	-800	-760	-700	-660	40	240	540	740	1040	1240	1540	1740	2040	2240	2740

Notes

The experimental work presented in this chapter was part of a concluded consulting project for a telecommunications operator that participated in the German DCS-1800 auction. Prior to and during the auction, the work is or was exclusively known to the advised bidder and no information is or was exchanged with other parties. None of the authors is or was affiliated to the bidder. As usual, all views expressed and all errors made are our own. We thank the experts and the executives of the advised bidder for providing valuable assistance in designing the experiment. We also gratefully acknowledge the financial and organizational support that was provided. We further thank Friedel Bolle, three anonymous referees, and the seminar participants of the CESifo conference on spectrum auctions, held in November 2001 in Munich, for helpful comments and suggestions.

1. For an earlier case study, see Salant (1997).

2. Other experiments motivated by spectrum auctions are reported in Plott (1997), Bolle and Breitmoser (2001a), Abbink et al. (2003), and Plott and Salmon (2001). The issue of multi-unit demand auctions has been experimentally analyzed by Kagel and Levin (2001).

3. Our theoretical considerations were restricted to the discussion of the strategic implications of various types of bidding behavior, especially those that emerged in our experiments. We did not analyze game equilibria. Other authors have taken theoretically more sophisticated approaches, investigating the equilibria of numerous specifications of multi-unit auctions; for example, see Menezes (1996), Ausubel and Schwarz (1999), Grimm, Riedel, and Wolfstetter (2003), Bolle and Breitmoser (2001b), Brusco and Lupomo (2002).

4. However, because of the different frequency range, the per MHz capacity of spectrum in the two bands is not exactly comparable.

5. For discussions of the FCC auctions and its European successors, see McMillan (1994), Cramton (1995), McAfee and McMillan (1996), Ausubel et al. (1996), Keuter and Nett (1997), van Damme (1999, 2002), Jehiel and Moldovanu (2000), and Klemperer (2002).

6. One DM is equivalent to €0.51.

7. There was an additional rule that whenever the price of a lot was DM 2bn or more, the lot would immediately be sold to the holder, and the offer could not be overbid. The motive behind this rule remains unclear.

8. The auction design provided the right of D band operators to withdraw from the purchase in cases where winnings were 2.4 MHz or less.

9. Even longer sessions may distort the results as subjects' ability to concentrate on the problem may decline.

10. Notice that full statistical independence for a comparison over the scenario combinations cannot be achieved. However, such a comparison between treatments was not the focus of our research anyway.

11. Of course, it was extremely unlikely that any of the student subjects had any connection to a person in charge of a competitor's preparations for the auction.

12. The scale of budget units is completely arbitrary, since it was used in the student sessions. The prices should not be taken as equivalent to any real world currency.

13. This is also emphasized by Grimm, Riedel, and Wolfstetter (2003). In a game-theoretic analysis of the German DCS-1800 auction, the authors find that similar outcomes are obtained in a completely noncooperative framework.

References

Abbink, K., and A. Sadrieh. 1995. "RatImage—Research Assistance Toolbox for Computer-Aided Human Behavior Experiments." SFB Discussion Paper B-325, University of Bonn.

Abbink, K., B. Irlenbusch, P. Pezanis-Christou, B. Rockenbach, A. Sadrieh, and R. Selten. 2003. "An Experimental Test of Design Alternatives for the British 3G/UMTS Auction." Forthcoming in *European Economic Review*.

Ausubel, L. M., and J. Schwartz. 1999. "The Ascending Auction Paradox." Mimeo., University of Maryland.

Ausubel, L. M., P. C. Cramton, P. R. McAfee, and J. McMillan. 1997. "Synergies in Wireless Telephony: Evidence from the Broadband PCS Auctions." *Journal of Economics & Management Strategy* 6(3): 7–71.

Bolle, F., and Y. Breitmoser. 2001a. "Spectrum Auctions: An Experimental Investigation." Mimeo., Europa-Universität Frankfurt/Oder.

Bolle, F., and Y. Breitmoser. 2001b. "Spectrum Auctions: How They Should and How They Should Not Be Shaped." *Finanzarchiv* 58: 260–285.

Brusco, S., and G. Lopomo. 2002. "Collusion via Signalling in Open Ascending Auctions with Multiple Objects and Complementarities." *Review of Economic Studies* 69(2): 407–436.

Cramton, P. C. 1995. "Money Out of Thin Air: The Nationwide Narrowband PCS Auction." *Journal of Economics & Management Strategy* 4: 267–343.

Dyer, D., J. H. Kagel, and D. Levin. 1989. "A Comparison of Naive and Experienced Bidders in Common Value Offer Auctions: Laboratory Analysis." *Economic Journal* 99: 108–115.

Esser, J. K. 1998. "Alive and Well after 25 Years: A Review of Groupthink Research." *Organizational Behavior and Human Decision Processes* 73: 116–141.

Grimm, V., F. Riedel, and E. Wolfstetter. 2003. "Low Price Equilibrium in Multi-Unit Auctions: The GSM Spectrum Auction in Germany." Forthcoming in *International Journal of Industrial Organization*.

Jehiel, P., and B. Moldovanu. 2000. "A Critique of the Planned Rules for the German UMTS/IMT-2000 License Auction." Discussion paper, University of Mannheim.

Kagel, J. H., and D. Levin. 2001. "Behavior in Multi-Unit Demand Auctions: Experiments with Uniform Price and Dynamic Auctions." *Econometrica* 69: 413–454.

Keuter, A., and L. Nett. 1997. "ERMES-Auction in Germany: First Simultaneous Multiple-Round Auction in the European Telecommunications Market." *Telecommunications Policy* 21(4): 297–307.

Klemperer, P. 2002. "What Really Matters in Auction Design." *Journal of Economic Perspectives* 16(1): 169–189.

McAfee, P. R., and J. McMillan. 1996. "Analyzing the Airwave Auction." *Journal of Economic Perspectives* 10: 159–175.

McMillan, J. 1994. "Selling Spectrum Rights." *Journal of Economic Perspectives* 8: 145–162.

Menezes, F. M. 1996. "Multiple-Unit English Auctions." *European Journal of Political Economy* 12: 671–684.

Plott C. R. 1997. "Laboratory Experimental Testbeds: Application to the PCS Auction." *Journal of Economics & Management Strategy* 6(3): 605–638.

Plott, C. R., and T. C. Salmon. 2001. "The Simultaneous, Ascending Price Auction: Dynamics of Price Adjustment in Experiments and in the Field." Mimeo., CalTech.

Salant, D. J. 1997. "Up in the Air: GTE's Experience in the MTA Auction for Personal Communication Services Licenses." *Journal of Economics & Management Strategy* 6(3): 549–572.

van Damme, E. 1999. "The Dutch DCS-1800 Auction." CentER Working Paper 9977, Tilburg University.

van Damme, E. 2002. "The European UMTS-Auctions." *European Economic Review* 46: 846–858.

IV

The German Auction Design

13   The German UMTS Design: Insights from Multi-Object Auction Theory

Christian Ewerhart and Benny Moldovanu

13.1   The Main Aspects of License Auction Design

The recent European 3G license auctions focused public attention and the debate among practitioners and academic economists on several issues pertaining to multi-object auctions. In fact, the most important issues in the design of license auctions are placed at the intersection of industrial organization and mechanism design (see the papers listed in Jehiel and Moldovanu 2000a). The point is that license auctions (or other procedures such as beauty contests) do not only allocate scarce goods, but also determine the nature of whole industries where entry is otherwise almost impossible. Hence the outcome of any allocation procedure influences the future interaction among winning firms, regulator (i.e., government), and consumers. This obvious effect should be taken in account for applications of auction theory to license auctions (it is interesting to note that many financial and telecom analysts explicitly took this effect into consideration in their reports[1]).

Because of the market structure effects, valuations (which depend on expectations about future market structure) are determined by the allocation procedure itself and are therefore endogenous. This creates another twist: Potential acquirers of licenses will anticipate the future scenarios as a function of the auction's outcome, and they will condition their behavior before and during the auction on those expectations. Failing to take into account these basic strategic motives at the design stage can have harsh consequences for governments and/or consumers.

13.1.1   Efficiency versus Value Maximization

Given the previous observation, a maxim such as "Put the licenses in the hands of those who value them most" is nonsense in the context of

European 3G auctions since the main goal of most license auctions is economic efficiency. But economic efficiency means that some weighted sum of firms' values and consumer surplus should be maximized. Thus, equating total welfare (efficiency) with firms' value maximization neglects the consumers. In fact, such an equation probably means that one should create either national monopolies or even a huge European one. Because of the well-understood and well-documented dissipation of rents in oligopoly, a potential monopolist may be willing to pay much more for a (monopoly) license than several oligopolists together. Most observers would rightly regard a recommendation to create a monopoly as ridiculous, since it is obvious to them that the impact on consumer welfare will be disastrous. But, the same observers seem to forget their Economics 101 when choosing among designs that yield the one or the other oligopolistic market structures: maximization of total welfare always means that, besides firms' valuations, the regulator must be concerned about the effects on consumers. Consumers' interest should have in fact a very high priority since this group does not participate at auctions, and therefore information about its "willingness to pay" is not revealed nor processed during the bidding process (nor during beauty contests that purport to care for consumers, but, in reality, tend to be determined by political interests, nationalistic preferences, lobbying, explicit or implicit bribes, etc.). Hence the only chance to incorporate consideration of consumers' welfare is at the auction design stage. Unfortunately, at this stage the regulators operate in the dark since information about consumer welfare in various future scenarios cannot be easily measured and anticipated.

One way (and probably the most effective one) to take into account consumer welfare is to encourage market entry. Although there is a myriad of industrial organization (IO) models with a myriad of results, as a rule of thumb it is probably wise to assume that in reasonable ranges concerning the number of firms, both consumers' surplus and overall efficiency increase with increased competition among firms. This means that market entry should be encouraged as long as it is economically viable (obviously, the duplication of fixed costs and other factors specific to network industries imply that new entry cannot be without limit). The most important variable for controlling entry is the number of licenses.[2] For example, many countries that opted for beauty contests adhered to a simple formula that made entry inevitable:

Number of 3G Licenses = Number of GSM Incumbents + 1

Moreover, several countries that organized auctions (most notably the U.K., which did not even allow GSM operators to bid on the additional license) adopted the above formula. The question is why should one choose a design where entry is inevitable or very likely? Why is it not enough to choose a fair design that gives all firms equal chances to acquire licenses? Because entry is encumbered by a basic asymmetry among the firms that already operate a GSM (2G) network in a given country (incumbents) and those that do not (entrants). This asymmetry (as reflected in the respective fixed costs needed to build a 3G system, financing costs, customer base, recognition and brand names, marketing know-how, etc.) means that incumbents will tend to have higher "pure" valuations for licenses than new entrants.[3] Besides the higher "pure" valuations mentioned earlier, incumbents' values will be even higher due to preemption motives: since per-firm industry profit in oligopoly decreases in the number of active firms, incumbents will be willing to pay large sums of money (even for a license that may be valueless to them!) simply to avoid entry and cannibalization of their existing profits. If potential entrants understand this logic,[4] they will either choose not to participate at the auction, or they will try to form consortia with incumbents. Both types of behavior have been amply observed in many of the UMTS auctions, with adverse effects on competitiveness (and hence ultimately on efficiency) and on revenue.

After a regulatory scheme that encourages entry has been chosen, it is possible to concentrate on an auction format that tries to maximize the value for firms. But, as we argue in the next section, there are many theoretical factors (including the asymmetry among bidders) that make this task rather difficult. Roughly put, value-maximizing multi-object auctions do not exist, and second-best mechanisms are not known.

13.1.2   *Value Maximization versus Revenue Maximization*

Maximization of revenue has been a secondary goal in the UMTS license auctions. Often this goal has been regarded as the main one by the media, by the public, and even by some academic commentators who tend to compare auction outcomes on the basis of the associated revenue. It is no wonder that, as the sequence of European auctions proceeded, several governments got very greedy, only to be thoroughly disappointed at a later stage. Revenue maximization seems a legitimate goal, particularly in the cases where it is believed that this form of taxing firms is more efficient (i.e., less distortionary) than other, more traditional taxation schemes.

A widespread idea is that "value and revenue maximization go hand in hand". The intuition is as follows: If a large pie is created (by maximizing value for the bidders), it will be possible to extract more revenue; conversely, a large willingness to pay reflected in high bids and revenue) means that a large value has been created. Based on this belief, it seems possible to use revenue maximization as a handy proxy for the more fickle value maximization. This belief is mostly based on powerful results from one-object auction theory. But nothing could be farther from the truth in auctions (even single-object ones) where the valuations are endogenous due to the external effects caused by market structure considerations, or in multi-object auctions with either exogenous or endogenous valuations: There is no general relation between efficiency and revenue! Not even in a completely standard multi-object model with no externalities whatsoever, no complementarities, no nothing, is it true that the auction that maximizes revenue is efficient or vice versa. *In particular, this means that multi-object auctions that maximize revenue will not necessarily put the objects in the hands of those that value them most.*

Since this last argument is exceedingly simple, it is worth it mentioning here (see also Jehiel and Moldovanu 2001b). Consider an auction for two objects A and B, and two bidders, 1 and 2. For both agents, the valuations for the bundle $\{A, B\}$ are given by the sum of the valuations for the individual objects, and assume these to be as follows:

$$v_1^A = 10; \quad v_1^B = 7$$

$$v_2^A = 8; \quad v_2^B = 12$$

The value-maximizing auction (which puts the objects in the hand of those who value them most) is simply given by two separate second-price auctions, one for each object. Then object A goes to bidder 1 for a price of 8, while object B goes to bidder 2 for a price of 7. Total revenue is 15. But, consider now a single second-price auction for the entire bundle $\{A, B\}$. Then the bundle will be acquired by bidder 2, for a price of 17! Hence, revenue is higher in the bundle auction, but object A is misallocated. Such a phenomenon occurs as soon as bidders do not have single unit demand (e.g., in the German setting where blocks of capacity were auctioned instead of licenses).

13.2   The Theory of Value and Revenue Maximization in Auctions

Given the previous widespread misconceptions, it is important to get an idea about the main auction-theoretical results concerning revenue and value maximization. This is surely not the place for an exhaustive survey, and we apologize to all authors whose important results are not included here. In particular, we consider only risk-neutral bidders.

Besides the obvious dependence on auction rules, the most important determinants of theoretical auction performance are related to the economics of demand in the underlying situation. Here are several crucial properties:

1. Bidder Symmetry. We say that bidders are (ex ante) symmetric if their utility functions have the same functional form.

2. Informational Externalities. We say that the economic situation displays informational externalities if the valuation of one agent depends on information available to another agent, that is, the valuations contain common components. (For example, consider two firms that bid for an oil field. If one firm has an adjacent field and has already conducted a geological survey, the information contained in the survey affects the valuations of both firms.)

3. Allocative Externalities. We say that the economic situation displays allocative externalities if the valuation of one bidder depends on the entire allocation of physical goods to herself and other bidders. (For example, in a license auction, the valuation of a monopolist incumbent may depend on whether one or two licenses are auctioned. In the latter case entry is possible, with an adverse effect on the monopolist's future profits.)

4. Homogeneity/Heterogeneity of Goods. In an auction where several objects are sold, we say that the objects are homogenous if they are indistinguishable from one another. Otherwise, objects are heterogenous.

5. Complementarities among Goods. In an auction where several objects are sold, we say that the objects are (positive or negative) complements if the value attached to a bundle is not equal to the sum of the values attached to the individual objects in the bundle.

6. Unit Demand/Multi-Unit Demand. We say that bidders have unit demand if, in a multi-object auction, their demand is satiated after they acquire one object. Otherwise, we say that bidders have multi-unit demand.

Generally speaking, the presence of asymmetries, heterogeneity, externalities, and complementarities all hinder value maximization in auctions.

13.2.1 Results for Single-Object Auctions

1. Classical auction formats (such as sealed-bid auctions, ascending, descending, all-pay, etc.) are both value maximizing and revenue maximizing (when augmented by simple instruments such as reserve prices or entry fees) if bidders are symmetric, and if there are no allocative or informational externalities (Vickrey 1961; Myerson 1981).

2. The so-called Clarke-Groves-Vickrey (CGV) mechanisms are value maximizing even if bidders are asymmetric and even if there are allocative externalities (Clarke 1971; Groves 1973; Vickrey 1961).

3. The English ascending auction is value maximizing even if there are asymmetric bidders and informational externalities, as long as there are no allocative externalities (Maskin 1992; Krishna 2000; Izmalkov 2001).

4. Modified CGV mechanisms are value maximizing even if there are asymmetric bidders, and even if informational and allocative externalities are present (Jehiel and Moldovanu 2001a).

5. In general, allocative or informational externalities drive a wedge between value maximization and revenue (Jehiel and Moldovanu 1996).

13.2.2 Multi-Object Auctions

1. CGV mechanisms are value maximizing as long as there are no informational externalities (Clarke 1971; Groves 1973; Vickrey 1961). In that case, the CGV mechanisms are revenue maximizing among value-maximizing mechanisms (Krishna and Perry 1998). With additional assumptions (e.g., either unit demand, or noncomplementarities, or homogenous goods), it is possible to implement the value-maximizing outcome by an ascending, multi-object auction (Ausubel 1997; Ausubel and Milgrom 2001; Demange, Gale, and Sotomayor 1986; Gul and Stacchetti 1999; Bikhchandani and Ostroy 2000a,b; Milgrom 2000).

2. Modified CGV mechanisms are value maximizing even if bidders are asymmetric and there are informational externalities as long as

there are no allocative externalities and no complementarities (Ausubel 1997; Cremer and McLean 1988; Dasgupta and Maskin 2000; Jehiel and Moldovanu 2001a,b). With additional assumptions (e.g., homogenous goods) bidding mechanisms can be constructed that attain the value maximizing outcome (Perry and Reny 1999).

3. Assume that either (1) bidders are asymmetric, objects are heterogenous, and there are informational externalities and complementarities, or (2) bidders are asymmetric and there are both informational and allocative externalities. Then value-maximizing auctions do not exist (Jehiel and Moldovanu 2001a). Moreover, constrained (i.e., second-best) value-maximizing auctions are not yet known.

4. In general, the multi-object revenue maximizing auction is not known. The maximization problem (which resembles the one for finding constrained value-maximizing mechanisms—see point 3) involves a complex integrability constraint (or, equivalently, a constraint that is represented by a complex partial differential equation) (Jehiel, Moldovanu, and Stacchetti 1999).

13.3   The German and Austrian Auctions

13.3.1   Design and Outcomes

The rather complex design (which was shared by both countries) involved two consecutive auctions.[5] The first auction allocated licenses together with so-called duplex or paired spectrum frequencies. The second auction allocated paired spectrum that has not been sold at the first auction, together with additional "unpaired" spectrum. Both auctions were of the "simultaneous multiple-round ascending" type. We focus initially on the first, main auction.

Bidders did not directly submit bids for licenses. Instead, the auctioned objects were twelve abstract blocks of paired spectrum. A bidder obtained a license only if he acquired at least two blocks, but a bidder was allowed to acquire (at most) three blocks. The number of licensed firms was therefore variable (between 0 and 6). If all blocks get sold, then there were bound to be at least four licenses (this equaled the number of GSM incumbents in both Germany and Austria).

Each block had a reserve price of DM 100 million in Germany and €50 million in Austria. At each round a bidder had to bid on at least two blocks. Strangely enough, although the blocks were abstract and identical, bids carried name tags![6] Bidding on only two blocks at round t precluded bidding on three blocks at all rounds $t' > t$.

A block could have remained unsold either because there were no bids for that block above the reserve price, or because the bidder who submitted the last highest bid on that particular block ultimately failed to acquire two blocks, in which case he was not required to make a payment.

In Germany there were seven bidders (including 4 GSM incumbents), after six other qualified bidders ultimately withdrew from the auction. The auction lasted for three weeks and 173 rounds of bidding, and resulted in six licenses being awarded (4 of them to the existing GSM operators). The licensed firms were the four incumbents and two new entrants (one of them already operating as service provider). Each licensed firm acquired two blocks of paired spectrum, paying approximately €8.4 billion (or €4.2 billion per block). The most interesting thing occurred after one of the potential entrants, Debitel, left the auction after 125 rounds and after the price level reached €2.5 billion per block. Since six firms were left bidding for a maximum of six licenses, the auction could have stopped immediately. Instead, the remaining firms (and, in particular, the two large incumbents) continued bidding in order to acquire more capacity. But no other firm was willing to quit, and bidding stopped in round 173. Compared to round 125, there was *no change* in the physical allocation, but firms were, collectively, *€20 billion poorer!*[7]

In Austria there were exactly six bidders (4 of them GSM incumbents) for a maximum of six licenses. Hence, in principle, the license auction could have ended immediately, at the reserve price (€100 million per license). Nevertheless, the auction continued for another sixteen rounds, before stopping with six licensed firms (4 of them to the existing GSM operators), each paying on average about €118 million per license. Hence, about €108 million has again been spent for nothing.

13.3.2 Benefits and Disadvantages of the German and Austrian Design

A main perceived advantage of the German auction was its flexibility. It has been argued that ex ante carving of spectrum in fixed chunks of capacity cannot be efficient, since the regulator is less informed about the precise operational needs of the involved firms. In the same vein, since the regulator does not really know how many firms are efficient, why not let firms themselves determine the number of licenses in a competitive bidding process? These arguments are not entirely correct, since they confuse value maximization (for the involved firms) with efficiency, thus neglecting consumers. From the point of view of value maximization, a design that allows for a variable number of small and large licenses seems more desirable than those designs where the number of licenses and their capacity were fixed ex ante. While this argument is correct, its implementation in the German and Austrian design mixed flexibility in that dimension with flexibility concerning the number of firms. Since the overall industry profits fall in the number of firms, while consumer surplus probably increases, it is obvious that letting the firms themselves decide how many of them will be able to operate in the market is very problematic from the point of view of consumers, and hence for overall efficiency.

Consider a hypothetical story where the regulator proposes the following regulatory scheme to existing firms in the market: Each firm has to pay a hefty fee to the state; depending on the paid fees, the regulator allows more or less (possibly none) new firms in the market, with higher fees meaning fewer firms. Sounds ridiculous? But this was, roughly speaking, how the German and Austrian designs operated, and this feature has been highly praised by some observers.

Despite this crucial caveat, it is instructive to judge the design in terms of its ability to achieve value and/or revenue maximization in light of the properties listed in the previous section:

1. By introducing bidding on 1, 2, or 3 blocks rather than directly on licenses, the auction artificially created a situation with multi-unit demand, and therefore offered scope for demand reduction gaming effects. While such effects usually lead to inefficiencies, here it may, in fact, have had some positive effect since they can partly combat the opposite demand-increasing effect due to allocative externalities (see point 3).

2. It is obvious that complementarities existed among blocks. The first block was worth nothing, the second a lot, and the third had a positive value.

3. By completely endogenizing the firms' valuations (since number of firms and capacities were endogenous), the auction focused most of the strategic behavior on the allocative externalities and created an

artificial demand-increasing effect. For example, the intrinsic value of a third block of capacity was greatly augmented in feasible scenarios where acquiring such a block leads to fewer firms in the market. It is impossible to say with certainty whether demand reduction was stronger than artificial demand increase or vice versa since the strengths of these effects depends on the levels of prices. Obviously, demand increase played the major role following Debitel's quitting, and demand reduction finally took place when prices reached very high levels.

4. In auctions with allocative externalities, a revenue-maximizing seller can extract revenue by "threats" to sell exactly to those agents that create negative externalities on others (Jehiel, Moldovanu, and Stacchetti 1996, 1999). I am happy to say that this argument was very well understood by the auction designers (see the demand increase effect mentioned in point 3). By allowing from four to six firms, such a threat to sell to newcomers was in effect operative, and, in principle, avoidable for a high enough price. Some commentators argued that the German design was therefore much better geared toward revenue maximization. If endogenous entry decisions are neglected, this argument is correct.

5. Last, the multi-unit demand and complementarity features created a massive exposure and regret problem for the involved firms (since exclusive combinatorial bids on entire packages were not allowed). It is therefore no wonder that €20 billion was spend on nothing in the German auction, and that firms quickly learned to avoid this catastrophe (by relatively fast demand reduction) in the Austrian auction. Generally speaking, auctions that create exposure and regret phenomena are not attractive for bidders that? who? may rationally decide to avoid bidding altogether.

In the next section we focus on this exposure problem, since it has been somewhat neglected in the debate so far.

13.4   The Exposure Problem in the German Design

13.4.1   Flexibility versus Risk

The presence of exposure risks in multi-unit license auctions has been identified before, for example, by Cramton (1997) in the context of the FCC spectrum auctions.[8] Cramton uses a simple example in order to show that, with increasing marginal valuations for several objects, bidders risk getting stuck with less of what they attempted to acquire. While the basic idea of the subsequent analysis is in the same spirit, we do not presuppose increasing marginal valuations. Indeed, our discussion shows that the exposure problem in the German design was a consequence of the fact that the flexible German design has been combined with a de facto uniform-price auction. Specifically, when a dominant incumbent tries to push the weakest entrant out of the market, he may be unsuccessful and suffer from regret. The attempt to create a more concentrated market structure may drive prices up for all acquired frequency blocks without changing the allocation.

This is the basic idea underlying Ewerhart and Moldovanu's (2001) analysis. The model used in this chapter combines elements of the complete information setting of Jehiel and Moldovanu (2000b) with existing models of uniform-price auctions, as analyzed by Noussair (1995) and Engelbrecht-Wiggans and Kahn (1998).

13.4.2   A Stylized Model

The model developed here abstracts from a number of facts that were present in the actual situation. First, we focus on the first stage of the German design. The bidders' valuations in the subsequent analysis should therefore be interpreted as valuations that the firms attribute to specific outcomes of the first stage. We discuss later why the second stage does not affect our arguments. We also abstract from the fact that the German license auction must be properly considered as a part of a more global process, in which international telecom firms have fought about the position in the European market. For example, it has been suggested by van Damme (2001) that the high prices in Germany resulted from a struggle mainly between KPN, represented by E-Plus, and Telefonica, represented by Group 3G. Moreover, while financial externalities and credit constraints might have played a significant role, we also abstract from these complications.

The formal analysis starts with a setting in which twelve frequency blocks are sold to $i = 1, \ldots, n$ bidders. Bidder i has valuations $v_m^i(k)$ for an m-block license in a k-player market, where $m \in \{2, 3\}$ and $k \in \{4, 5, 6\}$.[9] The auction is open and ascending and most easily viewed as a clock auction. Each bidder may bid for two or three blocks, and an activity rule specifies that demand may not increase during the auction.

The final price is the lowest price p^* at which aggregate demand drops to 12 or even lower. If aggregate demand drops to precisely 12, then the corresponding highest bids are satisfied. Otherwise a randomizing tie-breaking rule is applied, whose specification is of minor importance in the sequel. Essentially, each bidder submits a bid $b^i = (b_3^i, b_2^i)$, where b_3^i is the price level at which i's demand is reduced from three to two units, and b_2^i is the price level where bidder i drops out completely.

Considering "sealed bids" for modeling a dynamic auction is justified in view of our informational assumptions detailed here, because bidders do not learn new information during the auction.

13.4.3 Assumptions

Ewerhart and Moldovanu (2001) make a number of assumptions that focus the analysis on the case that had been observed. There are only $n = 6$ bidders (i.e., the analysis focuses on the main stage of interest that starts when the number of bidders precisely equals the maximal number of licenses and the auction could have been immediately stopped). Bidders are ordered according to their valuations, with bidder 1, the dominant incumbent, having the highest valuations. Thus, we require that $v_m^i(k)$ is decreasing in i. Moreover, we assume that valuations $v_m^i(k)$ are increasing in the number of blocks m and decreasing in the number of players in the market k.

The weakest bidder's (i.e., the weakest entrant's) valuation for a small two-block license is denoted by $v := v_2^6(6)$. We assume that v is uncertain ex ante and is distributed on an interval $[\underline{v}, \bar{v}]$ such that

$$\frac{\underline{v}}{2} < \frac{v_3^1(5)}{3} < \frac{\bar{v}}{2}. \tag{1}$$

This assumption generates an uncertainty about whether the per-block valuation of the dominant incumbent for a large license is higher or lower than the per-block valuation of the weakest entrant for a small license.

Finally, it is assumed that the value of the third block is not too large for bidders 2 to 6, namely, that

$$\frac{v_3^2(4)}{3} < \frac{\underline{v}}{2}. \tag{2}$$

Figure 13.1 illustrates the per-block valuations in the stylized model of the UMTS auction. On the left-hand side, one sees the per-block valuation of the weakest bidder 6 for a large license in a concentrated

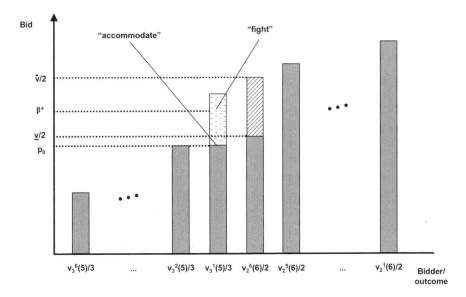

Figure 13.1
Equilibrium bids in the stylized UMTS auction (*Source:* Ewerhart and Moldovanu 2001.)

market, namely, in a market with five players. Going to the right, we have the corresponding valuations for bidders 5 to 1. Next, one has the uncertain valuation for the weakest entrant $v_2^6(6)/2$, which may vary between $\underline{v}/2$ and $\bar{v}/2$. Still further to the right we depict the per-unit valuations of the remaining bidders 5 to 1 for a small license in a less concentrated market.

13.4.4 Equilibrium

Ewerhart and Moldovanu (2001) show that the following bidding behavior constitutes an equilibrium in the stylized UMTS auction: With the exception of the strongest incumbent bid, each bidder i bids his true per-block valuations in the sense that he bids for three units up to $v_3^i(5)/3$, and for two units up to $v_2^i(6)/2$. Bidder 1, in contrast, bids only up to some price level β^* for three units. Equilibrium behavior is illustrated in figure 13.1. When prices increase, all six bidders first reduce their demand from three to two, one by one, and starting with the weakest bidders. It can be shown that, depending on the parameters of the model, each of the two alternative equilibria may occur:

1. ("accommodate") In this case $\beta^* = v_3^2(5)/3$, so that bidder 1 reduces his demand for the third unit in accordance with the second strongest bidder 2, and the auction ends at a price $p_0 = v_3^2(5)/3$ with a six-player market.

2. ("fight") In this case bidder 1 keeps up demand for three units up to a level of $\beta^* \in \lfloor \underline{v}/2, v_3^1(5)/3 \rfloor$ and tries to push the weakest entrant out of the market. In that equilibrium two things may happen. If $\beta^* > v/2$, the dominant incumbent wins the battle, and the auction ends with a price of $v/2$, allocating a large license to the dominant incumbent, and small licenses to bidders 2 to 5. Otherwise, the entrant wins the battle, and a six-player market results with a final per-block price of β^*. The optimal bid β^* for the incumbent maximizes the expected profit function

$$U_1(\beta) = \int_{\underline{v}}^{2\beta} \left\{ v_3^1(5) - \frac{3v}{2} \right\} dF(v) + \int_{2\beta}^{\bar{v}} \{ v_2^1(6) - 2\beta \} dF(v), \tag{3}$$

where $F(v)$ is the cumulative distribution function corresponding to the distribution of v. Hence, β^* is implicitly given by

$$\beta^* + \frac{1 - F(2\beta^*)}{F'(2\beta^*)} = v_3^1(5) - v_2^1(6). \tag{4}$$

Formula 4 shows that the dominant incumbent lowers his bid as a consequence of the exposure.

Both equilibria are stable with respect to the introduction of a second stage, under some additional assumptions. Specifically, when we assume that the marginal valuation of a fourth block is lower than the marginal valuation of a third block, then the second stage will always end with giving any remaining block to bidder 2. When the additional value that bidder 2 has from obtaining a third block in the second stage is taken into account in the first stage, this will increase the valuation of bidder 2 for a small license in a concentrated market with five players, but leave the valuations of both bidders 1 and 2 for a large license in a concentrated market unaffected. But then it is immediate from figure 13.1 that the second stage does not affect equilibrium behavior.[10]

13.4.5   Regret

The second equilibrium illustrates the exposure problem. Specifically, when the incumbent tries to push the entrant out of the market, but is ultimately unsuccessful, he increases the prices for the two blocks he could acquire for sure, so that regret may occur. Technically, this means that the outcome does not constitute an ex post equilibrium.[11] The regret can be made explicit by considering the difference in expected utility between fighting and accommodating:

$$\Delta U_1 = pr\left(\frac{v}{2} < \beta\right)\{v_3^1(5) - v_2^1(6) - p_0 - 3\Delta^w\}$$

$$+ pr\left(\frac{v}{2} \geq \beta\right)\{-2\Delta'\}, \tag{5}$$

where

$$\Delta^w = E\left[\frac{v}{2} \,\middle|\, \frac{v}{2} < \beta\right] - p_0 \tag{6}$$

$$\Delta' = \beta - p_0 \tag{7}$$

is the expected increment in the price per block in cases where the incumbent wins and loses the battle, respectively.

The previous expression captures the regret effect as follows: In a case where the incumbent wins, he earns an incremental utility that corresponds to the difference between his valuation of a large license in a concentrated market and his valuation of a small license in a less concentrated market. But he also has to pay the accommodating price p_0 for the additional block, and, for each of the three blocks, the expected price increment conditional on his winning the battle. In the other case, namely, when the incumbent loses the battle, he realizes a loss on each of the two remaining frequency blocks, which corresponds to the expected price increment conditional on his losing the battle. This second expression captures the regret outcome because Δ' is the per-block price increment that is spuriously paid when the battle is lost, and the outcome is the same as the one occurring at the lower price level.

13.5   Conclusion

This survey has reviewed a number of insights about value and revenue maximization objectives in multi-unit auctions. In the light of these insights, we have discussed several advantages and potential problems of the German UMTS auction. That design allowed a flexible allocation of capacity that is an advantage vis-à-vis less flexible designs. But, under incomplete information, and in the presence of externalities stemming from market structure considerations, this flexibility has caused a significant exposure for bidders, with the potential for inefficient nonparticipation and for shareholder value destruction. Because the flexible design allows incumbents to fight entrants, the prices paid in the flexible design can be strictly higher than those resulting from a less flexible design yielding the same outcome. Moreover, the flexible design included the risk of a concentrated market structure, with adverse effects on consumers. For this reason, and because the huge exposure problem affected the financial stability of the telecommunications industry, we question the efficiency gains obtained with a flexible design.

13.6 Summary

We briefly survey several insights about value and revenue maximization in multi-object auctions and apply them to the German (and Austrian) UMTS auction. In particular, we discuss in detail the exposure problem that caused firms in Germany to pay almost €20 billion for nothing.

Notes

C. Ewerhart thanks Mathias Meisel, portfolio manager at Zurich Invest, for many insightful discussions concerning the telecommunications industry. B. Moldovanu wishes to acknowledge the long cooperation with Philippe Jehiel. This cooperation has shaped several main ideas in this paper. We also wish to thank the participants at the CESifo conference on auctions and telecommunications for their many helpful comments.

1. For example, industry estimates amounted to per license values of €14.75 Bn, 15.88 Bn, and 17.6 Bn for a German symmetric market with 6, 5, or 4 firms, respectively (Deutsche Bank (2000), UBS Warburg (2000), and WestLB Panmure (2000)).

2. There are other regulatory instruments, such as mandatory roaming, mandatory site-sharing, and payment for license fees by installments, that reduce fixed costs and/or financing costs for entrants, and hence encourage entry.

3. In some cases, it is possible that entrants have higher valuations than incumbents. For example, a particular country may be the "last piece in the puzzle" for an entrant that operates globally. That firm may be willing to pay more than a small incumbent with only local interests. But such features are transient and hard to predict, and should not form the basis of auction design.

4. Klemperer (2002) points out that small perceived advantages ("toeholds") can be transformed in large advantages during the auction due to cautious behavior in order to avoid the "winner's curse."

5. For details on the design, see the official document by the RegTP (2000).

6. For example, the Italian design, which auctioned five identical licenses required from bidders just a bid (without specification to which license it applied).

7. The outcome was so unfortunate that Deutsche Telekom became apologetic after the auction. See *Financial Times* (2000).

8. See also and Ausubel and Cramton (1998).

9. In the actual setting, the second stage opened the theoretical possibility to obtain even four blocks. As mentioned before, for simplicity, we abstract here from the second stage.

10. In contrast, the second stage is strategically relevant in chapter 14, where it is assumed that two dominant incumbents have the potential to push out an incumbent.

11. In an ex post equilibrium, agents do not wish to change their actions even after learning the private information held by their competitors. This concept is stronger than the Bayes-Nash equilibrium, but weaker than the dominant strategy equilibrium.

References

Ausubel, L. 1997. "A Efficient Ascending-Bid Auction for Multiple Objects." Discussion paper, University of Maryland.

Ausubel, L. M., and P. Cramton. 1998. "Demand Reduction and Inefficiency in Multi-Unit Auctions." Working paper, University of Maryland.

Ausubel, L. M., and P. Milgrom. 2001. "Ascending Auctions with Package Bid." Mimeo., University of Maryland and Stanford University.

Bikhchandani, S., and J. Ostroy. 2000a. "The Package Assignment Model." Mimeo., UCLA.

Bikhchandani, S., and J. Ostroy. 2000b. "Ascending Price Vickrey Auctions." Mimeo., UCLA.

Clarke, E. 1971. "Multipart Pricing of Goods." *Public Choice* 8: 19–33.

Cramton, P. 1997. "The FCC Spectrum Auctions: An Early Assessment." *Journal of Economics & Management Strategy* 6(3): 431–495.

Cremer, J., and R. McLean. 1988. "Full Extraction of Surplus in Bayesian and Dominant Strategy Auctions." *Econometrica* 56(6): 1247–1257.

Dasgupta, P., and E. Maskin. 2000. "Efficient Auctions." *Quarterly Journal of Economics* 115(2): 341–389.

Demange, G., D. Gale, and M. Sotomayor. 1986. "Multi-Item Auctions." *Journal of Political Economy* 94: 863–872.

Deutsche Bank. 2000. "UMTS, The Third Generation Game." Deutsche Bank Equity Research.

Engelbrecht-Wiggans, R., and C. M. Kahn. 1998. "Multi-Unit Auctions with Uniform Prices." *Economic Theory* 12: 227–258.

Ewerhart, C., and B. Moldovanu. 2001. "A Stylized Model of the German UMTS Auction." Discussion paper, University of Mannheim.

Financial Times. 2000. "German 3G auction raises Euro 51bn." August 8.

Groves, T. 1973. "Incentives in Teams." Econometrica 41, 617–631.

Gul, F., and E. Stacchetti. 1999. "Walrasian Equilibrium with Gross Substitutes." Journal of Economic Theory 87, 9–124.

Izmalkov, S. 2001. "English Auctions with Reentry." Discussion paper, Penn State University.

Jehiel, P., and B. Moldovanu. 1996. "Strategic Non-Participation." *RAND Journal of Economics* 27(1): 84–98.

Jehiel, P., and B. Moldovanu. 2000a. "License Auctions and Market Structure." Discussion paper, Mannheim University and CEPR.

Jehiel, P., and B. Moldovanu. 2000b. "The European UMTS License Auctions." Discussion paper, Mannheim University and CEPR.

Jehiel, P., and B. Moldovanu. 2000c. "Auctions with Downstream Interaction among Buyers." *RAND Journal of Economics* 31(4): 768–791.

Jehiel, P., and B. Moldovanu. 2001a. "Efficient Design with Interdependent Valuations." *Econometrica* 69(5): 1237–1259.

Jehiel, P., and B. Moldovanu. 2001b. "A Note on Efficiency and Revenue Maximization in Multi-Object Auctions." *Economic Bulletin* 3(2): 2–5.

Jehiel, P., B. Moldovanu, and E. Stacchetti. 1996. "How (not) to Sell Nuclear Weapons." *American Economic Review* 86: 814–829.

Jehiel, P., B. Moldovanu, and E. Stacchetti. 1999. "Multidimensional Mechanism Design for Auctions with Externalities." *Journal of Economic Theory* 85: 258–293.

Klemperer, P. 2002. "What Really Matters in Auction Design." *Journal of Economic Perspectives* 16(1): 169–190.

Krishna, V. 2000. "Asymmetric English Auctions." Discussion paper, Pennsylvania State University.

Krishna, V., and M. Perry. 1998. "Efficient Mechanism Design." Mimeo., Pennsylvania State University.

Maskin, E. 1992. "Auctions and Privatizations." In *Privatization: Symposium in Honor of Herbert Giersch*, ed. H. Siebert, 115–136. Tübingen: Mohv(Siebeck).

McAfee, R. P., and J. McMillan. 1996. "Analyzing the Airwaves Auction." *Journal of Economic Perspectives* 10: 159–175.

McMillan, J. 1994. "Selling Spectrum Rights." *Journal of Economic Perspectives* 8: 145–162.

Milgrom, P. 2000. "Putting Auction Theory to Work." *Journal of Political Economy* 108: 245–272.

Myerson, R. 1981. "Optimal Auction Design." *Mathematics of Operations Research* 6: 58–73.

Noussair, C. 1995. "Equilibria in a Multi-Object Uniform Price Sealed Bid Auction with Multi-Unit Demands." *Economic Theory* 5: 337–351.

Perry, M., and P. Reny. 1999. "An Ex-Post Efficient Multi-Unit Auction for Agents with Interdependent Valuations." Discussion paper, University of Chicago.

Reg-TP. 2000. Entscheidung der Präsidentenkammer vom 18.02.2000 über die Regeln für die Durchführung des Versteigerungsverfahrens zur Vergabe von Lizenzen für UMTS/IMT-2000; Mobilkommunikation der dritten Generation—Aktenzeichen BK-1b-98/005-2. Official declaratory document.

UBS Warburg. 2000. "3G Hysteria! Not Everyone's Idea of Fun and Games." Mimeo., UBS Global Equity Research.

van Damme, E. 2000. "The Dutch UMTS Auction in Retrospect." cpb Report 2001/2.

Vickrey, W. 1961. "Counterspeculation, Auctions, and Competitive Sealed Tenders." *Journal of Finance* 16: 8–37.

WestLB Panmure. 2000. "UMTS. The Countdown Has Begun." Mimeo., WestLB Panmure, Pan European Equity.

14   The Third Generation (UMTS) Spectrum Auction in Germany

Veronika Grimm, Frank
Riedel, and Elmar Wolfstetter

14.1   Introduction

In 2000 several European countries auctioned licenses for third generation (UMTS) mobile telecommunications, the new standard that is expected to revolutionize mobile communications.[1] Among other benefits, UMTS offers enormously higher transmission rates (up to 200 times faster than the current GSM standard). This allows mobile phone operators to supply an abundance of new services, from virtual banking, credit card transactions, and information and booking services to fast Inter- and Intranet access, audio and video clips on demand, and video conferencing, that promise to surpass the quality of the most advanced fixed line telephony.

Building third generation networks and marketing, handling, and billing the new services is enormously costly. The UMTS technology works at a higher frequency than GSM (the current industry standard in Europe) to transmit and receive information; therefore, each base station has a much shorter range. Roughly, UMTS networks require four to sixteen times as many base stations to manage a given data flow as the established GSM networks. In addition, the higher data flow associated with the new services that become available with UMTS requires even more stations to serve customers in a given area. More stations also raise health concerns about radio emissions and objections to the littering of the environment with transmitters and radio masts.

Nevertheless, the auctioning of UMTS licenses generated an unsurpassed amount of revenue. The U.K. treasury alone earned €37.5 billion, and the German finance minister cashed in the record sum of €50.8 billion. However, in some countries the UMTS auctions were disappointing. Revenue was remarkably low in the Netherlands and

Table 14.1
UMTS auctions in Europe in the year 2000

Where	When	# Bidders	# Licenses	# Incumb	€/Pop	€/(Pop/Lic)
UK	03/04	13	5	4	630	3150
Netherlands	07	9/6	5	5	170	850
Germany*	07/08	12/7	4–6*	4	615	3690
Italy	10	8/6	5	4	210	1050
Austria*	10	6	4–6*	3	103	618
Switzerland	11/12	10/4	4	3	19	76

in Italy, which has one of the most profitable mobile phone markets in Europe. And the year ended with a complete flop in Switzerland, where only four bidders showed up to bid for four licenses, and the regulator desperately (though in vain) tried to patch up last-minute changes in auction rules. That anticlimax continued well into the year 2001, when the auction had to be called off in Belgium and Israel.

Putting the German auction into perspective, table 14.1 summarizes the European UMTS auctions in the year 2000 in chronological order. The first column states the country (a star indicates that the German auction design was applied; all other countries applied the U.K. rules). The second column states the month(s) when the UMTS auction took place, the third the number of bidders, the fourth the number of licenses (when a range is given, an asterisk indicates the final number of licenses), the fifth the number of incumbents, the sixth the revenue per population unit, and the last the revenue divided by the population units per license, which is a more meaningful performance measure.

In all third generation (UMTS) spectrum auctions in Europe the supply of spectrum was roughly the same. A total band of 2×60 MHz (paired) spectrum,[2] plus some 20 MHz of unpaired spectrum. Moreover, everybody employed the same simultaneous, ascending price auction format, which is well known ever since the first successful spectrum auctions took place in the United States.

However, there was one important broad difference: Whereas the English auctioned a fixed number of licenses, each prepackaged with fixed amounts of radio spectrum (and restricting bidders to bid on one license only), the German regulator broke down the supply of paired spectrum into identical blocks and allowed bidders to aggregate spectrum blocks into a variable number of licenses, ranging from 4 to 6 licenses. With the exception of Austria, which followed the German example, all other European regulators copied the U.K. design.

While the U.K. design earned high praise, the competing German design was harshly criticized by Jehiel and Moldovanu (2000) and Moldovanu (2000a,b) as "an error with serious consequences (Moldovanu 2000b)." Essentially, it was claimed that, due to their cost advantage, the four incumbents would outbid all new entrants, and that "the auction would most likely lead to four licenses in the hands of the four incumbents."

However, the results of the auction proved these critics wrong. The UMTS auction in Germany resulted in a more competitive market structure than in other European countries—altogether six licenses were issued, of which two went to new entrants—and yet earned the highest revenue.

In Germany seven bidders competed for twelve blocks of paired spectrum that could be aggregated into either four, five, or six licenses. Since a license had to include at least two blocks, the auction could not possibly end before one bidder quit the auction. That point was reached in round 126. Here, the auction could have ended, but only if all remaining six bidders had reduced their demand to two blocks each. However, all six bidders maintained a demand for three blocks.

As the auction continued, the small incumbents and new entrants reduced demand to two blocks, one after another. And so, effective in round 147, the two major incumbents (Mannesmann and T-Mobil) found themselves at the crucial phase of the auction, where they alone had to decide whether to end the auction. The predicted four license outcome was already a bygone; the choice was only one between either five or six licenses.

Both major incumbents chose to maintain a demand for three blocks in order to acquire a "large" license of 2×15 MHz (equal in size to the large licenses A and B in the U.K.) each. However, several rounds later they both aborted that attempt, and the auction ended with six "small" licenses, acquired by the four incumbents and two new entrants.

That outcome, and the preceding behavior during the crucial phase of the auction, has puzzled several observers. Indeed, Jehiel and Moldovanu (2001) describe it as "bizarre," and question whether it can be consistent with equilibrium. Similarly, Klemperer (2001, fn. 52) equates the aborted attempt to acquire large licenses and thereby crowd out one bidder with the allegedly irrational behavior of his father-in-law (who apparently tended to quit standing in line, if it moved slowly).

This chapter explains the rules of the German UMTS auction, gives an account of events, and attempts a rational reconstruction of the play observed during the crucial phase of the auction. We proceed as follows: section 14.2 explains the auction rules; section 14.3 gives a summary of events, section 14.4 introduces key assumptions of our analysis, and section 14.5 proposes a game-theoretic explanation. Section 14.6 discusses the merit of the German auction design, and the paper closes with conclusions (section 14.7).

14.2 Auction Rules

Late in 1999 the regulator proposed rules for the upcoming UMTS auction. These were subjected to a hearing process with industry representatives and subsequently changed. The first proposed rules stipulated some form of discrimination in favor of new entrants. However, on February 18, 2000, the regulator decreed an entirely new format that involves a sequence of two auctions and excludes all forms of discrimination. The highlights of these rules are as follows.[3]

For sale were 2×60 MHz paired spectrum in the 1900–2025 MHz band. These were broken up into twelve identical, individual blocks of 2×5 MHz each, numbered 1 to 12. In addition, the regulator offered five blocks of 1×5 MHz unpaired spectrum also in the 2 GHz range, the utility of which was still somewhat dubious at the time of the auction, which is why we ignore them here.

The two auctions were simultaneous, open, and ascending. The first auction was dedicated to selling the paired spectrum and to determining who gets a license. The second auction was devoted to selling leftover paired spectrum, in case anything was left over from the first auction, and to selling the unpaired spectrum. Participation in the second auction was restricted to those who survived the first auction.

In the first auction, bidders were restricted to bid on "at least two" and "at most three" blocks. Any bidder who, at the end of the first auction, held either three or two high bids was assured a license and permitted to participate in the second auction. Those who held fewer than two high bids were excluded from the auction and relieved from any obligation, even if they held one high bid.[4]

In the second auction, the surviving bidders could only bid for at most one block, in the event anything was left over from the first auction. Bidding for unpaired spectrum (which will be ignored here) was unrestricted.

Given these restrictions, the feasible number of licenses was between zero and six, each endowed with from two to four blocks.[5] Ignoring unlikely events, the relevant outcomes were either four, five, or six licenses, endowed with two to three blocks.

An *activity rule* stipulated that bidding rights had to be exercised or would be lost forever. Specifically, the number of bidding rights in round $n + 1$ was equal to the number of blocks on which that bidder placed a bid or had already held a high bid in the previous round n. Therefore, once a bidder had reduced his demand to two blocks, he could never return to demand three.

In both auctions, only the high bids were made public after every round. Thus, bidders could not directly observe their rivals' bids and did not know exactly their number of bidding rights. However, when only a few high bids change, it is possible to infer bidding rights, as we explain in section 14.3.

The minimum bid was DM 100 million per block, and the minimum increment was 10 percent. However, the regulator was free to change this, and he actually reduced it toward the end of the auction. If there were any leftover spectrum, the minimum bid was reset in the second auction to DM 100 million per block.

All blocks were "abstract" in the sense that bidders did not buy the right to obtain concrete spectrum, defined by a particular location within the 2 GHz band. Instead, the regulator made a pledge to choose the best allocation of spectrum, which minimizes interference, after the results of the auction are known. In principle, this intelligently eliminated the coordination problems that plagued earlier spectrum auctions in the United States.

We close our account of the auction rules with some straightforward yet important implications:

1. There can be no more than six licenses; therefore, *the first auction cannot end before one of the seven bidders has quit.*

2. When only six bidders are left, *one bidder alone can force out one other bidder by maintaining three bidding rights,* thus driving up the prices of all licenses.

3. When only five bidders are left, *one more bidder can only be forced out if at least three bidders maintain three bidding rights.*

4. *The second auction is potentially appealing,* because the minimum bid for leftover blocks of paired spectrum is set back to DM 100 million, and rival bidders are already "jam-packed."

14.3   Summary of Events

The auction was scheduled to begin on July 31, 2000, and it lasted 173 rounds of bidding, until August 17, 2000. Initially, twelve bidders registered to participate. However, one bidder was not approved by the regulator, and five bidders withdrew successively prior to the auction. As a result, only seven bidders showed up to bid for four to six licenses. These were the four incumbent mobile phone operators: *T-Mobil* (a subsidiary of Deutsche Telekom) (T), *Mannesmann-Vodafone* (M), *E-Plus* (e+), and *Viag Interkom* (Viag), backed by British Telecom, and three new entrants: *Mobilcom* (mobi), backed by France Telecom, *debitel* (debi), backed by Swisscom, and *3G*, backed by Telefonica and Sonera.[6]

Among the four incumbents, M and T each serve 40 percent of customers in the German mobile phone market, whereas e+ and Viag have only a market share of 15 percent and 5 percent, respectively. Among the new entrants, debi and mobi are already present in the market as service providers (with their own customers and billing system). Only G3 has no prior role in the market. However, the firms that back G3 were already strong and well-established European providers of mobile phone services. Also mobi has a strong backing, whereas debi did not succeed in finding strong partners.

At the auction, bidding started cautiously. All bidders opened with the minimum bid and then used small increments, except for mobi, who started with a jump bid of DM 501 million on two blocks (see table 14.2). It took forty-five rounds until the other bidders caught up with that initial jump bid.

From the high bids during subsequent rounds, it was clear that initially all bidders maintained three bidding rights. Thus, in the early

Table 14.2
Cautious beginning (High bids per round in DM million)

Round	Frequency block											
	1	2	3	4	5	6	7	8	9	10	11	12
1	100	100	100	501	501	150	100	—	100	—	—	—
	T	T	T	mobi	mobi	M	3G		e+			
2	100	100	100	501	501	150	100	100	100	100	150	150
	T	T	T	mobi	mobi	M	3G	e+	e+	viag	M	M
3	110	110	100	501	501	150	111	111	110	100	150	150
	3G	3G	T	mobi	mobi	M	viag	viag	debi	viag	M	M

rounds of the auction, total demand was twenty-one blocks, while supply was only twelve blocks.

As long as excess demand remains high, bidders cannot typically find out whether another bidder has reduced demand, since only high (and not all) bids were published. However, there are circumstances in which such an inference can be drawn beyond doubt. In particular, one can be sure that a rival bidder has reduced demand to two blocks if that bidder

• held no high bids in the previous round, and only two high bids have changed;

• held one high bid in the previous round, and only one high bid other than his own has changed;

• held two high bids in the previous round, and only those bids have changed.

The first bidder who gave up one bidding right was debi. This was announced after day nine of the auction (round 115); however, the last round where debi was seen to have three high bids was round 70. All key events described in the remainder of this section are illustrated in table 14.3.[7]

The auction could not possibly end before one of the seven bidders quit the auction. This precondition was met when debi finally gave up, when the price per block had reached roughly DM 5 billion (the announcement came at the end of day 10 (round 127)).

At this point, all remaining six bidders still maintained three bidding rights (except possibly viag). Therefore, the full range of market structures, either four of five or six licenses, was still within reach.

As the auction continued, all bidders, except the two major incumbents, reduced their demand to two blocks, one after another. Viag was last seen to have three high bids in round 110 and reduced demand not later than in round 134.[8] 3G was seen to be active on three blocks until round 132, and reduced demand to two blocks not later than in round 138. Both demand reductions were announced after day 11 of the auction (round 138). On the following day, the auctioneer reduced the minimum increment from 10 percent to 5 percent.

The last round where e+ and mobi had three high bids was 136. In rounds 140 and 146, respectively, e+ and mobi followed suit and reduced demand as well (this was announced in press interviews after day 12 of the auction).

Table 14.3
Summary of demand reductions (High bids in DM million)

Round	Frequency block											
	1	2	3	4	5	6	7	8	9	10	11	12

Round 126: Debitel exits

Round	1	2	3	4	5	6	7	8	9	10	11	12
125	5117.2	5129.7	4989.0	4897.0	4730.0	4700.0	4880.0	4870.0	4872.3	4992.1	4947.2	4987.3
	e+	*e+*	*e+*	*debi*	*viag*	*mobi*	*mobi*	*debi*	*M*	*viag*	*T*	*M*
126	5117.2	5129.7	4989.0	5400.0	5203.0	5200.0	5368.0	5357.0	4872.3	4992.1	4947.2	4987.3
	e+	*e+*	*e+*	*mobi*	*3G*	*mobi*	*T*	*3G*	*M*	*viag*	*T*	*M*

Round 134: VIAG drops third bidding right

Round	1	2	3	4	5	6	7	8	9	10	11	12
133	6200.0	6207.0	6060.0	5940.0	5723.6	6296.6	6060.0	5892.7	5895.6	6040.6	6060.0	6050.0
	mobi	*viag*	*3G*	*M*	*M*	*M*	*3G*	*e+*	*T*	*e+*	*T*	*mobi*
134	6200.0	6207.0	6060.0	5940.0	6296.1	6296.6	6060.0	5892.7	5895.6	6040.6	6060.0	6050.0
	mobi	*viag*	*3G*	*M*	*e+*	*M*	*3G*	*e+*	*T*	*e+*	*T*	*mobi*

Round 138: 3G drops third bidding right; Round 140: E-Plus drops third bidding right

Round	1	2	3	4	5	6	7	8	9	10	11	12
137	6200.0	6207.0	6060.0	6666.0	6296.1	6296.6	6666.0	6482.0	6485.3	6644.7	6060.0	6666.0
	mobi	*viag*	*3G*	*T*	*e+*	*M*	*T*	*mobi*	*e+*	*viag*	*T*	*M*
138	6200.0	6207.0	6696.0	6666.0	6296.1	6296.6	6666.0	6482.0	6485.3	6644.7	6696.0	6666.0
	mobi	*viag*	*3G*	*T*	*e+*	*M*	*T*	*mobi*	*e+*	*viag*	*3G*	*M*
139	6510.0	6517.4	6696.0	6666.0	6296.1	6296.6	6666.0	6482.0	6485.3	6644.7	6696.0	6666.0
	T	*mobi*	*3G*	*T*	*e+*	*M*	*T*	*mobi*	*e+*	*viag*	*3G*	*M*
140	6510.0	6517.4	6696.0	6666.0	6611.1	6296.6	6666.0	6482.0	6485.3	6644.7	6696.0	6666.0
	T	*mobi*	*3G*	*T*	*e+*	*M*	*T*	*mobi*	*e+*	*viag*	*3G*	*M*

Round 146: Mobilcom drops third bidding right

145	6835.5 M	6843.6 M	6696.0 3G	6666.0 T	6941.8 e+	6950.0 mobi	6999.4 viag	7146.6 M	6809.7 e+	6644.7 viag	6696.0 3G	6999.5 T
146	6835.5 M	6843.6 M	6696.0 3G	6999.6 mobi	6941.8 e+	7297.5 T	6999.4 viag	7146.6 M	6809.7 e+	6644.7 viag	6696.0 3G	6999.5 T
147	6835.5 M	6843.6 M	6696.0 3G	6999.6 mobi	6941.8 e+	7297.5 T	6999.4 viag	7146.6 M	6809.7 e+	7001.7 T	6696.0 3G	6999.5 T

Round 170: Telekom drops third bidding right

169	8310.4 viag	8170.0 mobi	8166.6 T	8141.7 M	8200.0 mobi	8206.6 viag	8141.4 3G	8274.3 e+	8277.9 T	8143.9 e+	8143.8 M	8141.4 3G
170	8310.4 viag	8170.0 mobi	8330.0 M	8141.7 M	8200.0 mobi	8206.6 viag	8141.4 3G	8274.3 e+	8277.9 T	8143.9 e+	8143.8 M	8141.4 3G

Round 173: Final allocation

173	8310.4 viag	8170.0 mobi	8330.0 M	8304.6 3G	8200.0 mobi	8206.6 viag	8304.3 T	8274.3 e+	8277.9 T	8143.9 e+	8143.8 M	8141.4 3G

From this point on, it was no longer possible to end the auction with four licenses (recall: "it takes at least three bidders with three bidding rights to crowd out two more bidders"). It was also impossible to immediately terminate the auction with six licenses, since in round 146 M held three high bids, while mobi only held one.

However, effective in round 147, the two major incumbents, M and T, found themselves at the crucial phase of the auction, where they alone had to decide whether to end the auction or maintain a demand for three blocks, and thus continue the attempt to crowd out one more bidder from the auction. They both chose to maintain a demand for three blocks, but when it turned out that they had not succeeded in crowding out one more bidder after many more rounds of increasingly costly bidding, T reduced its demand to two packages in round 170, and M followed suit as soon as possible in round 172.

And so the auction ended in round 173 with six "small" (2×10 MHz) licenses, acquired by the four incumbents, and the two new entrants: mobi and 3G. The price per block was roughly DM 8 billion, and total auction revenue DM 98,807.2 million. Since no paired blocks were left over, in the second auction only unpaired spectrum was sold. There, each licensee, except viag, got one block, adding DM 561 million to the auction revenue.

As in other spectrum auctions, bidders occasionally used the last digits of feasible bids (the smallest money unit was DM 100.000) to signal their intentions or to attempt a coordination of actions. Such coordination can be useful to determine who shall get which block if excess demand has vanished and, perhaps, to suggest to other bidders that bidding may come to a quick end if they reduce their demand.

It has been claimed that such signaling occurred already before the crucial phase of the auction, in rounds 133 to 146. Indeed, in these rounds one observes an abundance of the digit 6, which we indicate by bold-faced entries in table 14.3, and which cannot be explained by the minimum increment requirement. If it is correct to interpret these bids as signals, one would conclude that bidders M, T, and 3G signaled that they would be willing to settle with a market structure of six licenses. However, one should probably only consider those bids, if any, where the six occurred in the last digit, because it is hard to believe that bidders would waste millions and more to convey a signal of dubious value.

An unequivocal case of signaling occurred during and shortly before the crucial phase of the auction. During the rounds 130 to 150, M sent the signal "6" in seven out of eight of their visible new (high) bids, indicating that they would settle with a market structure of six licenses. During rounds 130 to 140, T repeatedly sent the same signal. However, on two occasions, in rounds 144 and 146 they used a "5" as the last digit of their high bids (while bidding higher than the required increment). This has been interpreted to mean that T indicated to M that they did not consent to a market structure of six licenses, and instead were suggesting to continue the attempt to crowd out another bidder.[9] However, this interpretation is not entirely convincing, on several grounds. First of all, T obviously sent contradictory signals, if their actions were signals at all. Second, it is not clear why T should convince M to maintain a demand for three blocks, since it did not require any coordinated effort to crowd out one more bidder, by the "one is enough to crowd out one bidder" principle.

14.4   Basic Assumptions

To prepare the game-theoretic analysis of the crucial phase of the UMTS auction in Germany, we now introduce some assumptions and notation. These are geared to the analysis of the relevant subgames, and they use some characteristics of the participating bidders, along with the German mobile phone market.

Specifically, we assume that bidders have some idea of the ranking of bidders' valuations, have a preference for a less competitive market structure, which reflect in valuations that depend on the number of licenses, and are subject to incomplete information. In addition, we allow for stochastic dependencies, due to some form of affiliation between valuations.

At the given auction rules, a license is endowed with at least two and at most four blocks. Therefore, the marginal valuations for two, three, and four blocks matter. We denote the marginal valuations of bidder i for each of the first two blocks by V_i, and those for the third and fourth block by V_{i3}, V_{i4}, respectively. Capital letters V_i, V_{ij} denote random variables, and small letters v_i, v_{ij} denote realizations. Marginal valuations are not increasing.

Bidders have some common beliefs about each other's relative strength. In particular, the two major incumbents, M and T, are viewed as considerably stronger than their competitors and as identical. The weaker bidders are ranked by their strength (in this order) and called bidders 3 to 7. In the industry, one had a pretty clear understanding of the ranking of their marginal valuations.

Specifically, we assume the following for all states in the world:

$$v_M = v_T > \max\{v_3, \ldots, v_7\}, \tag{1}$$

$$v_{M3} = v_{T3} > v_{33} \geq \cdots \geq v_{73}, \tag{2}$$

$$v_{M4} = v_{T4}. \tag{3}$$

A bidder's total valuation for two and three blocks is denoted by w_i, w_{i3}, respectively:

$$w_i := 2v_i, \quad w_{i3} := w_i + v_{i3}. \tag{4}$$

All these valuations v, w are defined for a mobile phone market with six licenses, which is used as a reference point. Of course, bidders prefer to operate in a market with fewer competitors. We capture this by assuming that successful bidders earn higher valuations, represented by a bonus $b > 0$, which applies if the number of licenses is reduced from six to five.[10]

In order to capture the uncertainty concerning the marginal valuation of the weakest among six bidders (called bidder 6), which plays a pivotal role, we assume that V_6 has two possible realizations (weak and strong): $V_6 \in \{v_6, v_6'\}$, with $v_6' > v_6$, and $0 < \Pr\{V_6 = v_6\} =: \rho_6 < 1$.

At some stage in the auction game, the only new information that becomes available to the relevant players is the fact that bidder 6 is strong. Since we allow for stochastically dependent valuations, in this case we assume that bidders update their valuations. We capture this updating by denoting valuations conditional on $V_6 = v_6'$ by primed v and w. The valuations that are conditional on $V_6 = v_6$ are denoted by v and w (without primes). We assume $v' \geq v$, $w' \geq w$, and that the stochastic ordering (1) is preserved. Expected values of v and w are denoted by $\bar{v} := v' - \rho_6(v' - v)$ and $\bar{w} := w' - \rho_6(w' - w)$, respectively. Of course, our analysis permits, but does not require, stochastically dependent valuations.

An important detail of the German UMTS auction, which plays a key role in our understanding of events, is the fact that any blocks that are left over in the first auction are auctioned in the second auction. There, the minimum bid is set back to DM 100 million, only those who bought at least two blocks in the first auction are permitted to participate, and participants can bid on at most one block. The latter implies that the second auction has all the essential features of a single-unit auction (see Weber 1983), and therefore is easily predictable. In particular, truthful bidding is a (weakly) dominant strategy in that second auction. It follows immediately that if one player, say T, has acquired three blocks in the first auction, while all other five licensees have acquired only two blocks, one block is left over, and player M will win it in the second auction and pay a price equal to

$$P_2 := \max\{V_{T4}, V_{33}\}. \tag{5}$$

Of course, if the price in the first auction is already sky-high, it may be very appealing for player M to make sure that one block is left over, and becomes relatively low-cost "prey" in the second auction, whenever that player has a chance to do so.

14.5 Game-Theoretic Explanation

We now analyze the crucial phase of the game, from round 148 onward. At that point only two of the remaining six bidders—the two dominant incumbents, M and T—have three bidding rights left. The only feasible market size is either five or six licenses; an outcome of four licenses is already bygone. M and T can now also reduce demand to two blocks, and thus end the auction with a market size of six licenses or attempt to crowd out one more bidder. Predation succeeds if M or T maintain(s) a demand for three blocks, until bidder 6 quits the auction, by the "one bidder alone can force out bidder 6" principle.

As we already pointed out in section 14.3, in the actual course of events during that phase of the auction, both M and T attempted predation. However, at round 170 T reduced demand to two blocks, and M followed suit as soon as possible so that the auction ended in round 173 with six licenses. The goal of our analysis is to find necessary and sufficient conditions to explain the observed play as a perfect equilibrium, and to assess the plausibility of this explanation.

At this phase of the game the main strategic players are M and T. We assume that bidders 3 to 5 maintain their demand for two blocks at least as long as the weakest bidder 6. Since bidder 6 has the weakly dominant strategy to maintain two bidding rights as long as the price for two blocks is below his valuation, only the valuation of bidder 6 matters for the strategic decisions of M and T. Therefore, we can view this situation as a game played between the two strong bidders, M and

T, taking the behavior of bidders 3 to 6 as given, yet facing significant uncertainty about the valuation of the weakest remaining bidder.

In the following, we slightly simplify the remaining first auction game by condensing it to a two-stage game. In the first stage, bidders M and T simultaneously choose either the action "r(esign)" (reduce demand to two blocks, immediately) or the action "t(ry predation)" by bidding prices up to the level v_6. The auction ends immediately, at the current price p, if both M and T play r. If M or T plays t, prices go up to level v_6. At this point bidder 6 quits and the auction ends with a market size of five licenses in the event when bidder 6 is weak ($V_6 = v_6$). Whereas if bidder 6 is strong ($V_6 = v_6'$), the game enters into the second stage. At this stage, valuations are common knowledge because it is clear by exclusion that bidder 6 is strong. Bidders who played t now have the choice between the actions "pr(edation)" (drive up prices further to the level v_6') and "r(esign)" (reduce demand to two blocks immediately). If M or T plays pr, prices go up to the level v_6', at which point bidder 6 quits, and a market size of five licenses is reached.

When predation has succeeded, but either M or T has reduced demand to two blocks, one block is left over.[11] That leftover block is then sold in the second auction, and, given our assumptions, it will be acquired by the one dominant bidder who had reduced demand in the first auction, at the expected price $p_2 := E[\max\{V_{14}, V_{33}\} \mid V_6 = v_6]$ if bidder 6 is weak, and $p_2' := E[\max\{V_{14}', V_{33}'\} \mid V_6 = v_6']$ if bidder 6 is strong, respectively. The game tree of the first auction is depicted in figure 14.1.

A strategy for a player is given by three actions at the three information sets in which the player has to move. So the strategy (t, r, pr) of player M means that he maintains three bidding rights in the first stage, reduces demand in stage 2 if the other player has reduced demand in stage 1, and maintains three bidding rights in stage 2 if the other player has also maintained three bidding rights in stage 1.

The payoffs are as follows. If both M and T play r in stage 1, their payoff is $\bar{w}_{12} - 2p$, where p denotes the current price, at the beginning of stage 1. If one bidder has played t and bidder 6 is weak, then bidder 6 quits, and prices are equal to v_6. The bidder who played t earns the payoff $w_{13} + b - 3v_6$, and the bidder who played r gets two blocks in the first auction and a third block in the second auction, at the expected price p_2; his payoff is thus $w_{13} + b - 2v_6 - p_2$.

If at least one bidder plays t and bidder 6 happens to be strong, the game continues. If one bidder has reduced demand, the other bid-

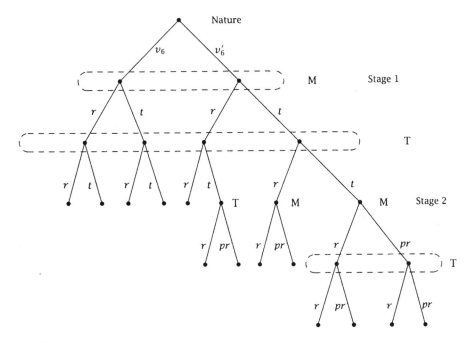

Figure 14.1
Game tree of the crucial phase of the UMTS auction

der has the option to crowd out bidder 6 by increasing prices up to v'_6 or to give up. If he gives up, both bidders obtain $w'_{12} - 2v_6$. Otherwise, he gets $w'_{13} + b - 3v'_6$, whereas the other bidder obtains the payoff $w'_{13} + b - 2v'_6 - p'_2$. If both bidders have maintained three bidding rights, we are in a subgame with complete information in which both players can choose two actions. The payoffs of bidder M are summarized in table 14.4, where Δ^2_{pr} denotes the gain from unilateral predation, and Δ^2_{fr} the gain from free riding (playing r while the rival plays pr).

We begin the analysis with the stage 2 subgames that are reached if at least one bidder has tried predation, but player 6 has not quit, because he happens to be strong. When these subgames are played, prices are already at the level v_6, and it is common knowledge that bidder 6 is strong ($V_6 = v'_6$). Since the valuations of bidders 3 to 5 do not matter, it follows that these games can be viewed as games of complete information.

LEMMA 14.1   Consider all stage 2 subgames. Demand reduction is an equilibrium of these subgames iff "unilateral predation" does not pay:

Table 14.4
Payoff matrix of stage 2 subgame

		Bidder 2 (T)	
		r	pr
Bidder 1 (M)	r	$(w'_{12} - 2v_6)$	$[\ldots] + \Delta^2_{fr}$
	pr	$(\ldots) + \Delta^2_{pr}$	$[w'_{13} + b - 3v'_6]$

$$\Delta^2_{pr} := v'_{13} + b - (3v'_6 - 2v_6) \leq 0. \tag{6}$$

That equilibrium is unique iff the inequality (6) is strict and, in addition, free riding pays:

$$\Delta^2_{fr} := v'_6 - p'_2 > 0. \tag{7}$$

Proof In a first step consider the particular stage 2 subgame in which both M and T have three bidding rights. Its payoff matrix is given in table 14.4. From this one can see immediately that (r, r) is an equilibrium iff unilateral predation (playing pr while the rival plays r) does not pay, that is, iff $\Delta^2_{pr} \leq 0$. If the latter inequality is strict, (r, pr) cannot also be an equilibrium. This leaves only (pr, pr) as another candidate for an equilibrium. However, if the rival plays pr, playing r entails that one block is left over, and acquired in the second auction at the expected price p_2. Evidently such free riding on predation pays iff a third block is cheaper in the second than in the first auction, namely, iff $\Delta^2_{fr} > 0$.

Now consider those stage 2 subgames in which only one of the two players has three bidding rights. Evidently, if $\Delta^2_{pr} \leq 0$, it is optimal for that bidder to also reduce demand. If that inequality is strict, this is the unique optimal decision. Note that if these conditions for uniqueness of equilibrium are satisfied, r is actually a dominant strategy in all stage 2 subgames.

Using these results we arrive at the following necessary and sufficient conditions for existence and uniqueness of a subgame perfect equilibrium that conforms with the observed pattern of behavior.

THEOREM 14.1

i. The strategies (t, r, r) for both players are a subgame perfect equilibrium iff free riding does not pay in stage 1:

$$\Delta^1_{fr} := p_6(v_6 - p_2) \leq 0, \tag{8}$$

Table 14.5
Reduced form payoff matrix of stage 1 subgame

| | | Bidder 2 (T) | |
		r	T
Bidder 1 (M)	r	$(\bar{w}_{12} - 2p)$	$[\ldots] + \Delta^1_{fr}$
	t	$(\ldots) + \Delta^1_t$	$[\bar{w}_{12} - 2v_6 + p_6(v_{13} + b - v_6)]$

and $\Delta^2_{pr} \leq 0$ (unilateral predation does not pay in the stage 2 subgames).

ii. That subgame perfect equilibrium is unique iff the inequality concerning Δ^1_{fr} is strict, unilaterally trying predation pays:

$$\Delta^1_t := p_6(v_{13} + b - v_6) - 2(v_6 - p) > 0, \tag{9}$$

and $\Delta^2_{pr} < 0$, $\Delta^2_{fr} > 0$ (r is a dominant strategy in all stage 2 subgames).

Proof The payoff matrix for bidder M of the reduced game in stage 1 is given in table 14.5, assuming that r is played in all stage 2 subgames by both M and T. There the gain from free riding on predation (playing r while the rival plays t) is $\Delta^1_{fr} = p_6(v_6 - p_2)$ because one gets a third block, at the expected price p_2, in the second auction only in the event when bidder 6 is weak. Similarly, the gain from unilaterally trying predation (playing t while the rival plays r in stage 1) is $\Delta^1_t = p_6(v_{13} + b - v_6) - 2(v_6 - p)$, because one obtains a third block at the higher price v_6 when the sixth bidder is weak, and one incurs the cost of raising prices to the level v_6, with no benefit, in the event when bidder 6 is strong.

By Lemma 14.1 it is known that r is an equilibrium strategy in stage 2 if $\Delta^2_{pr} \leq 0$. Therefore, table 14.5 applies, and it follows immediately that (t, r, r) is an equilibrium iff $\Delta^1_{fr} \leq 0$ and $\Delta^2_{pr} \leq 0$.

The stronger conditions assure uniqueness of equilibrium in all stage 2 subgames, and uniqueness of equilibrium in the stage 1 reduced form game represented by table 14.5.

As we have shown, the rational reconstruction of the observed play requires that, at stage 2, bidders have an incentive to free-ride on predation and yet do not gain from unilateral predation, whereas, at stage 1, just the opposite must hold true. Therefore, one may wonder whether the necessary and sufficient conditions spelled out in theorem 14.1 are compatible.

p v_6 $E[P_2]$ v_6'

Figure 14.2
Illustration of Theorem 14.1

However, notice that these conditions refer to different price levels and relevant price changes. At stage 2, the price per block is already at the level v_6, and predation involves a price hike by the amount $v_6' - v_6$. At this point, unilateral predation does not pay if $v_6' - v_6$ is sufficiently large, and free riding pays if the expected price in the second auction, $E[P_2]$, is in between v_6 and v_6', as illustrated in figure 14.2. Whereas, at stage 1, given the equilibrium continuation play in stage 2, free riding does not pay, since the price at which crowding out bidder 6 may occur, V_6, is below $E[P_2]$, but the unilateral attempt of predation (t) pays, since $v_6 - p$ is relatively small, provided the probability of $V_6 = v_6$ is sufficiently high.

One may object on the grounds that in the actual auction there were many rounds of bidding between the two stages considered in this model. Incorporating multiple rounds does not lead to fundamentally different results. However, it leads to slightly stronger requirements than those spelled out in theorem 14.1. Indeed, the observed play is an equilibrium only if, in addition to theorem 14.1 (i), condition (9) is satisfied as well. The reason is that without (9), both (r, r) and (t, t) are an equilibrium of the stage 1 subgame, and (r, r) always payoff-dominates (t, t). Each bidder knows that if he plays r, the other follows suit. Therefore, in the presence of multiple rounds of bidding, each bidder can unilaterally prevent (t, t) from being played, and only (r, r) survives, unless condition (9) is satisfied in addition to the conditions spelled out in theorem 14.1 (i).

Is this rational reconstruction of the observed events in the German UMTS auction plausible? A first objection might be that bidders do not engage in such complicated strategic reasoning as required in the preceding model. After all, why should they not bid in a straightforward way up to their valuation as in an ascending single unit auction? Now, one must note that such straightforward bidding is an ambiguous thing in the present multi-unit framework because the valuation of the bidders depends on the final number of licenses. So, keeping three bidding rights up to $v_{13} + b$, for example, can easily lead to a winner's curse problem in case the attempted predation is not successful. On the other hand, keeping three bidding rights just up to v_{13} is also not convincing because one does get the bonus if one gets three blocks. So, already the definition of straightforward bidding leads to complicated reasoning.

Moreover, there is by now ample theoretical evidence that straightforward bidding need not be an equilibrium in multi-unit auctions because bidders have an incentive to strategically reduce demand in order to keep prices low.[12] In any case, straightforward bidding is not a weakly dominant strategy, unlike in the single unit case.

Finally, M and T have already shown during the German GSM auction in 1999 that they understand very well the strategic issues of such auctions. There, M first outbid the two weaker bidders, and then equally shared the ten blocks with T, without further driving up prices (see our account of these events in Grimm, Riedel, and Wolfstetter 2003b, where we also show that this play is the unique perfect equilibrium of that game). Summing up, there is strong evidence that M and T did not use straightforward bidding.

Given that M and T behaved strategically, one may ask whether the conditions necessary to explain the observed behavior are plausible. When M and T give up the attempted predation, the (conditional expected) valuation of the sixth bidder must be relatively high compared to the bonus from predation and the additional value of a third block. This seems plausible since prices had already reached a high level when M and T gave up.

Ex ante, it must have been worth trying predation for M and T. A necessary condition for this is that there was no incentive for free riding, that is, no incentive to reduce bidding rights to two and let the other player attempt predation. This means that the expected price p_2 of a block in the second round is higher than the valuation of a weak bidder 6. Now, under which conditions is p_2 high? Since it is determined by the maximum of V_{14} and V_{33}, either the valuation for a fourth block must be high for M and T, or the valuation for a third block must be high for the third bidder. Now, V_{14} might be high when the value of being the unique leader with double capacity compared to the opponents is considered as high. V_{33} is high when the third bidder is willing to pay a lot for reaching the capacity of the two leading firms. Both cases are, of course, plausible.

One may object that V_{33} must have been low because the third bidder had already reduced his bidding rights. However, as we argued earlier, straightforward bidding is generally not optimal behavior for the third bidder either. Therefore, it is quite plausible that the third bidder had an incentive to reduce demand before prices reached the level of his marginal valuation. This is in particular the case when the third bidder thinks that a market size of four cannot be reached.

Finally, one may ask whether it was reasonable to assume that the weakest bidder may quit at a price below the level at which the auction ended. A rough estimate can be derived from the U.K. auction data. There, a small license raised roughly €109 per population unit. Therefore, if the U.K. and the German markets are similar, one should have $2\hat{v}_6 + \hat{b} \leq €109$ (where $\hat{v}$ and $\hat{b}$ are per population unit). The German auction raised €100 per (small) license. Therefore, using the U.K. data, one should have expected that bidder 6 quits early whenever the bonus for a smaller market $\hat{b}$ is at least €9, which is not at all unreasonable.

14.6   Merit of the German Auction Design

Should future spectrum auction designers borrow some key ingredients of the design employed in the German UMTS auction?[13] While one may debate whether the German regulator should have assured at least one new entry into the mobile phone market, the idea of allowing some flexibility by letting bidders aggregate their own licenses is appealing. Indeed, starting from the U.K. style rules, which broke down the available 60 MHz of paired spectrum into five fixed licenses in the United Kingdom, it might have been better to break down the available supply into individual blocks, and allow bidders to aggregate these blocks into either five or six licenses. By thus borrowing from the German auction rules, the British would have assured *at least* five licenses, and yet reached *more competition or more revenue*.

A defendant of the U.K. rules might respond that revenue cannot be lower if one excludes that flexibility and sticks to the U.K. rules. For if the German style rules lead to six licenses, revenue must be lower (bidders prefer a market of 5 licenses to one of 6), whereas if it results in only five licenses, revenue should be just the same as in the U.K. design. Therefore, one is led to conclude that allowing bidders to aggregate spectrum into either five or six licenses, in the spirit of the German design, may give rise to more competition but never to more revenue, and thus never more competition and more revenue.

However, this argument misses one important point: It assumes that bidder participation is the same under both rules, and that there are more bidders than licenses. Once bidders know the ranking of their valuations, which they did after the battle for the pan-European field was settled, low-ranking bidders know that they will always be outbid in an open ascending auction, and therefore do not even bother to participate. This suggests that the U.K. design poses a serious bidder participation problem: As a tendency, the number of participating bidders converges to the number of licenses, as it did in Switzerland (see table 14.1), and thereafter in Belgium and in Israel (where the auction was subsequently called off).

Competition is not a free good. In order to participate, bidders must have some reasonable chance to obtain a license. The flexibility offered by the German-style auction design does offer such an incentive. If it is effective and raises bidder participation, the German-style auction design may, paradoxically, give rise to more competition and more revenue.

The two last UMTS auctions in the year 2000, in Austria and Switzerland, are a case in point. Austria employed the German and Switzerland the U.K. design. The enthusiasm of the market concerning the prospects of the UMTS technology had already cooled off, and the main battles for the pan-European field were already settled. Nevertheless, the performance was quite different. After the usual "bidder meltdown," in Austria six bidders showed up to bid for four to six licenses; whereas in Switzerland four bidders showed up to bid for four licenses; exactly as one would expect it to occur, after bidders know their ranking of valuations. In the end, both auctions earned relatively low revenues; however, Austria achieved considerably more competition (2 vs. 1 new entries) and more revenue (see table 14.1).

Another interesting feature of the German auction was the sale of "abstract" spectrum, already mentioned in section 14.2. In principle, this may eliminate the coordination problems that plagued earlier spectrum auctions in the United States. However, while this worked well in the 1999 German GSM auction, it was apparently not as successful in the German UMTS auction. Indeed, it took the regulator and licensees more than a year to reach an agreement on the allocation of the spectrum.

In one regard, the German design was unnecessarily complicated. Instead of asking for bids on the numbered abstract licenses, it would have been better to employ an "ascending price clock auction" format. There, the auctioneer announces a uniform price per block and asks bidders to state their demand at that unit price. If demand is equal to or below the given supply, the auction ends, and bidders get what they demanded at that price; whereas if demand exceeds supply, the unit price is raised by one increment, and the procedure is repeated. This format would have eliminated bidder coordination problems. Moreover, there would have been no need for the "at least two" restriction, because in that auction format no bidder is ever left with just one spectrum block, unless he finds it profitable to operate with one block.

14.7 Conclusions

In this chapter we explained the rules of the German UMTS auction, and proposed a rational reconstruction of the observed play. Our results suggest that the outcome of that auction is not at all bizarre, contrary to what some of the critics of the German auction design have claimed. Moreover, we could not confirm the critics' other contention, that the auction design used in Germany is inferior to that used in England and in most other European countries. On the contrary, we pointed out that the design used in Germany tends to give rise to more competition or more revenue than the competing U.K. design, which indeed it did in the European spectrum auctions in the year 2000. This suggests that the designers of future spectrum auctions may be well advised to borrow some ingredients of that design.

At the same time, we would like to stress that the design of good spectrum auction mechanisms is still subject to many open questions. Neither the English nor the German design is geared to achieve efficiency in the sense of maximizing the weighted sum of consumer and producer surplus; our understanding of multi-unit auctions is still insufficient; and the design of optimal mechanisms that implement an efficient market structure is still in its infancy.[14] Moreover, bidder participation will remain a concern, even if one alleviates it by introducing the kind of flexibility in the aggregation of licenses that was used in Germany. In this regard, a major improvement can only be expected if one replaces the auctioning of the portions of the radio spectrum set aside for mobile telecommunications by auctioning the entire radio spectrum, the bulk of which is used or reserved for TV and satellite TV broadcasting, in one auction.

Notes

The authors served as consultants to prepare bidding for one bidder at the German UMTS auction. Financial support for this research was received by the Deutsche

Forschungsgemeinschaft, SFB 373 ("Quantifikation und Simulation Ökonomischer Prozesse"), Humboldt-Universität zu Berlin, and the Norwegian Ruhrgas Fund. We wish to thank Barry Allan, Winand Emons, Gerhard Illing, Byoung Heon Jun, Paul Klemperer, Achim Wambach, Chang-Ho Yoon, and seminar participants at the universities of Bergen, Bern, Frankfurt, Graz, Kiel, München, Tübingen, the Berlin Internet Economics Workshop, the CESifo workshop, and the Korean Association for Telecommunications Policy for useful comments.

1. UMTS means Universal Mobile Telecommunications System; it was introduced by the International Telecommunications Union as part of the IMT-2000 family of third generation mobile standards.

2. Spectrum is paired because one is used to send and the other to receive information. To see why this is important, just listen to radio communication in a taxicab; there, only one party is able to speak, until the line is freed for the other party to respond.

3. The complete auction rules can be found in RegTP (2000).

4. The rationale for the "at least two" restriction was that building a network of radio stations is not economically feasible with a capacity of only one block of radio spectrum.

5. In order to acquire four blocks, a bidder would have to acquire three blocks in the first auction, and one leftover block in the second auction.

6. The bidder who was not approved, due to insufficient funding and experience, was Nets AG; the bidders who withdrew prior to the auction were (in this order): Hutchison (who formed an alliance with E-Plus and thus, had to back out), MCI Worldcom, Vivendi, and Talkline.

7. We have compiled the high bids in all rounds in an Excel file, and make this available for download at ⟨http://www.wiwi.hu-berlin.de/wt1/papers/umts.zip⟩. Unfortunately, the German regulator does not release information on all bids.

8. In round 133 Viag held only one high bid, and in rounds 133 and 134 only the high bid on block 5 changes. Thus, one can infer that Viag holds at most two bidding rights effective round 135.

9. See Jehiel and Moldovanu (2001), who suspect that T may have driven up prices in the interest of its majority shareholder, the German government.

10. We do not make assumptions concerning a market with four licenses, because this outcome could not have occurred in the phase of the game that we study here.

11. 4×2 plus 1×3 makes eleven blocks; since twelve blocks are available, one is left over.

12. See Ausubel and Schwartz (1999), Menezes (1996), Grimm, Riedel, and Wolfstetter (2003b), and Engelbrecht-Wiggans and Kahn (1998).

13. For a detailed discussion of the deficiencies of the U.K. auction design, and a number of further recommendations for changing spectrum auction rules, see Wolfstetter (2003). For a very careful critical assessment of the U.K. auction design, and some puzzling features of actual bidding in the U.K. auction, see Börgers and Dustmann (2002).

14. Some first contributions in this direction, in the optimal mechanism design tradition, are Dana and Spier (1994), Auriol and Laffont (1992), and Grimm, Riedel, and Wolfstetter (2003a).

References

Auriol, E., and J. J. Laffont. 1992. "Regulation by Duopoly." *Journal of Economics and Management Strategy* 1: 507–533.

Ausubel, L., and J. Schwartz. 1999. "The Ascending Auction Paradox." Working paper, University of Maryland.

Börgers, T., and C. Dustmann. 2002. "Strange Bids: Bidding Behavior in the United Kingdom's Third Generation Spectrum Auction." Discussion paper, University College, London.

Dana, J. D., and K. E. Spier. 1994. "Designing a Private Industry. Government Auctions with Endogenous Market Structure." *Journal of Public Economics* 53: 127–147.

Engelbrecht-Wiggans, R., and C. Kahn. 1998. "Low Revenue Equilibria in Simultaneous Auctions." Working paper, University of Illinois.

Grimm, V., F. Riedel, and E. Wolfstetter. 2003a. "Implementing Efficient Market Structure." *Review of Economic Design* 7: 443–463.

Grimm, V., F. Riedel, and E. Wolfstetter. 2003b. "Low Price Equilibrium in Multi-unit Auctions: The GSM Spectrum Auction in Germany." Forthcoming in *International Journal of Industrial Organization*.

Jehiel, P., and B. Moldovanu. 2000. "A Critique of the Planned Rules for the German UMTS/IMT-2000 License Auction." Working paper, University of Mannheim.

Jehiel, P., and B. Moldovanu. 2001. "The European UMTS/IMT-2000 License Auctions." Discussion paper, University of Mannheim.

Klemperer, P. 2001. "Collusion and Predation in Auction Markets." Working paper, Nuffield College, Oxford University.

Menezes, F. M. 1996. "Multiple-Unit English Auctions." *European Journal of Political Economy* 12: 671–684.

Moldovanu, B. 2000a. "Für ein Plätzchen am Himmel der Funker." *Frankfurter Allgemeine Zeitung*, July 29.

Moldovanu, B. 2000b. "Kleiner Verfahrensfehler mit großen Folgen." *Financial Times Deutschland*, June 4.

RegTP. 2000. Entscheidung der Präsidentenkammer vom 18.02.2000 über die Regeln für die Durchführung des Versteigerungsverfahrens zur Vergabe von Lizenzen für UMTS/IMT-2000; Mobilkommunikation der dritten Generation, Official document, Aktenzeichen: BK-1b-98/005-2. Available online at ⟨http://www.regtp.de⟩.

Weber, R. J. 1983. "Multiple-object auctions." In R. Engelbrecht-Wiggans, M. Shubik, and J. Stark, eds., *Auctions, Bidding, and Contracting*, 165–191. New York: New York University Press.

Wolfstetter, E. 2003. "The Swiss UMTS Spectrum Auction Flop: Bad Luck or Bad Design?" In *Regulation, Competition, and the Market Economy. Festschrift for C. C. V. Weizsäcker*, 281–294. Göttingen: Vandenhoeck & Ruprecht.

\

15

Some Observations on the German 3G Telecom Auction: Comments on Grimm, Riedel, and Wolfstetter

Paul Klemperer

Grimm, Riedel, and Wolfstetter (chapter 14) have developed an intriguing explanation for the apparently puzzling bidding in the 2000 German 3G telecom auction. In this chapter, I discuss why I do not find their explanation fully satisfactory and suggest alternative explanations, including a relative-performance-maximizing theory. I also comment briefly on issues about several other 3G auctions.

15.1 Introduction

The German 3G spectrum auction was undoubtedly a success from the government's viewpoint. Indeed, it was probably one of only three successes among the nine Western European 3G auctions. The measure of success most commonly used is total revenue raised per capita, with some adjustments for the level of the telecommunications stock index as a reflection of sentiment toward 3G's prospects.[1] (We assume governments have no ability to time the market, and therefore deserve neither credit nor blame for selling when market sentiment is unusually positive or negative.) Based on this, figure 15.1 suggests the U.K., German, and Danish auctions were successes, while the Netherlands, Austrian, and Swiss auctions were the biggest failures.

To be sure, the figure flatters larger countries (especially Germany; conversely it underrates tiny Denmark), flatters centrally located countries (Germany, again, and also Austria and Switzerland), flatters countries with lightly regulated telecommunications industries (Germany, again, among others)—since larger, centrally located, lightly regulated markets are worth more—but it also ignores the fact that Germany and Austria sold more licences than other countries, reducing the total profitability of those markets. However, the more systematic discussion of the relative performance of the different auctions in Klemperer (2002a) comes to very similar conclusions.

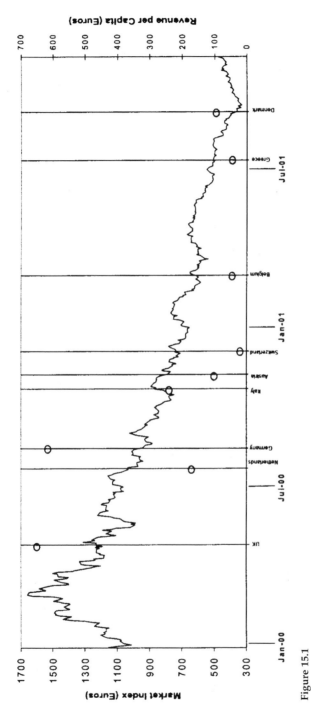

Figure 15.1

European 2000–2001 3G Mobile spectrum auctions (*Note:* Per capita revenues, by country o (right-hand scale); (auctions are shown on the dates at which they finished); Dow Jones European Telecom Stock Price Index (left-hand scale).)

So, since the German auction was both successful and of a novel and complex design, it clearly deserves study, and chapter 14 would be welcome for that reason alone; Grimm, Riedel, and Wolfstetter give very valuable detail about the auction, and their chapter is a key reference for anyone studying it. But more than that, the chapter is extremely interesting and makes acute observations about both the German and other 3G auctions.

I have learned a lot from the chapter, and I agree with much of it. However, these comments naturally focus on the disagreements. Section 15.2 summarizes why I think Grimm, Riedel, and Wolfstetter's explanation of the bidding in the German auction is not fully satisfactory, and section 15.3 develops this point more fully (the latter section can be omitted by readers who do not want too much detail). Section 15.4 suggests other explanations for the bidding, and Section 15.5 develops a relative-performance-maximizing theory for it. Sections 15.6 and 15.7 briefly comment on some other 3G auctions, and stress (as Grimm, Riedel, and Wolfstetter also do) the importance of attracting entry into an auction.

15.2   The German Auction

In particular, I disagree with Grimm, Riedel, and Wolfstetter's central claim that their model, as it stands, rationalizes the behavior of the two strongest bidders—T-Mobil and Mannesman, or "T" and "M," in the authors' terminology.[2] These bidders initially pushed up the price in the hope of driving out the sixth-strongest bidder, "bidder 6" in GRW's terminology, but then gave up pushing the price up so that the auction did actually end with six winners but at a much higher price than was necessary to end the auction with this number of winners. This seems bizarre. To put the point simply, consider T's and M's decision about whether to end the auction with six winners at some given price, or whether to push the price up further. Raising the per-block price by 1 euro costs T and M 2 euros each, since they would each win two blocks in a six-winner outcome. Their gain is the probability that bidder 6 quits times their benefit from bidder 6 quitting. If it is worthwhile for T and M to push the price up in one round, but to stop pushing the price up in the next round, then the perceived probability of bidder 6 quitting in the next round must be both low and also lower than it was in the last round. However, most observers thought the probability of bidder 6 quitting in the next round, conditional on not having previously quit, was high and increasing around the time T and M ended the auction (when per capita price levels were approaching those achieved in the UK) and was much lower earlier (a six-player conclusion for the auction became possible at 55% of the U.K. price levels). So any rationalization of T and M's behavior must explain this apparently irrational behavior of theirs. But Grimm, Riedel, and Wolf-stetter's model sidesteps this basic issue, as I now explain.

15.3   GRW's Analysis of the German Auction

(This section can be omitted by readers who do not want too much detail.)

To understand Grimm, Riedel, and Wolfstetter's argument—and why I believe it is incomplete in this context—consider the preferences of either one of the two strong bidders, M and T. At any point of time, a bidder would like to end the auction only if it prefers this to waiting until the price has risen a small further amount, $\Delta price$, before the auction ends.

The gain from waiting is the probability, ρ_6, that bidder 6 will quit in the price interval, $\Delta price$, times the value of driving bidder 6 out. This value is itself the benefit, β, of winning a third block, including the benefits from excluding bidder 6 from the industry (leading to a more concentrated, and hence more profitable, market), less the current price of buying an additional block. That is, the total gain from waiting equals $\rho_6[\beta - price]$.

The cost of waiting is the extra price, $\Delta price$, paid on the two units that the bidder will win anyway, namely, $2(\Delta price)$. That is, the bidder would prefer to plan to end the auction if a further price rise of $\Delta price$ fails to drive out bidder 6, rather than end it now if

$$\rho_6[\beta - price] > 2[\Delta price] \tag{1}$$

The bidder would prefer to end the auction now if

$$\rho_6[\beta - price] < 2[\Delta price]. \tag{2}$$

In Grimm, Riedel, and Wolfstetter's model, bidder 6's value can only take one of two possible values, v_6' (strong type) and v_6 (weak type), and the auction cannot be ended before price p ($< v_6$), so the only conceivably sensible strategies for the strong bidders are (a) to end the auction as soon as possible at p; (b) to push the price up a further $\Delta price = v_6 - p$ to v_6 to drive out the weaker type of bidder 6, but then to end the auction; or (c) to push the price up further still, by an additional $\Delta price = v_6' - v_6$ more to v_6', to drive out both types of bidder 6.

The observed behavior in the actual auction corresponded to case (b) of Grimm, Riedel, and Wolfstetter's model.

The condition for (b) to be preferred to (a) is the appropriate version of (1) or equivalently is Grimm, Riedel, and Wolfstetter's equation (9).[3] The condition for (b) to be preferred to (c) is the appropriate version of (2), or equivalently Grimm, Riedel, and Wolfstetter's equation (6).[4] So these are the key conditions in their theorem 15.1.[5] If (6) holds there is an equilibrium in which outcome (b) arises. (If (6) fails, both strong bidders prefer (c), and either can unilaterally implement it.) If (9) holds, the equilibrium is unique. If (9) fails, outcome (b) can still be an equilibrium of the model if (6) holds, since neither strong bidder can unilaterally end the auction, but the equilibrium is neither unique nor plausible.[6] So for the observed play to correspond to a plausible equilibrium of their model, both (9) and (6) are required.[7]

Noting that (9) and (6) are just my equations (1) and (2) suggests why Grimm, Riedel, and Wolfstetter's theory seems unlikely to describe reality. Of course, (9) and (6) correspond to (1) and (2) evaluated at different values of p_6, β, price and $\Delta price$, reflecting the different stages of the game at which (9) and (6) are computed. So the observed play can correspond to an equilibrium of their model. But this requires that $[p_6/(\Delta price)]$ not be too much lower when the strong bidders could first have ended the auction (when (1) must be satisfied) than at the actual end of the auction (when (2) must be satisfied).[8]

Furthermore, the tension between conditions (9) and (6) is more severe when the game is generalized to many small stages since the values of $[p_6/(\Delta price)]$, β, and price to be substituted into (1) and (2) cannot then vary much between stages, and related conditions must then hold at all the stages—an issue that Grimm, Riedel, and Wolfstetter do not address.[9] In particular, (1) must hold just before the auction ends, and (2) must hold at the price at which the auction ends. So if, as was the case in the actual auction, the price is changing only slowly between rounds, it is required that $[p_6/(\Delta price)]$ is falling (or at least not much increasing) at the end of the auction.

So, summarizing the two previous paragraphs, Grimm, Riedel, and Wolfstetter's equilibrium requires that, at the end of the auction, the probability of bidder 6 quitting conditional on not yet having done so is both not much increasing, and not much larger than at the lower prices at which the strong bidders could earlier, if they had both wished, have ended the auction.

And these two conditions seem implausible. A six-player conclusion to the auction became possible when Debitel quit at prices that were just 55 percent of the final U.K. prices (per capita).[10] The German auction actually finished at 94 percent of the final U.K. prices. The weakest of the six remaining bidders was generally thought to be either Mobilcom or "Group 3G," the joint venture between Telefonica and Sonera, so p_6 represents the probability that one of these would quit in the next round, conditional on their not yet having quit. But Telefonica and Mobilcom had quit the U.K. auction when the price levels had reached 94 percent and 100 percent of the final U.K. price level, respectively.[11] Mobilcom (at least) had made public statements that suggested that it was likely it would bid as far as it had in the United Kingdom,[12] and outside observers also thought that these bidders would probably go a lot further than 55 percent of the U.K. auction price but might quit at around the final U.K. price levels. Certainly, the most plausible distribution of valuations implied that at the end of the auction the probability of bidder 6 quitting was both much higher than earlier, and increasing, and either of these implications is sufficient to rule out Grimm, Riedel, and Wolfstetter's equilibrium.[13]

In brief, their equilibrium requires, roughly, that the strong bidders thought it relatively likely that Mobilcom or Group 3G would quit while prices were well below U.K. levels but then, having seen that Mobilcom and Group 3G did not quit at such low prices, the strong bidders thought it both relatively unlikely and increasingly unlikely that they would quit while prices were close to U.K. levels. And this seems unreasonable.

15.4   What Actually Happened in the German Auction?

While no one can be certain, it seems that other factors are required to explain the behavior of T-Mobil and Mannesman in the German auction. Some of these factors are discussed in Klemperer (2002a,b).[14]

They include the complexity of the rules and the opacity of the information available to bidders about others' bids, which made it hard for bidders to figure out optimal strategies (T may simply have made a mistake in failing to heed M's signal suggesting that they both reduce demand early on) or to understand their rivals' thinking. Klemperer (2002b) stresses the apparent lack of trust and understanding between the two strong bidders and discusses why this mistrust might have arisen.

Furthermore, the strong bidders may not simply have been maximizing expected profits. M and T may have focused more on their performances *relative* to each other, as might be rational behavior for managers who had private career concerns, or were concerned that their firm seemed well managed, deserving of further investment, and so forth. Relative-performance concerns may explain the auction's outcome, especially in conjunction with the mistrust between the bidders, as I explain in more detail in the next section.

It has been suggested that other contributory factors to T's behavior include that T felt pressured by the stock market's response to the rising auction prices (and that T had not fully anticipated this), and even that T's objectives were affected by the fact that it was majority-owned by the German government.

15.5   A Relative-Performance-Maximizing Theory of the German Auction

Grimm, Riedel, and Wolfstetter explain that if, for example, M reduced demand to two blocks while T did not, and T then won three blocks by driving out bidder 6, there would then have been a second auction for the remaining block that would most probably have been won by M at an expected price p_2 (in GRW's terminology) so both M and T would have ended with three blocks but having paid different prices for them.

Recall also from the discussion above that when prices are still low (e.g., around 55% of the final U.K. auction price), the probability of bidder 6 quitting is low, so it probably maximizes both firms' expected profits to reduce demand to two blocks and end the auction at low prices. However, if one firm, say M, reduces demand while T fails to do so and continues to push the price up, there is some—perhaps small—probability that bidder 6 will be driven out at a price $\tilde{p} < p_2$, in which case T and M will both end up with three blocks (assuming that M wins the block in the second auction), but T will on average pay less for its blocks than M (since T pays $3\tilde{p}$, but M expects to pay $2\tilde{p} + p_2$). Even in this case T and M may both be worse off in absolute terms than if T and M had both reduced demand to win two blocks at low prices. And because the chance of driving out bidder 6 at a low price is not that high, the more probable result would simply be that T would eventually reduce its own demand to two blocks later on, in which case both T and M would be much worse off than if they had both reduced demand earlier. But note that T always improves its performance relative to M by failing to reduce demand at prices below p_2.

Furthermore, even if each firm is actually an ordinary profit maximizer, but each firm expects the other is likely to maximize relative performance, then neither firm will reduce demand first (since being the only firm to reduce demand when prices are low risks paying $2\tilde{p} + p_2$ rather than $3\tilde{p}$).[15]

Similarly, when prices are higher (e.g., close to the final U.K. levels), it may maximize both M's and T's expected profits to push up the price to drive out bidder 6. But if one of the firms, say T, reduces demand to two blocks and lets M push up the price on its own to drive out bidder 6 at a price $p^* > p_2$, then again T and M will both end up with three blocks (assuming that T wins the block in the second auction) but T will pay less on average for its blocks than M pays (since T expects to pay $2p^* + p_2$, but M pays $3p^*$). So T would improve both its relative and its absolute performance if it could reduce demand alone, and M would then improve its relative performance by reducing demand along with T, even though M might increase its (and T's) absolute profits by continuing to raise price to drive out bidder 6.

The story told thus far is extreme. True, there is anecdotal evidence that firms' managers cared about relative performance, and concerns about relative performance also seem to have played at least some role in other European 3G auctions (see, e.g., chapter 10). But M and T were surely not concerned only with relative performance. So one might have expected M and T to attempt to coordinate their behavior to reduce their demands at low prices to maximize both of their absolute profits. Indeed it seems that M did initially try to signal to T that they should do just this (see chapter 14 and Klemperer 2002a,b). But T could not know whether M was sincere, and the firms apparently mistrusted each other's intentions (see Klemperer 2002b) and, as I have demonstrated, there are very strong relative-performance arguments (it suffices that each feared that the other might maximize relative-performance) why neither was prepared to be the first to reduce demand while prices were still low.

T then reduced demand later when prices were higher, perhaps for relative-performance reasons,[16] and/or because this could also improve its absolute performance if M failed (or was unable) to follow its demand reduction.[17] And once T had reduced demand, there are several possible reasons why M followed straightaway. First, M had a strong relative-performance incentive to follow immediately, as explained earlier. Second, M may have wanted to develop a reputation for cooperative behavior in which M and T parallel each other's behavior—a kind of "relative-performance" effect but strictly driven by M's long-run absolute-performance goals (see Klemperer 2002b). Third, M might have been concerned only with its (short-run) absolute performance, but it might all along have taken the view that this would be maximized by both M and T reducing demand, and it might have stuck to this view (i.e., M may have been extremely pessimistic about driving out bidder 6 at low prices and, even though driving out bidder 6 seemed more likely at high prices, remained fairly pessimistic; see Klemperer 2002a); this is consistent with M's early behavior (signaling T to reduce demand but not unilaterally reducing demand) if it feared that T might place a large weight on relative performance.

Of course, there may be other reasons for the observed behavior in the auction. For example, fear that one's rival has very different perceptions from one's own about the chance of driving out bidder 6 can have similar effects to fear that one's rival is a relative-performance maximizer,[18] and Klemperer (2002b) emphasizes the mistrust and misunderstanding between the bidders. But the point is that the apparently puzzling behavior can be explained by postulating only a limited concern with relative performance. To explain why M and T failed to reduce demand early on, it suffices that each firm thought its rival put some weight on relative performance; it is not necessary that either firm actually did so, and even the conjectured weights on relative performance need not have been large if firms were also uncertain about their rivals' perceptions about bidder 6's behavior, and so forth. And not much more concern with relative performance is needed to explain the firms' later behavior in the auction.

15.6 The Austrian and Swiss Auctions

Turning to other 3G auctions, I disagree with Grimm, Riedel, and Wolfstetter's assertion that the Austrian auction design was superior to the Swiss, except to the extent that the Austrian reserve price was somewhat more realistically chosen than the Swiss reserve. Neither auction attracted more bidders than there were winners, and neither involved any significant bidding. (Although there was a semblance of serious bidding in the Austrian auction, the bidders there were put under considerable pressure from the authorities to continue the bidding, and it was widely believed that the bidding only lasted the few rounds it did in order to create some public perception of genuine competition and reduce the risk of the government changing the rules.) Neither auction achieved more than 11 percent more than the reserve price that had been set. The only important difference is that the Swiss reserve price had been set ludicrously low at 20 euros per capita, while the Austrian reserve price, although still far lower than it should have been, was 90 euros per capita.[19] But revenues in excess of 300 euros per capita should probably have been attainable in both auctions (see Klemperer 2002a). So both of these auctions were failures, and both were intensely embarrassing to their respective governments. Indeed there was no successful European 3G auction after the U.K. and German auctions until the Danes switched to a sealed-bid design. I have discussed all these auctions in more detail in Klemperer (2002a).

15.7   The Importance of Entry and the U.K. Auction

Where I do agree very strongly with Grimm, Riedel, and Wolfstetter is on the importance of attracting entry into an auction.[20] As they say, "competition is not a free good" and auctions must be designed with this in mind. However, this does not imply that there is any single best design. Often a sealed-bid design is best for attracting entry, as is suggested by the Danish example in the previous paragraph. But this need not be the case. The U.K. design was appropriate in its context, because the U.K. auction was the first 3G auction and was therefore unlikely to suffer from entry problems. (See Klemperer 2002a,b for more discussion of why being first was so important.) Indeed the U.K. auction attracted thirteen bidders compared with the seven that entered the German auction. It seems improbable that the German design would have usefully increased competition in the British auction, and the British design had other advantages over the German design[21] (see Binmore and Klemperer 2002 and Klemperer 2002a, though my view may be colored by my having been the principal auction theorist for the U.K. auction[22]). In another context, when Peter Cramton, Eric Maskin, and I advised on the United Kingdom's 2002 auction for greenhouse gas emission reductions, we chose a uniform-price ascending design as being most likely to attract "small" bidders who did not have the resources to work out how to bid correctly in a discriminatory price auction.[23] Nor, of course, is entry always the key issue. As I discuss further in Klemperer (2002c), good auction design is not "one size fits all," but must always be tailored to its context.

15.8   Summary

Grimm, Riedel, and Wolfstetter (chapter 14) have developed an intriguing explanation for the apparently puzzling bidding in the 2000 German 3G telecom auction. These comments on their chapter discuss why I do not find their explanation fully satisfactory and suggest alternative explanations, including a relative-performance-maximizing theory. I also comment briefly on issues about several other 3G auctions.

Notes

I was the principal auction theorist advising the U.K. government's Radiocommunications Agency, which designed and ran the U.K. mobile phone license auction, but the views expressed in this chapter are mine alone. I do not intend to suggest that any of the behavior discussed in this chapter violates any applicable rules or laws. I am grateful for comments from Elmar Wolfstetter and to the representatives of the firms involved in the German auction to whom I showed an earlier draft, and I am also very grateful to Marco Pagnozzi for our collaboration in the study of the 3G auctions, and for his helpful suggestions about this essay.

1. Although efficiency was generally the primary objective, there is no evidence that efficiency differed much across the different countries' auctions. Hence the focus on revenues.

2. T-Mobil and Mannesman were subsidiaries of Deutsche Telekom and Vodafone, respectively.

3. In Grimm, Riedel, and Wolfstetter's (hereafter GRW's) notation, $\beta = v_{13} + b$ for the case of successfully driving out bidder 6 at price v_6.

4. In GRW's notation, $\beta = v'_{13} + b$ for the case of driving out bidder 6 at price v'_6, but $\rho_6 = 1$ in GRW's model at stage c).

5. GRW rename (6) as "$\Delta^2_{pr} \leq 0$" in their statement of Theorem 15.1.

6. This equilibrium is not plausible if (9) fails because in this equilibrium both strong players prefer outcome (a) to outcome (b), but both follow the strategy corresponding to (b) because each expects the other to do this. This logic can only hold in the two-stage model: With more stages, each strong player would know that if it followed the strategy corresponding to (a), then the other strong player would follow just one round of the auction later (if (9) fails)—that is, the players could trivially coordinate on strategy (a) in the actual multi-round auction, which eliminates this equilibrium. This equilibrium is, of course, also Pareto dominated by the more natural equilibrium for the players in GRW's two-stage model, and GRW also eliminate this equilibrium in their limited extension to multiple rounds (see note 9). However, an equilibrium of this kind becomes more plausible if M and T are each uncertain that its rival shares its assessment of the parameters, or are uncertain about the rival's objectives (see section 15.5).

7. GRW note that Theorem 14.1 requires other conditions too.

8. It does not seem likely that $(\beta - price)$ ever became very small because β includes both the value of a third block to a strong bidder and the value, b, in GRW's terminology, of excluding bidder 6 from the industry, leading to a more concentrated and hence more profitable market. Therefore, β must be greater than $p_2 + b$, where p_2 is the expected maximum of the value of a fourth block to a strong bidder and a third block to a less strong bidder. And, as GRW point out, p_2 must itself be quite high for the GRW equilibrium to make sense—the logic of GRW's equilibrium requires p_2 to at least equal the final German auction price. (The very limited anecdotal evidence suggests that p_2 might have been, very roughly, in the region of the final German auction price.)

9. GRW do briefly consider extending their model to many rounds of bidding, but when they do this they maintain the extreme assumption that bidder 6's valuation can take only two possible values, v_6 and v_6'. Thus in their extension there is no possibility of bidder 6 quitting before v_6, or between v_6 and v_6', so the additional rounds of bidding are mostly irrelevant and (1) and (2) are relevant only at the same points at which they matter in the two-stage game; that is, GRW's conditions (9) and (6) suffice as before. In a proper multiple-round extension of GRW's game in which it is also recognised that bidder 6's valuation is not restricted to just two possible values, conditions related to (1) or (2) must hold at each round of the game. (One difference that arises even in GRW's simplified multiple-round version is that (9) and (6) are both required for GRW's result to be an equilibrium.)

10. Ending the auction at these prices would have required the cooperation of all six bidders, but this could probably have been obtained. And even if this seemed hard, M and T could together have ended the auction once the other four bidders had stopped bidding for three blocks; none of the other bidders had high bids for three blocks beyond round 136 when the prices were 70 percent of the final U.K. price, and all could be proved to have lost eligibility for three blocks shortly thereafter.

11. Mobilcom was in large part owned by France Telecom, which was also part owner of NTL Mobile, the last bidder to quit the U.K. auction.

12. It may be objected that such statements were cheap talk. But following through on them may be necessary to maintain management credibility; they probably reflected an availability of finance, and—what matters—they seemed credible to observers at the time.

13. Although GRW argue (in the last paragraph of section 14.5) that it was reasonable to expect that bidder 6 might quit at some point before the final German auction price, they fail to consider the crucial questions about the *relative* likelihoods of bidder 6 quitting at a very low price, or at close to the final U.K. prices.

14. Ewerhart and Moldovanu (2001) make interesting points about the German design but in a model in which there is only a single strong bidder, so they cannot address why initially both strong bidders pushed up the price, then both stopped doing so. Also they do not model the second auction that would have taken place if just one strong bidder had pushed up price and subsequently driven a weak bidder out, and this possible second auction may have played an important role in behaviour in the main auction, as we discuss in section 15.5.

15. A similar argument is that if all firms are known to be ordinary profit maximizers, but firms are unsure that their rival has the same estimates of parameters such as ρ_6, then firms may be unwilling to reduce demand first.

16. It might seem that a firm could protect its relative performance by following a strategy of quitting only if its rival quits when prices are above p_2. However, it takes time to

be sure the rival has quit (because the auctioneer gave the bidders only limited information about their rivals' bidding), and it also takes time to respond. Furthermore, some of the weaker players may have been staying in the auction in the hope of being a winner in a five-firm industry, which would have been the outcome if M and T had successfully driven one of them out; in particular, each of Mobilcom and Group 3G might have hoped that the other (or possibly E-Plus or Viag) was the "bidder 6" who might have been driven out. In this case, when one of M and T quits bidding for a third block, these weaker players may expect the other of M and T to try to follow suit and may therefore try to quit first rather than find themselves stuck as winners in a much-less-profitable six-firm industry. So if either M or T failed to quit first when prices became high, it might have risked being stranded buying a third block at a higher price than its opponent, and achieving a very poor relative performance.

17. If T thought M was not too concerned with relative performance, T could improve both its relative and absolute performance by reducing demand once the price exceeded p_2, and free-riding on M continuing to push price up to drive out bidder 6. And even if M was concerned with relative performance, there was the possibility that M would have been unable to follow T (see note 16). Of course, there may be other reasons, such as T being influenced by stock market pressure or its government ownership (see section 15.4). It might be argued that another possibility was that β was not in fact that high. However, this seems less likely since β must have substantially exceeded p_2 (see note 8), and if p_2 were low then both firms would have been willing to reduce demand early on for relative-, as well as absolute-, performance reasons.

18. In particular, either fear can make a bidder unwilling to reduce demand first when prices are low, because of the perceived risk that the rival will not follow. See note 15.

19. Of course, Switzerland sold four licenses while Austria sold six, but the Swiss could obviously have used their same design to sell six licenses if they had preferred that outcome.

20. I emphasized this in Bulow and Klemperer (1996), and Klemperer (1998, 2002c, 2003).

21. One advantage is identified in note 16: In the German design, a bidder might rationally follow a strategy that could mean that it felt sorry to have won as soon as the auction finished.

22. I was the principal auction theorist advising the Radiocommunications Agency, which designed and ran the U.K. auction. Ken Binmore had a leading role and supervised experiments testing the proposed designs. Other academic advisors included Tilman Börgers, Jeremy Bulow, Philippe Jehiel and Joe Swierzbinski.

23. Larry Ausubel and Jeremy Bulow were also involved in the implementation of this auction. Strictly this was a descending auction, since the auctioneer was buying reductions in emissions rather than selling permits to emit, but the auction corresponded to an ascending auction to sell emissions.

References

Binmore, K., and P. Klemperer. 2002. "The Biggest Auction Ever: the Sale of the British 3G Telecom Licences." *Economic Journal* 112(478): C74–C96. Available online at ⟨http:// www.paulklemperer.org⟩.

Bulow, J., and P. Klemperer. 1996. "Auctions vs. Negotiations." *American Economic Review* 86(1): 180–194.

Ewerhart, C., and B. Moldovanu. 2001. "A Stylized Model of the German UMTS Auction." Working paper, University of Mannheim, Germany.

Klemperer, P. 1998. "Auction with Almost Common Values." *European Economic Review* 42(3–5): 757–769.

Klemperer, P. 2002a. "How (Not) to Run Auctions: The European 3G Telecom Auctions." *European Economic Review* 46(4–5): 829–845.

Klemperer, P. 2002b. "Using and Abusing Economic Theory (2002 Alfred Marshall Lecture to the European Economic Association)." Forthcoming in *Journal of the European Economic Association* 1 (2003). Forthcoming in *Advances in Economics and Econometrics: Theory and Applications*, ed. R. Becker and S. Hurn. Cheltenham, U.K.: Edward Elgar. Available online at 〈http://www.paulklemperer.org〉.

Klemperer, P. 2002c. "What Really Matters in Auction Design." *Journal of Economic Perspectives* 16(1): 169–189.

Klemperer, P. 2003. "Why Every Economist Should Learn Some Auction Theory." In M. Dewatripont, L. Hansen, and S. Turnovsky, eds., *Advances in Economics and Econometrics: Invited Lectures to Eighth World Congress of the Econometric Society*, 25–55. Cambridge, UK: Cambridge University Press. Available online at 〈http://www.paulklemperer.org〉.

V

Closing the Circle:
The Dutch Auction and
the Interplay among the
Political Process, Market
Structure, and Strategic
Behavior in Auctions

16 The Dutch UMTS Auction

Eric van Damme

16.1 Introduction

Shortly after the United Kingdom had organized "the biggest auction ever," the Netherlands was the second European country to auction UMTS licenses. The auction took 306 rounds to complete and lasted from July 6 to July 24, 2000. In contrast to the U.K. auction, which was viewed as a big success, the Dutch auction was generally considered to be a major flop. In an opinion piece in the *Financial Times*, published two days after the closing of the Dutch auction, Paul Klemperer forcefully argued that the Dutch had failed. As Klemperer posed the question: "So why did the Netherlands' auction, using similar bidding rules to the UK one, attract so few competitors and such feeble bidding, and raise barely a quarter of the per capita revenue of the UK auction?" (Klemperer 2000).

In Klemperer's view, the Dutch had done two things wrong. Most important, they had used the wrong auction design: in a market with five incumbent 2G operators, they should not have sold the five 3G licenses in a simultaneous multi-round ascending auction because such an auction gives newcomers little chance to win a license. A different auction format, such as the "Anglo-Dutch" design, would have been more favorable for newcomers; hence, it would have led to more auction participants, to more aggressive bidding, and to higher revenues for the government. Second, through a tougher competition policy, the Dutch should have prevented competitors from teaming up with each other before the auction. While these points may be valid, they need not, however, be relevant. The Dutch auction should be judged on the basis of whether it achieved the goals that it was supposed to achieve. Moreover, neither attracting many bidders nor establishing new market entry nor obtaining high revenue were official goals of the Dutch

Table 16.1
Auction revenues in € per capita

Country	2G	3G	Revenue
United Kingdom	4	5	650
Netherlands	5	5	170
Germany	4	6	620
Italy	4	5	210
Austria	4	6	105
Switzerland	3	4	20
Belgium	3	4	45
Denmark	4	4	95

government. Of course, one may question whether the goals that were specified are the appropriate ones, and one might argue that revenue maximization and generating entry *should* have been explicit goals. Be that as it may, in retrospect, in terms of revenue, the Dutch government did not do so badly after all, as the European comparison in the table 16.1 shows.

Unfortunately, answering the question of whether the goals were achieved is somewhat difficult since these goals were never stated explicitly. In its reaction to the evaluation of the auction that researchers of Erasmus University did on behalf of the Dutch parliament (Janssen, Ros, and van der Windt 2001), the government states that policy was supposed to achieve two goals; the auction should (1) efficiently allocate the available spectrum, and (2) contribute to having a competitive telecommunications market.[1]

The first goal relates to the spectrum that is allocated and to the allocation process that is used for doing this; the second relates to the market resulting from the allocation. Both these goals are stated in vague terms and, as I discuss in more detail in what follows, in the policy documents of the Dutch government, the term "efficiency" was not always used in a consistent way. Furthermore, many of these documents contain generic reference to the auction mechanism, and frequently there is an implicit belief that any auction will produce an efficient outcome, no matter how efficiency is defined. As a consequence, even though information is lacking to judge whether the stated goals were achieved, I can definitely state that the designers of the Dutch auction showed insufficient awareness of the precautions that needed to be taken to assure the achievement of these goals.

In this chapter, I review the Dutch UMTS auction and discuss those aspects on which there has been extensive debate in Dutch newspapers and journals.[2] The chapter builds on my previous publications on this topic in Dutch and makes these arguments available to a larger audience.[3] At the same time the chapter adds to the earlier material by making some of the bidding data available and by analyzing them. While most of the discussion in the popular press has concentrated on the supposedly low revenue that was generated, several other aspects of the Dutch auction are really more interesting and, hence, deserve more attention. In this chapter I discuss and explain the following six aspects:

1. The auction attracted only six bidders, of which only one was not yet active on the Dutch mobile market.

2. The auction did not allocate a license to a new entrant.

3. There were "strange bids" in the opening phase of the auction, with all bidders but one issuing waivers, so as to drive the minimum price to zero, and this led to questions of whether there was coordinated behavior (tacit collusion).

4. There were allegations of collusion in the auction with the Dutch competition authority investigating this issue after the auction.

5. There were allegations that in the auction's final phase at least one bidder could benefit from "insider information," hence, that there was not a level playing field and that the auctioneer should have suspended the auction.

6. The auction ended in turmoil with the newcomer claiming that it could no longer bid because it was threatened by one of the incumbents (predation).

This long list suggests that indeed a lot may have been wrong with the Dutch auction. This makes it an interesting object for study since it may contain several useful lessons for other auction design problems. By providing a detailed overview and analysis of the Dutch UMTS auction, this chapter indeed allows me to draw several such lessons.

The remainder of the chapter is organized as follows. Section 16.2 describes the Dutch 2G market and the goals of Dutch spectrum policy. It focuses on the question of whether revenue should be a goal when auctioning spectrum, on different aspects of efficiency, and on how to obtain an efficient outcome in case asymmetries exist between incumbents and entrants. Section 16.3 describes the process leading to the

Dutch 3G auction, with special emphasis on asymmetries between incumbents and entrants, and on the lobby of incumbents for auction rules that favor them. This section explains the first two observations from our list. Section 16.4 describes the playing of the 3G auction and the simultaneous developments outside the auction; it provides a detailed discussion of points 3–6 mentioned earlier. Section 16.5 concludes by making several recommendations for practical auction design problems.

16.2   The Dutch DCS-1800 Auction and the Dutch 2G Market

Within Europe, the Netherlands was rather late in introducing second generation (2G) mobile telephony. In March 1995, two licenses to operate 2G networks using frequencies in the 900 MHz band were given out. One license was given to the incumbent monopolist, KPN; the second one was awarded by means of a beauty contest and was won by Libertel, at that time a joint venture of Vodafone and ING-Bank. At the same time, the Dutch government decided that it was desirable to quickly license additional mobile operators using spectrum in the 1800 MHz band, and that it was desirable to award such additional licenses by means of an auction. In July 1995, the government took the decision that auctions were the preferred mechanism for allocating spectrum. Since a change in the telecommunications law was needed to award licenses through auctions rather than by means of beauty contests, considerable time elapsed (until February 1998) before the DCS-1800 auction actually took place. In van Damme (1999) I provided a detailed description of the process that led to that auction, the auction rules, and the auction outcome. I now review the salient aspects that are relevant for a proper understanding of the Dutch 3G auction.

16.2.1   Why Auction the Spectrum?

During the parliamentary year 1996–1997, extensive discussion took place on the pros and cons of using auctions to allocate spectrum. The major advantage that the government saw was that an auction is a transparent allocation mechanism that guarantees that the spectrum is efficiently used. Using auctions as the allocation mechanism may thus contribute to reaching the main goal of Dutch spectrum policy, which is to allocate spectrum so as to have a communications market that contributes optimally to overall Dutch welfare. The government realized that auctions may lead to considerable revenue, but revenue as such was said not to be a goal. Parliament agreed on the pros of auctions, but fueled by concerns voiced by the European Commission (1994) that auction prices might be passed on to consumers and that high prices might delay innovation, it expressed a preference for low revenues. While the government argued that these fears were not justified, it did not insist too much, and a consensus position was then adopted that revenue generation, let alone revenue maximization, should not be a goal. When specifically asked about the goals associated with spectrum allocation, the Minister responded that it was to create a strongly competitive mobile telecommunications market.

Dutch economists did not challenge the stated government objective; they did not point out that raising revenue could be a valid goal.[4] The argument in favor of this position, of course, is that, since auction prices are sunk cost, auctions might be the least distorting way of raising taxes; hence, raising taxes in this way might contribute to higher welfare (see, e.g., Klemperer 2002a). In other words, just as a competitive telecommunications market contributes to the overall Dutch welfare, so might high auction revenue, and therefore both objectives should be considered. It is to the discredit of Dutch economists that, up to this very moment, they have not yet gotten this message across.

When reading the Dutch parliamentary documents about spectrum auctions and telecommunications policy that have appeared during the period 1995–2002, one notices three things:

1. The objectives are described in vague terms ("creating a competitive and innovating market").

2. The goals are linked to (economic) efficiency, but it is not always clear what type of efficiency one has in mind, especially not since the term efficiency appears to be used in an inconsistent way.

3. There is generic reference to the auction mechanism.

For example, even in the evaluation of the 3G auction that the government sent to Parliament on September 4, 2000, one reads statements like "In general the auction mechanism is to be preferred as it is economically efficient and generates optimal revenue."[5] Similarly, in the response of the government to the evaluation of the 3G auction in Janssen, Ros, and van der Windt (2001) one reads: "The auction is an open, transparent and non-discriminatory allocation instrument which ensures that the object is allocated to that bidder that values it most. It is assumed that this bidder will then also make the most efficient use of that object."[6]

Note that the last sentence from the quoted passage makes reference to what might be called "spectrum efficiency": An auction will select a party that uses the spectrum efficiently. In the preceding sentence, the reference, instead, is to "value efficiency": An auction will select that party that attaches the highest value to a license. Both these efficiency concepts, however, are different from "market efficiency" (an auction will select those parties that contribute most to total welfare), which, given the overall policy goal stated previously, is the only one that is relevant. In the policy documents, there seems little appreciation for the possibility that one type of efficiency need not imply another, that whether or not a certain type of efficiency is reached might depend on the type of auction that is used, or that efficiency might not be reached at all. The impression that remains after having read these government documents is that those who wrote them have studied papers about standard auctions and that they believe that the statements made in those papers (about efficiency and revenue equivalence) apply to the context at hand, hence, that there is little need to devote much energy to the question of how the auction should be designed.

16.2.2   How to Auction the Spectrum?

There are, however, at least two reasons why the standard auction model need not be relevant in the context of allocating spectrum.[7] First, in this case no end products are auctioned but rather licenses to be active on a market, and the bidders are firms, not the final consumers of the product. To put it differently, this is not an auction of consumer products, but of licenses, in which bidders are guided by shareholder value and not by consumer surplus, or total welfare. Hence, at best one can expect an auction to produce an allocation that is "value efficient"; it need not be "market efficient." Second, while in practical situations there may be strong asymmetries between incumbents and newcomers, the basic auction model assumes symmetry between the bidders. For both these reasons the standard auction model does not apply, an auction need not produce an "efficient" outcome, and the government needs to carefully think about what instrument it should use to reach its objectives.

Gilbert and Newbery (1982) appears to be the first paper that stresses that, in license auctions, if there are asymmetries between incumbents and entrants, market efficiency may be nontrivial to achieve. The intuition is easily conveyed. Consider a monopolistic market and suppose a second license is auctioned. For the incumbent monopolist, the value of the license is his future monopoly profit; for the entrant, the value is the profit that he can obtain when competing with the monopolist. Because the latter is smaller, in an ordinary ascending auction, the monopolist will win the second license, the monopoly will remain, and the benefits of competition will not be realized. Furthermore, the higher the potential benefits of competition, the lower the value to the entrant, hence, the lower the auction price. In fact, since he knows he cannot win, a forward-looking entrant may not participate in the auction and the monopolist might get the second license for free. In this situation, if the government really wants to achieve market efficiency, then it may have to discriminate against the monopolist: If the playing field is not level, the rules of the game have to favor the weaker players in order to reach the efficiency goal. This point is extremely important in this special case at hand, and I return to the issue in the next section.

16.2.3   The Dutch DCS-1800 Auction

At the beginning of 1998, the Dutch DCS-1800 auction took place. Spectrum in the 1800 MHz band was sold by using a variant of the simultaneous multi-round ascending auction. Important for my discussion here is that the number of licenses that could be won in this auction was endogenous and that the auction produced three winners. Dutchtone and Telfort won the two large lots (of 15 MHz each), and Ben was able to acquire 16.8 MHz of spectrum by buying several smaller lots in the auction and by buying spectrum from losing parties after the auction. Note, therefore, that while other European countries typically have either three or four 2G operators, the Netherlands is special in that it has five of them. The 2G licenses were given out in the spring of 1998. At the time of the 3G auction, these DCS-1800 operators had been on the market for only two years, so that, in a certain sense they were still relative newcomers. This is also reflected in their market shares. In the summer of 2000, KPN had 49 percent of the subscribers, Libertel 31 percent, Telfort 7.3 percent, Dutchtone 6.9 percent, and Ben 5.8 percent.[8]

   In van Damme (1999), I have argued that this auction was badly designed and that, because of the large variation in prices, it might not have achieved the efficiency goal that was specified. In the evaluation of the auction that the Dutch government sent to Parliament on January, 11, 1999, the responsible Minister rejected my criticism and instead concluded that the simultaneous multi-round format had functioned well and that the goal of the auction, "to allocate scarce spectrum in a transparent way" had been achieved.[9] Note that the goal that is mentioned here is a very minimal one. It is fair to say that the civil servants, having prior beliefs based on their reading of the auction literature, being satisfied with the outcome of the 2G auction, and expecting there to be a lot of demand for the 3G licenses, did not see much need to change a design that had already proved itself.

16.3   The Process to the 3G Auction

Immediately, after the 2G auction had taken place, the government started preparing for the 3G auction. A consultation document was published on July 16, 1998, and discussed with market parties later that year. These discussions led to a policy proposal that was published on March 25, 1999. In line with the recommendation of the UMTS Forum (Report number 5, September 1998), the plan was to allocate four licenses, each containing 2×15 MHz of paired spectrum and 5 MHz of unpaired spectrum. These licenses would last fifteen years, incumbents (i.e., existing 2G operators) would not be excluded from participating in the auction, no license would be reserved for a newcomer, and newcomers would not receive special roaming rights on existing 2G networks. The document did not specify details about which auction mechanism would be used; however, it was stated that the design would take into account the lessons learned from the DCS-1800 auction. Note that this proposal would have made a simple multi-unit auction (of 4 identical, abstract lots) possible. Of course, the proposal would also have implied that at least one of the existing players would have to leave the market.

16.3.1   The Goal of the 3G-Auction

Quite interestingly, the UMTS policy proposal formulates a very general goal "to give the Netherlands a leading position in Europe." Equally interesting is the observation that, during the process leading to the auction, this goal was never discussed explicitly, nor made more specific. One may thus conclude that the overall goal of spectrum policy that had been formally agreed upon before, "maximizing welfare," remained the relevant one. In the previous section, we have, however, seen that asymmetries between incumbents and newcomers may make this goal nontrivial to reach and, hence, may make the auction design problem an interesting one.

A simple back-of-the-envelope calculation may indicate how large in this context the value differences between incumbents and entrants can be.[10] Assume, for example, that ARPU (average 3G revenues per subscriber) is €40 per month and that the discount rate (WACC) is 1 percent per month. If it takes two years to roll out the network, hence, before revenue starts to flow in, total discounted revenue is about €3,000 per subscriber. If one counts on six million subscribers and a market share of one-third, then one gets expected revenue of €6 billion. From this one has to subtract the cost of actually building and maintaining the network, say €1 billion, to get to the value of €5 billion. The value is lower for an entrant because he can expect only a smaller market share, can start later, and has higher cost for constructing the network. Fortis Bank (2000) estimates that network cost for an entrant to be one-third higher. Then with an expected market share of 10 percent, which is on the high side, one can calculate value to be €0.5 bln, hence, an order of magnitude less.

This calculation raises the question of why any newcomer would want to participate in a symmetric ascending auction in which at most five licenses are offered, a question that I answer later. An even more important question is whether a new entrant winning a license is a necessary condition for "maximizing welfare" or for "giving the Netherlands a leading position in Europe." There are several reasons why a new entrant might be a more aggressive player on the market: It has to gain market share and does not cannibalize its own existing 2G product. On the other hand, capital market constraints might inhibit new entrants, hence may make them less aggressive. Furthermore, the three DCS-1800 operators had entered the market only relatively shortly before the 3G auction; they were fiercely competing for market share, and hence, in a certain sense they were still relative newcomers. Given this market situation, I am not able to answer this second question.

In its advice on the policy proposal, the Dutch telecom regulator, OPTA, hinted at the desirability to favor newcomers to the market in the auction. OPTA actually criticized the government proposal on two points. First, it argued that, if feasible, it would be desirable to allocate more than four licenses, in order not to create a (too) tight oligopoly.

Second, it recommended giving newcomers explicit rights to roam on existing 2G networks. The government, however, was convinced that new entrants did not need special roaming rights since EU regulations would force 2G operators with significant market power to honor reasonable requests for special access, and since requests for roaming would fall under these regulations.

16.3.2 Lobbying for Favorable Rules

Within economics two different theories of regulation are distinguished. According to the public interest theory, the government supplies regulation to correct for market failures. The private interest theory holds that regulation is demanded by incumbents to protect against entrants. The equilibrium on this market for regulation determines the actual regulations. In the Netherlands, this market is organized in a somewhat formal way, and this is known as the Dutch "poldermodel." In line with the customs of the poldermodel, the Dutch government consulted with the sector about its March 25 proposals. The discussions took place within the OPT, the consultation group of operators in the post and telecommunications sector. The minutes of the OPT meetings, which were published after the 3G auction, give detailed insight into how this market worked in this special case.[11] In these minutes, one sees lobbies in action and one can see how successful lobbies work. Obviously, one may expect the sector to lobby in favor of rules from which it will benefit. Furthermore, one may also expect differences of opinion between incumbents and entrants. The incumbents in the Dutch market were very effective in keeping newcomers out of the formal lobby process; at one point it was simply argued that the OPT meeting room was already very crowded, and hence, too small for newcomers to be admitted to the market.

One can imagine that the proposal to auction only four licenses was not greeted with great enthusiasm by the incumbents. Because NMa (the Dutch competition authority) and OPTA were not happy with the prospect of a rather concentrated market, the discussion moved to whether five or six licenses could and should be offered. Most parties actually favored awarding six licenses, presumably based on the idea that a larger supply would imply a lower price. The better economists, or at least the more experienced ones, were to be found with KPN and they lobbied for five licenses. Because KPN had had an interest in acquiring a license in the United Kingdom, it had participated in the preparations of the U.K. auction a year before. From the U.K. discussion of the problems associated with a 4-to-4 scenario (4 incumbents, 4 licenses), KPN had learned that a situation with as many licenses as incumbents was very unfavorable for newcomers and, hence, most desirable for incumbents. Consequently, KPN argued strongly in favor of five licenses, two large ones and three small ones, and in the end, that proposal was adopted. It is noteworthy that, while the U.K. discussions about the 4-to-4 scenario had been very open and extensive, and had taken place almost a year before the Dutch came to discuss the 5-to-5 scenario that presents equal difficulties, the Dutch government officials never showed any awareness of this problem, let alone of the possible ingenious way out (the Anglo-Dutch auction) that had been identified by the academic advisors to the U.K. government. As a result, alternative auction designs were never discussed, and the outcome of the lobby game was very favorable for the Dutch incumbents.

Based on the consultation rounds and the advice received, the government published its definite plans on January 26, 2000. The decision was to award five licenses (two of $2 \times 15 + 1 \times 5$, and three of $2 \times 10 + 1 \times 5$), to have a license duration of fifteen years, to not reserve a lot for a newcomer, and to not attach special roaming rights to a license. This plan was discussed in Parliament in March 2000, where no major comments were made. At that point, the details of the auction rules were not yet revealed; however, given the positive evaluation of the DCS-1800 auction, one could expect that a simultaneous multi-round auction would be used. Indeed, in the end, the adopted auction format was ascending and symmetric and, not surprisingly, no newcomer won. As I have already stated, since three of the incumbents had entered the market only relatively shortly before the 3G auction, this by itself does not prove that the goals of the auction have not been achieved.

16.3.3 The Auction Design Stage

After the Parliament had given the go-ahead, the actual preparations for the auction started. When making the design, the people in the ministry relied on their own past experience with the DCS-1800 auction and on the evaluation of that auction. It is fair to say that the civil servants, being satisfied with the outcome of the 2G auction and expecting there to be a lot of demand for the 3G licenses, did not see much need to change a design that had already proved itself. They nevertheless asked economists associated with the Center for Research in Experimental Economics and Political Decision Making (CREED), University of Amsterdam, for advice on the optimal extent of transparency, on the best minimum bid, and on the proper size of the bid increment. The request for advice was, however, stated in very general terms; hence, the response was rather general as well. I discuss here the minimum opening bid in some detail, since it played an important role in the auction.

A positive minimum price is desirable because it may shorten the duration of the auction. On the other hand, a minimum price that is too high may deter potential bidders from participating, and hence, may have a negative effect on efficiency or revenue. Obviously, imposing a minimum price can also have the consequence that some frequencies are left unsold. In the reading of the government, the Dutch Telecommunications Law forced it to always allocate all available spectrum, which ruled out imposing a hard minimum price. Indeed, in one parliamentary discussion, the Minister openly acknowledged that the licenses would go for free in case there were only five interested parties. In order not to risk violating the law, the government thus adopted a soft minimum price: There was a minimum price in round 1, but this would be lowered (ultimately to zero) if there would be no bidding on the lot. While the reader may wonder about this peculiar feature of the law, he can now at least better understand the opening phase of the Dutch auction. I note that meanwhile the Dutch government has adopted a law that makes a hard minimum bid possible.

The detailed auction rules were discussed in at least one OPT meeting, that of March 28, 2000. Parties were concerned about having a transparent procedure; that is, in contrast to the earlier DCS-1800 auction, the identities of the parties having the highest bids should be revealed. Furthermore, the parties argued against having a final auction round. It is also interesting to note that Dutchtone advocated using the German design, and that KPN volunteered to develop software to assist the government in detecting flaws in the design. One such (serious) flaw, which was discussed extensively, was the proposal concerning the re-auction that would be used in case one of the first winners did not honor its commitments. The NextWave situation in the United States shows how serious the difficulties can be if one of the

winners does not honor its commitments. As a result of these discussions, the design was changed somewhat, although the final design
did not fully allay the concerns.

16.3.4   The 3G Auction Rules

The auction rules were published in April 2000. For my purpose, the
following aspects of the rules are relevant:

1. Five licenses are auctioned; licenses A and B involve 2 × 15 MHz of
paired spectrum, and 1 × 5 MHz of unpaired spectrum, the licenses C,
D, and E each involve 2 × 10 MHz of paired spectrum, and 1 × 5 MHz
of unpaired. The license duration is fifteen years.

2. The licenses are sold in a simultaneous multi-round auction.

3. Each bidder can bid on each license, however, in each round one
can bid on at most one license, and if one is standing high on lot L one
is not allowed to bid on a different lot; hence, each bidder can acquire
at most one license.

4. In the first round, the minimum required bid on the lots A and B is
f100 million; it is f90 million on the lots C, D, and E. If there is no bid
on a lot, the minimum price for the next round is reduced to 70 (resp.
60) and if also in the next rounds there is no bid, this minimum is further reduced to 35 and next to 0 (resp. 30 and 0).

5. Each bidder has three waivers (or pass cards); waivers can only be
used in one of the first thirty rounds of the auction.

6. A bidder who is not standing high on a lot, and who is not bidding
or not using a waiver, is no longer eligible to bid.

7. Bidders know who is standing high on each lot.

8. For each lot, the auctioneer determines the minimum bid that is relevant for the next round; the bid increment is at most 10 percent of the
previous highest bid on the lot, or 200,000 guilders if the latter amount
is higher.

9. Bidders are not allowed to disturb the proper course of the auction;
they are not allowed to prevent competition from taking place in the
auction.

10. The auction ends when no more bids are made, with parties having the highest bids at that time winning the licenses; the winners have
to pay their final bid.

16.3.5   The Interest in the Auction

Parties that wanted to participate in the auction had to register before June 5. Ten parties expressed such an interest. In addition to the five incumbent mobile operators, these were NTL, Hutchison, T-Mobil, Sonera, and Versatel. The latter is a small firm that at the time was investing in a high-speed fixed (glass fiber) data network connecting the major cities in western Europe. The Dutch competition authority was asked for advice concerning the "independence" of several of these parties. France Telecom, who is the major shareholder in incumbent Dutchtone, is also a minority shareholder in NTL. Furthermore, at the time France Telecom had an interest in Vodafone (resulting from the sale of Orange). The competition authority didn't see any problems in the links between these companies; hence, all parties were eligible to bid. A couple of days after filing its application, Sonera, however, withdrew.

Of course, frequently it is better to cooperate rather than compete. On June 27, T-Mobil announced its cooperation with (takeover of) the incumbent Ben, while at the same time withdrawing its independent application. Because Ben was generally considered to be the financially weakest incumbent, this move substantially reduced the chance of a newcomer winning a license.[12] On July 3, KPN and Hutchison formally announced that they were considering cooperation in UMTS auctions in Germany and Belgium, and two days later Hutchison withdrew its independent application. In the morning of the first auction day, twenty minutes before the auction was about to start, NTL announced that it would not bid. This left only six bidders for five licenses.

Given that the design adopted by the Dutch government was unfavorable for new entrants, why did any entrant take the trouble to participate in this auction? Why did the auction take place? Why wasn't the government forced to give the licenses to the incumbents for free? These are the questions that the government should have been thinking about in the months before the auction. All signs, however, are that, after the U.K. auction raised revenues so high, the Dutch government was thinking about exactly the opposite "problem" of how to prevent an excessive price (Bennett and Canoy 2000). At least one economist had warned the government that an unfavorable scenario, with only five bidders for five licenses might become reality (Maasland 2000), but this possibility seems not to have been taken seriously.

16.3.6   Versatel

So why then did Versatel participate? I note that also Versatel was well aware that, under normal conditions, it could not win a license in the auction. In fact, Versatel had clearly communicated to the other parties that it was aware of having no chances to win in the auction: It had started formal legal complaints about the auction design against the Dutch government. In these legal procedures, which were taking place both in the Netherlands and at the EU level, Versatel had given the full arguments for why it could not win.[13] Hence, Versatel did not participate to win a license. Instead it participated since it had not yet gotten the concessions from the incumbents that it wanted. Just to make completely sure that the incumbents understood its motivation to play, Versatel openly displayed its motives for participation on its Web site the day before the auction started. Versatel's CFO is quoted there as saying: "Versatel fears it is defining the success or failure of the auction. We would however not like to see that we end up with nothing whilst other players get their licenses for free. Versatel invites the incumbent mobile operators to immediately start negotiations for access to their existing 2G networks as well as entry to the 3G market either as a part owner of a license or as a mobile virtual network operator."[14]

The message should be clear: Versatel was willing to share a license (and, hence, not participate as a bidder in the auction) provided that the terms were right and that access to an existing 2G network was offered at reasonable terms. Incumbents might thus have expected Versatel to drop out of the auction if an agreement were reached. As part of its strategy, Versatel had also provided itself an exit option. In the days before the auction, it had stated in several press releases that it would bid only if it had found a strategic partner, and on the day the auction started, such a partner had not yet been announced.[15] With other newcomers withdrawing from the auction, the scenario obviously developed in the way most favorable to Versatel. Being the only entrant, Versatel had bargaining power over the incumbents, which it was fully aware of, as the opening sentence of the press release makes clear. The longer Versatel stayed in the auction, the higher the price the incumbents would have to pay; if an agreement were reached immediately, only five bidders would be left for five licenses, and the incumbents could get their licenses for free. Note, however, the free rider problem on the side of the incumbents: All of them would benefit from

Versatel dropping out, but only one party had to conclude an agreement. Which party should this be? Note that Ben, Dutchtone, and KPN each had already taken out a newcomer, which left Libertel and Telfort as obvious candidates. On the morning of Friday, July 7, the Internet journal *Planet Multimedia* was openly speculating on Versatel sharing with Dutchtone; this journal was excluding Libertel because Vodafone wanted to focus on mobile telephony while Versatel had its main interests in fixed. (Planet Multimedia 2000).

16.4   The 3G Auction

The auction started on Thursday, July 6. That morning, the government was surprised by there being only six bidders, but it was too late to call off the auction. The auction lasted for thirteen days and had a total of bidding rounds. It came to a halt when, in round 306, Versatel decided not to bid again. For the largest part, the auction was uneventful. In what follows, I analyze in some detail the more interesting stages in which there was bidding on the larger lots. This includes the beginning and the end of the auction. Throughout this section, I use the following abbreviations:

K = KPN

L = Libertel

B = Ben

D = Dutchtone

T = Telfort

V = Versatel

With the exception of former monopolist KPN, all the incumbents are affiliated with major European players: Vodafone is the majority shareholder in L; for B, one may read Deutsche Telekom; for D, France Telecom; and for T, British Telecom.

16.4.1   The Opening

Since the government was of the opinion that it could not charge a strictly positive price in case there was no scarcity, the rules specified that players could use "pass cards" at the beginning of the auction and that, on lots receiving no bids, the minimum price would be (stepwise)

Table 16.2
The opening phase of the auction

Rounds	A	B	C	D	E
1	— —	L 100	— —	— —	— —
2	— —	L —	— —	— —	— —
3	— —	L —	— —	— —	— —
4	K 0	L —	B 0.1	T 0	V 0
5	K —	L —	D 0.3	T —	V —

reduced to zero. At the start of the auction, the players faced considerable uncertainty about the actual number of serious bidders. Possibly there were only five serious bidders for five licenses; hence, by using the pass cards, it might be possible to actually get a license for free. All players, apart from Libertel, realized that it was sensible (a dominant strategy?) to use the pass cards in the opening rounds and to first drive the minimum prices to zero, instead of starting to bid immediately. Table 16.2 gives the bids that were made in these opening rounds, with all prices listed in millions of Dutch guilders.[16] (In round 4, there were two bids on A, and also two on C.) In effect, since Versatel turned out to be an active player as well, the bidders were in a kind of prisoners' dilemma; the only effect of using the waivers was that the auction lasted a week longer than it would otherwise have. (Of course this also gave the parties more time to come to an agreement.)

In rounds 6, 7, and 8 there is then some activity on the small lots, but in round 9, Telfort switches to lot A to compete with KPN. In light of the talks (negotiations?) that are taking place between T and V (see later), this is understandable: Since K is the largest player on the market, since L is occupying a large license, and since lot A is cheap, T may expect K to stay bidding on A, which implies that the price on the small lots remains low, and hence, that, if the negotiations are successful, a large cake can be divided between T and V. In the next rounds, K and T then drive up the price on lot A. With a minimum increment of 0.2 (million) or 10 percent of the previous highest bid, it obviously takes a long time before the price is back at its original level. In fact, it takes until round 60 before Libertel is eventually outbid by KPN. Table 16.3 describes the state of the auction at that time.

The table should be read as follows: on lot A, T has made the highest bid up to now and the current minimum bid on that lot is 110.1; and similar for the other lots.

Table 16.3
Round 60 of the auction

State	A	B	C	D	E
60	T 110.1	L 110	D 0.5	B 0.4	V 0.6

Table 16.4
Rounds 60–62 of the auction

State	A	B	Bidder	Lot	Bid
60	T 110.1	L 110	K	B	110
61	T 110.1	K 121	L	A	110.1
62	L 121.1	K 121	T	B	121

Table 16.5
Round 96 of the auction

State	A	B	C	D	E
96	L 612.2	K 611.6	D 0.5	B 0.4	V 0.6

In the following rounds, there is then bidding on the large lots A and B. Table 16.4 provides details.

The pattern that is displayed in table 16.4, with K, L, and T driving up the prices on A and B is maintained in all rounds until round 95, when K outbids T on lot B (with a bid of 556). The state that T faces in round 96 is as follows.

The prices on the small lots are still the same as they were in round 8, and, with this large price difference, T decides not come back on A or B, but instead to switch to the smaller lots. In fact, T bids on the cheapest lot, D, and this then starts a process in which B, D, T, and V drive up the prices on the smaller lots by bidding only on these. As a result of this, K and L do not have to bid again until round 177.

16.4.2   The Middle Play

Something very interesting and surprising happens on Friday June 26, when the auction has been going on for a week. Versatel has to bid and is confronted with the state shown in table 16.6.

Even though the price difference between the small and the large lots is still very large, V decides to bid on A and to replace L there. What is

Table 16.6
Round 176 of the auction

State	A	B	C	D	E
176	L 612.2	K 611.6	D 14.1	T 12.2	B 11.1

Table 16.7
Round 177 of the auction

State	A	B	C	D	E
177	V 673.4	K 611.6	D 14.1	T 12.2	B 11.1

Table 16.8
Round 219 of the auction

State	A	B	C	D	E
219	V 673.4	K 611.6	D 96.8	B 88	L 66

Versatel trying to achieve? One possibility is that it is signaling its willingness to pay; it is communicating that it could possibly drive up the prices of the smaller lots to more than 600 million. Hence, the signal might be that now it is still possible to get these small lots cheaply, but they might get very expensive as well. Being overbid by V, L is confronted in the next round with the state depicted in table 16.7 and, quite interestingly, L bids on E. In the next rounds, the game that was played on the small lots from rounds 96 to 176 is continued, but with L replacing V as an active player. It takes until round 219 when T is confronted with the state shown in table 16.8 and decides to displace K by bidding (the minimum needed) on B.

In round 220, K immediately takes back B, by bidding the required minimum amount 672.7. In the next round, 221, T then takes A from V by bidding 673.4. In round 222 (table 16.9), V is then confronted with the state displayed in the following line, and it decides to switch back to the smaller lots: It bids the minimum on E.

V thus displaces L and L decides to continue bidding on the smaller lots. This has the consequence that there is only bidding activity on the smaller lots until round 248 when Libertel is confronted with the state shown in table 16.10 and decides to bid on B.

For a couple of rounds, there is then activity on the large lots again. This lasts until round 253, when K overbids T on A, whereafter, in

Table 16.9
Round 222 of the auction

State	A	B	C	D	E
222	T 740.7	K 740	D 96.8	B 88	L 66

Table 16.10
Round 248 of the auction

State	A	B	C	D	E
248	T 740.7	K 740	D 302.5	V 223.9	B 277.2

Table 16.11
Rounds 248–253 of the auction

State	A	B	Bidder	Lot	Bid
248	T 740.7	K 740	L	B	741
249	T 740.7	L 815.1	K	A	740.7
250	K 814.8	L 815.1	T	A	814.8
251	T 896.3	L 815.1	K	B	815.1
252	T 896.3	K 896.6	L	B	896.6
253	T 896.3	L 986.2	K	A	896.3

Table 16.12
Round 254 of the auction

State	A	B	C	D	E
254	K 985.9	L 986.2	D 302.5	V 223.9	B 277.2

round 254, T switches to the small lots. The details of the rounds 248–253 are given in table 16.11.

The following line (table 16.12) gives the situation that T is faced with in round 254.

In this situation, T decides to enter a (minimum) bid on D, starting another bidding war on the smaller lots, which K and L can watch until round 275. In round 275, the auction is in this state, as table 16.13 shows.

T decides to bid 985.9 on A. For a couple of rounds, there is then again activity on the larger lots. The details are given in table 16.14.

Note the jump bid by K in round 276, which is one of the few really serious jump bids that occur throughout the game. From this bid one

Table 16.13
Round 275 of the auction

State	A	B	C	D	E
275	K 985.9	L 986.2	D 539	B 588.5	V 489.7

Table 16.14
Rounds 275–281 of the auction

State	A	B	Bidder	Lot	Bid
275	K 985.9	L 986.2	T	A	985.9
276	T 1084.4	L 986.2	K	B	1080
277	T 1084.4	K 1188	L	A	1084.4
278	L 1192.8	K 1188	T	B	1188
279	L 1192.8	T 1306.8	K	A	1192.8
280	K 1312	T 1306.8	L	A	1312
281	L 1443	T 1306.8	K	B	1306.8

may infer that K was not completely indifferent between the lots A and B. Confronted with this situation in round 282 (see table 16.15), T then decides to move again to the small lots: T bids on C.

This again leads to bidding only on the small lots in the rounds 282 up to and including 300. At that time, we are already in the end game, which in my opinion starts around round 297, which is the final round that is played on Friday and in which Versatel overbids Telfort on lot D.

Before moving to this end game, however, I briefly discuss some aspects of the players' strategies.[17] I have already outlined Versatel's strategy and will come back to it. From the previous description, it is clear that the market leader, K, bids only on the large lots. As may be inferred from K's behavior in round 276 (a jump bid that is approximately 10% above the required minimum), K is not indifferent to the lots A and B. Of the smaller players, B and D only bid on the smaller lots. With few exceptions, B always bids on the cheapest of these lots. On the other hand, D expresses a clear preference for lot C: throughout the auction, it makes only two bids on a different lot, and both these bids are on E. The explanation may be that D wants to signal that it is (or that it wants to be perceived as) the third player in the market; license C is the third license and D is willing to pay a price to get it, but this price should not be too high. Indeed, in the two rounds in which D bids on E, this price difference between C and E is relatively large; in

Table 16.15
Round 282 of the auction

State	A	B	C	D	E
282	L 1443	K 1437	D 539	B 588.5	V 489.7

round 286 it is 111.5 and in round 296 it is 76.6. Libertel and Telfort bid on both the small and the large lots. From the previous description it can be inferred that, up to round 278, T prefers to bid on a large lot as long as this is not more than (approximately) 600 more expensive than bidding on a small one; however, in round 278, the price difference is approximately 700 and T still bids on B, indicating a somewhat larger premium. In the first part of the middle phase of the auction, L bids on the smaller lots when A and B are not more than 535 more expensive; when prices reach higher levels, L is, however, willing to pay a premium of more than 800 for a large lot. Hence, it is somewhat difficult to pin down this player's indifference curve.

16.4.3   The End Game

I now analyze the end game in greater detail. The following table provides the play of the game. Although it is not evident from table 16.16, this part of the game beyond doubt is the most interesting part of the Dutch auction.

The reason that the table does not reveal why the end game was so interesting is that most of the action actually took place outside of the formal auction. On Friday, July 21, 2000, around 4:00 p.m., just when Versatel was about to overbid Telfort on lot E in round 293, the bidding team of Versatel received a letter from one of Telfort's lawyers, which stated, among other things:

Expert opinion indicates to Telfort that you will soon reach a bid level that is not in the interest of your company and its shareholders. If a bid at or above such a level would succeed, it might possibly be considered misconduct vis-à-vis these shareholders and could lead to personal liability of the directors of Versatel ... Telfort is of the opinion that the only conceivable reason why Versatel would place a bid at or above such level is that your company believes that its bids will always be surpassed by bids of the other participants in the auction. Press statements and your appeal against the government's decision to hold this auction support this view. As a result, the ulterior motive for such a bid must be that Versatel is attempting to either raise its competitors cots or to get access to their 2G or future 3G networks. Versatel's own press release of

Table 16.16
The end game of the auction

State	A	B	C		D		E		Bidder	Lot	Bid
296	L 1443	K 1437	B	867.9	T	861.5	V	791.3	D	E	791.3
297	L 1443	K 1437	B	867.9	T	861.5	D	870.4	V	D	861.5
298	L 1443	K 1437	B	867.9	V	947.6	D	870.4	T	C	867.9
299	L 1443	K 1437	T	953	V	947.6	D	870.4	B	E	870.4
300	L 1443	K 1437	T	953	V	947.6	B	955	D	C	960
301	L 1443	K 1437	D	1045	V	947.6	B	955	T	B	1437
302	L 1443	T 1567	D	1045	V	947.6	B	955	K	A	1443
303	K 1573	T 1567	D	1045	V	947.6	B	955	L	A	1573
304	L 1703	T 1567	D	1045	V	947.6	B	955	K	B	1567
305	L 1703	K 1697	D	1045	V	947.6	B	955	T	D	947.6
306	L 1703	K 1697	D	1045	T	1042	B	955	V	—	—

July 5 even appears to link its behaviour in the auction to gaining concessions from other participants. A bid strategy with such a motive constitutes a tort towards Telfort, who will hold Versatel liable for all damages as a result of this ... To conclude, Telfort intends to treat the matter as strictly confidential in the interest of the proper course of the auction.[18]

Hence, Telfort claims that Versatel is bidding only to raise its rivals' costs or to get concessions from them, that such behavior constitutes a tort toward Telfort, and that Telfort will hold Versatel and its managers liable for all damages resulting from this. Perhaps it is not surprising that Telfort intends to keep this letter secret, but the argument given ("in the proper course of the auction") is remarkable.

Versatel, however, did not keep the letter secret. Immediately after having received it, Versatel informed Telfort that it considered this letter to be a violation of the auction rules, intended to influence Versatel's bidding behavior, and that it was considering informing the Minister about this letter. The same day, Telfort responded that Versatel had misread the letter, that it had not been the intention to influence Versatel's behavior, and that the letter had been sent confidentially precisely not to damage Versatel and to keep Versatel's options open. It took until Sunday when Versatel took formal action, and one may wonder what happened over the weekend. That evening, around 10:40 p.m., Versatel sent the letter to the Minister and to the auctioneer (with a copy to Telfort). It was accompanied by the request to exclude Telfort from the auction. Specifically, Versatel argued that Telfort's intention was to deter Versatel from further bidding ("Deze brief heeft tot doel

of effect om Versatel te verhinderen verder in de veiling te bieden")
and that this threat was very serious (and hence, that competition in
the auction has been damaged), that Telfort had violated the rules and
should, therefore, be punished by exclusion from the auction.

The auctioneer and the representatives of the Dutch state studied the
material received from Versatel on Monday morning. At 9:33 a.m. they
sent a fax to Versatel announcing that they would study the case. In
the meantime, they decided to let the auction continue, and in the first
round on Monday morning, round 298, Telfort bid on C. When Versatel learned that the auction had continued, it wrote the auctioneer that
it was now no longer in the position to bid, and that it considered all
bids made on Monday to be vacuous. Somewhat later, around 10:00
a.m., the Minister informed Versatel and Telfort that it did not consider
Telfort's behavior to be a violation of the auction rules. Around 12:20
p.m., Versatel appealed the decision not to exclude Telfort. Simultaneously, Versatel requested the suspension of the auction. At 1:40 p.m.
the auctioneer responded that a party could be excluded from the auction only after a formal warning had been issued first and that such a
warning had not yet been given. At 2:06 p.m., when Versatel had to
bid, it informed the auctioneer that it was not in a position to bid,
which ended the auction.

Note that on Monday morning, Telfort could infer that Versatel
would no longer bid. Now that the negotiations had obviously broken
down, Versatel's only chance of winning a license was by having Telfort eliminated from the auction. Since Versatel's case now rested on
demonstrating that Telfort's threat was credible, Versatel had to act as
if it were deterred by the threat.[19] The auctioneer and the Minister
were informed directly that Versatel would no longer bid. This crucial
piece of information, however, was not available to the other bidders.
Furthermore, neither the auctioneer nor the government informed
these bidders of the fact that Versatel would no longer bid; they did
not even inform them of the communication that had taken place
between Telfort and Versatel. On the contrary, they let the auction
continue as if nothing had happened. Hence, on Monday, July 24, Telfort could profit from insider information. In fact, Telfort's bid on lot C
in round 298 can be interpreted as an attempt to profit from this additional piece of information.

Recall from the previous discussion that Libertel had shown a willingness to move to the smaller lots in order not to have a too large
price difference between the small and the large lots, but that it was

unclear what price difference it was willing to accept. It is reasonable to assume that, if Libertel moved to the smaller lots, it would bid on the cheapest of these. Consequently, T's strategy of first (in round 298) bidding on C and next (in round 301) on B might be interpreted as first making Versatel's lot, D, the cheapest and next inducing L to end the auction by bidding on it. This strategy is also risk free, since, if Libertel remains on the large lots, the prices on the small lots remain unchanged; hence, T can still buy C cheaply. This theory of manipulation is supported by T's behavior in round 298. Recall that T is willing to bid on a large lot, provided that the premium is not more than 600 to 700. In round 298, however, while the price difference is only 570, T nevertheless bids on a small lot. This behavior is not in line with that earlier on in the auction. In contrast, the behavior in rounds 301 and 305 is consistent with the original plan: In round 301, the difference is 490 and T bids on a large lot; in round 305, when Telfort has seen the plan failed, the difference is 750 and T bids on a small lot.

Whether or not one accepts this theory of insider trading, it is clear that bidding behavior is distorted during the last day, and that the auctioneer should have suspended the auction and should have created a level playing field as far as information is concerned. It is still very surprising that that course of action was not taken, especially since bidders suffered considerably: at the close of the auction total revenue was $f857$ million (22%) higher than it was on Monday morning. Apparently, the auctioneer and the government were not well prepared well for this contingency.

16.4.4   Collusion?

It is unclear how closely the Dutch competition authority, NMa, has watched the bidding process. The NMa did not act at the start of the auction, apparently it did not view Versatel's July 5 press release to be a violation of the competition law. On the final day of the auction, the Ministry asked the NMa for its opinion on Telfort's letter, and the NMa concluded that this letter did not violate the rules. When after the auction, during a hearing at the Ministry on November 1, 2000, Telfort voluntarily revealed that on the day the auction started, talks had already taken place between representatives of Telfort and Versatel, the Dutch competition authority became active.[20] Two days later, on November 3, it raided the offices of both companies to search for evidence. A large collection of documents were confiscated, but in the end

the NMa concluded that no evidence was found that the talks had as
their aim or effect to influence competition in the auction. Hence, there
was no proof of violation of the competition act, and meanwhile the
file had been closed. (See NMa 2001.) In other words, even if the case
does not smell well, it is not clear that it was rotten. What is surprising is that the NMa became active only four months after the event.
Clearly, after such a long time, it would have been very difficult to
find any evidence. Given the small number of bidders, the high stakes
involved, and the press release of Versatel, the Dutch competition
authority should have monitored the game much more closely.

To an economist, the conclusion reached by the NMa that there was
no collusion may appear surprising. However, it is not clear that the
behavior that Telfort and Versatel engaged in was a violation of the
competition law. To be specific, suppose Telfort had made the following proposal to Versatel: "I offer you the opportunity to become an
MVNO on my network, as well as access to my 2G-network on such
and such conditions, provided that the price I pay for my license is not
more than €0.1 mln." Suppose Versatel decides not to participate in the
auction, prices drop to zero, and Versatel accepts Telfort's offer. Is this
collusion? The question is for lawyers to answer, but personally, I
think it is not. What the example shows is that the competition law is
not sufficiently powerful to prevent all behavior that one might consider anti-competitive, or undesirable. If one wants to prevent such
behavior, it has to be done through the auction rules. It is at this
point that the Dutch auction rules were especially weak; they provided
almost no way to exclude players from the auction in the case of anti-
competitive behavior. In any case, players suspected for such behavior
had to be given warnings first by the Minister, and he obviously would
have been reluctant to issue warnings since eliminating players would
have reduced revenue. The lesson for the government is that it should
commit itself by writing stronger penalty clauses in the auction regulation. Given the allegations of collusion in several other European
UMTS auctions, this lesson appears to have broader relevance.

16.5   Conclusion

One way to summarize the Dutch UMTS auction is that it was a game
between a somewhat naive government and sophisticated market
players. The government was naive in its belief that, in order to realize
its goals, it did not have to pay much attention to the details of the
auction rules, nor to assuring that the game was being played accord-

ing to these rules. For the bidders, this auction was just one subgame of a large overall game with high stakes. At least one market party was sophisticated in that it realized that, even though it could not win in the auction, it could use the auction as a means of trying to achieve its overall goal. There are two general lessons. First, a license auction such as this one is not an isolated event; it takes place in a certain context and this context should be taken into account when designing the auction rules. Second, auction design is an art in itself of which the difficulty should not be underestimated.

At a more detailed level, based on this specific case, one can draw the following conclusions and make several recommendations:

1. The goal to be achieved by this auction was said to be efficiency, not generating revenue. There are, however, good arguments for why revenue might be a valid goal. Since these two goals might conflict, choices have to be made. The goals should be explicit so that the auction design can be targeted toward reaching it.

2. Market efficiency was confused with cost efficiency and value efficiency. These concepts, however, are very different in nature, and one type of efficiency need not imply another. In particular, if a license auction awards the licenses to those bidders that value them most (value efficiency), the resulting allocation is not necessarily market efficient, that is, it need not maximize welfare or consumer surplus.

3. Asymmetries between incumbents and newcomers may drive a wedge between value efficiency and market efficiency. While consumers may prefer a newcomer to win the auction, symmetric rules favor incumbents. These value differences may be surprisingly large and may make it virtually impossible for newcomers to win licenses in ordinary ascending auctions.

4. Policy makers are not (yet) fully aware of the richness of the set of auctions, that is, of the many degrees of freedom that the auction mechanism allows. Furthermore, there appears too little recognition of the fact that it is important to get the details right in order to ensure that the goals are reached.

5. Market parties lobby for those auction rules that suit them best, and the lobby game is biased in favor of incumbents. In order not to become a puppet of the vested interests, the government should ask independent experts for advice on the auction design.

6. An auction is not an isolated event, but it typically is a subgame of a larger game. Players bid in the auction not necessarily to win the

auction, but rather to reach their goal in the overall game. Participating in an auction may make sense, even if one cannot win in the auction, as long as it yields benefits elsewhere in the game.

7. Because competition in an auction is very intense, participants have strong incentives to reduce this intensity, either through cooperation (merging, or making agreements) before the auction or collusion within the auction. Special attention of the competition authorities is therefore warranted, but the general competition laws may be too weak to effectively prevent all anti-competitive behavior. Collusion could be tackled through specific auction provisions, but it seems very difficult to prevent cooperation and contracts before the auction.

8. Since, being the seller, the government will not always have the correct incentives to strictly enforce the auction rules, an independent auctioneer should conduct the auction. Of course, the auctioneer should be knowledgeable so that it is well prepared for the different contingencies that may arise during the auction.

While one may definitely conclude that several things were wrong with the way the Dutch UMTS auction was designed and conducted, the large amount of criticism that it has drawn has had at least two positive consequences. First, in the "official evaluation" of the UMTS auction that was done on behalf of Parliament (Janssen, Ros, and van der Windt 2001) several recommendations for improvement were made, and in its reaction to that evaluation, the government stated that it would take the lessons to heart.[21] Second, within its overall project of structural reform, the government has started a general project on auctions and beauty contests that aims to provide a general framework for how to select and implement the appropriate instrument for allocating licenses and scarce commodities.[22] The report, prepared by a committee that includes both policy makers and academics, and incorporating input from leading auction experts, is scheduled to appear this spring. Hence, it may be expected that the Dutch will do better next time. It is only somewhat unfortunate that the UMTS auction was such an expensive occasion to learn the lesson that auction design matters.

Notes

Based on my presentation given at the conference on Spectrum Auctions and Competition in Telecommunication, CESifo Munich, November 22–23, 2001. The author thanks Emiel Maasland (Erasmus University) for detailed comments on an earlier version.

1. See Tweede Kamer (2001b).

2. For reviews of the European UMTS auctions, see Jehiel and Moldovanu (2003), Klemperer (2002b) and van Damme (2002).

3. Specifically, this chapter builds on van Damme (2000a,b) and van Damme (2001).

4. An exception is van Damme (1997, 19), but there the argument was not forcefully made.

5. Tweede Kamer (2000).

6. Tweede Kamer (2001b, 4).

7. Also see Jehiel and Moldovanu (2000) and Klemperer (2002a).

8. Data from Mobile Communications (2001).

9. Ministry of Public Works and Transport (1999).

10. The numbers used in the calculation correspond to "realistic (lower end) estimates" of market analysts at the time of the auction. Note that for incumbents I have not included the value of business lost, while I have also assumed that newcomers and incumbents can start at the same point in time; hence, if anything, the extent of asymmetry is underestimated.

11. See Appendices 8, 11, 14, 16, 21, and 23 to Tweede Kamer (2000).

12. Given, as argued earlier, that incumbents will attach a higher value to a license, only budget constraints can tilt the competition in favor of an entrant.

13. For example, see Versatel (2000a).

14. Versatel (2000b); an MVNO is a mobile operator that does not have its own network, but that in all other respects appears to the consumer as a regular operator.

15. See Versatel (2000c) and Financieel Dagblad (2000).

16. 1 € = 2.20 guilders.

17. I follow the approach first outlined in Börgers and Dustman (2003).

18. The letter has been published by the Ministry of Public Works and Transport; see Tweede Kamer (2000), Appendix 26.

19. In my view, Telfort's letter cannot be viewed as a credible threat. First, it is hard to see how getting concessions in this way could be against the interests of Versatel's shareholders. Second, according to Versatel's own information, the letter was received shortly before Versatel had to bid in round 293, so that Versatel had to bid twice after having received Telfort's letter: in round 293 and in round 297. This behavior considerably weakens Versatel's position that it could no longer bid, and it might be classified as a strategic mistake. To counter, Versatel might, perhaps, argue that, upon receiving the letter, these bids had already been prepared, that it was too late not to bid.

20. It has remained somewhat unclear who took the initiative for these talks (Telfort points to Versatel and vice versa) and what exactly was discussed there.

21. Tweede Kamer (2001b).

22. Tweede Kamer (2001a).

References

Bennett, M., and M. Canoy. 2000. "Auctions and Precautions: Overbidding in Spectrum Auctions and Its Possible Impact." Working paper 127, CPB, June.

Börgers, T., and Chr. Dustmann. 2003. "Awarding Telecom Licenses: The Recent European Experience." *Economic Policy* 36: 216–268.

Damme, E. van. 1997. *Aanbesteding en Veilingmechanismen: Economische Theorie en Toepassingen.* Onderzoeksreeks Directie Marktwerking, Ministry of Economic Affairs, January.

Damme, E. van. 1999. "The Dutch DCS-1800 Auction." In: *Game Practise: Contributions from Applied Game Theory,* ed. Fioravante Patrone, I. García-Jurado, and St. Tijs, 53–73. Boston: Kluwer Academic Publishers.

Damme, E. van. 2000a. "Afspraken en voorkennis in UMTS-veiling." Economisch Statistischen Berichten 85: 680–683.

Damme, E. van. 2000b. "Het spel van Versatel." *Nederlands Juristenblad* 33, 22 September, pp. 1666–1671.

Damme, E. van. 2001. "The Dutch UMTS-Auction in Retrospect." *CPB Report* 2: 25–30.

Damme, E. van. 2002. "The European UMTS auctions." *European Economic Review* 46: 846–858.

European Commission. 1994. "Green Paper on a Common Approach in the Field of Mobile and Personal Communication in the European Union." Office for Official Publications of the European Communities, Luxembourg.

Financieel Dagblad. 2000. "Without a Partner, Versatel Cannot Participate in UMTS-Auction." *Financieel Dagblad,* July 3.

Fortis Bank. 2000. "Putting UMTS in Perspective." Brussels, September.

Gilbert, R., and D. Newbery. 1982. "Preemptive Patenting and the Persistence of Monopoly." *American Economic Review* 72: 514–526.

Janssen, M., A. Ros, and N. van der Windt, eds. 2001. *De draad kwijt? Onderzoek naar de gang van zaken rond de Nederlandse UTMS-veiling.* Erasmus Universiteit Rotterdam.

Jehiel, Ph., and B. Moldovanu. 2000. "License Auctions and Market Structure." Discussion paper, University College London and Mannheim University.

Jehiel, Ph., and B. Moldovanu. 2003. "An Economic Perspective on Auctions." *Economic Policy* 36: 271–308.

Klemperer, P. 2000. "The Flaws of a Dutch Auction." *Financial Times,* July 26, p. 19.

Klemperer, P. 2002a. "What Really Matters in Auction Design." *Journal of Economic Perspectives* (Winter): 169–189.

Klemperer, P. 2002b. "How (Not) to Run Auctions: The European 3G Telecom Auctions." *European Economic Review* 46: 829–845.

Maasland, E. 2000. "Veilingmiljarden zijn een fictie." *ESB,* June 9, p. 479.

Ministry of Public Works and Transport. 1999. "Letter DGTP/98/2517." January 11. (Included as Appendix 4 in the appendices to *Tweede Kamer* (2000).)

Mobile Communications. 2001. *Mobile Communications*, Issue Number 310, June 26.

NMa. 2001. "Geen overtreding mededingingsregels geconstateerd bij veiling UMTS-frequenties." Press Release 22-02-2001, The Hague.

Planet Multimedia. 2000. "Versatel kan samen met Dutchtone; Analyse van eerste veilingdag; artikelen uit de Pers." *Planet Multimedia*. July 7 (9:00 a.m.).

Tweede Kamer. 2000. "Frequentiebeleid. Brief van de Staatssecretaris van Verkeer en Waterstaat en de Minister van Financiën met Procesbeschrijving en verantwoording UMTS." *Kamerstukken* 1999–2000, 24 095, Nr. 55.

Tweede Kamer. 2001a. "Startnotitie Veilen en Alternatieve Allocatiemechanismen." *Kamerstukken* vergaderjaar 2000–2001, 24 036, Nr. 223.

Tweede Kamer. 2001b. "Brief van de Staatssecretaris van Verkeer en Waterstaat en de Minister van Financiën." *Kamerstukken* vergaderjaar 2001–2002, 24 095, Nr. 86.

Versatel. 2000a. "Versatel Pursues UMTS Courtcase Against Dutch Government." Press release, July 4.

Versatel. 2000b. "Versatel Disappointed with Dutch UMTS Auction Tomorrow." Press release, July 5.

Versatel. 2000c. "Versatel Remains in Auction for Dutch 3G Mobile Internet License." Press release, July 6.

17 Comments on "The Dutch UMTS Auction" by Eric van Damme

Christian Ewerhart

Chapter 16 documents and discusses bidding behavior during the Dutch UMTS auction as part of the political process among government, regulatory authorities, and telecom firms. The background information provided in the discussion is impressively comprehensive, and so the chapter makes a very interesting case study. The chapter is also part of a larger research program (see, e.g., van Damme 2001a,b) in which the author describes and analyzes various aspects of the Dutch mobile phone license auctions.

The main contribution of chapter 16 is probably that it puts the design of license auctions into the necessary broader context. As a matter of illustration, I mention only two examples here, both of which are related to the unfortunate fate of market newcomer Versatel, but both of which also point toward questions that, as I believe, call for clarification. To start, it is reported that, once the decision in favor of the five-license design had been made—which was apparently at least in part due to lobbying efforts by the market leader in the 2G market KPN—the entrant Versatel had no chance whatsoever to profitably outbid any opponent. From a naive point of view, this is just unfair. However, from a more critical perspective, this example puts into question an ingredient of the standard methodology of auction theory, at least for the case of license auctions. As the case study shows, when he stakes are sufficiently high, it is not always realistic to assume that the design of an auction is performed—or an "independent" consultant is chosen—by a benevolent government.

Another story illustrating my previous claim is the description of Versatel's cold-blooded strategy to increase the price level in the auction to the detriment of the other bidders. This story is probably interesting just for anybody who is intrigued by ingenious strategic behavior. However, I found this story interesting because it illustrates very clearly the vulnerability of noncooperative theory with respect to "collusive" behavior.

While van Damme's chapter touches upon so many more interesting issues, such as signaling, insider trading, and so forth, I focus in the rest of this discussion on just one somewhat unexpected feature of the bidding behavior that is well documented in the chapter, but for which no explanation is offered! The reader recalls that there were two types of licenses, large and small, for sale in the Dutch UMTS auction. So bidders, when being asked to submit a new bid, had to decide whether to bid on a small or on a large license. This decision may not be straightforward because, at any given round, the price level P_L that is necessary to acquire a large license will in general differ from the price level P_S that is necessary to acquire a small license.

In many settings, the following "benchmark strategy" seems appropriate to facilitate this decision. Let ΔV_i denote the additional value of a large license over the value of a small license for bidder i. Then it appears plausible that bidder i should place a bid on a large licence whenever $P_L - P_S \leq \Delta V_i$, and bid on a small license otherwise. This strategy, which is very much in line with economic intuition, has been suggested first by Börgers and Dustmann (2002). Somewhat surprisingly, however, bidders in the Dutch auction did not follow this rule. Rather, the valuation spread, especially for Telfort and Libertel, turned out to grow over the course of the auction.

To cite the relevant passages from chapter 16: "up to round 278, T[elfort] prefers to bid on a large lot as long as this is not more than (approximately) 600 more expensive than bidding on a small one; however, in round 278, the price difference is approximately 700 and still T bids on [a large license]" (284). And then: "In the first part of the middle phase of the auction, L[ibertel] bids on the smaller lots when [the larger licenses] are not more than 535 more expensive, when prices reach higher levels, L is, however, willing to pay a premium of more than 800 for a large lot" (284). According to van Damme, "it is somewhat difficult to pin down this player's indifference curve" (284).

As I now argue, the observed behavior may be rationalized when bidders are uncertain about their valuations and make some simplifying assumptions about their strategic problem. Specifically, firms might have had a comparatively accurate idea about the size of the investments that the new technologies would require, but a less clear picture on prospective demand. Let C_L and C_S be the expected net present value of investments necessary to realize a 3G business on the basis of a large and a small license, respectively. Similarly, let $\tilde{R}_L$ and $\tilde{R}_S$ denote the net present value of uncertain future revenues that would result for an owner of a large and a small license.

For simplicity, I assume—in the spirit of Milgrom's (2000) notion of straightforward bidding—that at any stage, a bidder maximizes utility conditional on the case that his bid will end the auction. In the simplest case, when $\tilde{R}_L$ and $\tilde{R}_S$ are independently distributed, the benchmark strategy is in fact optimal in the previous sense, where

$$\Delta V_i = E[\tilde{R}_L] - C_L - (E[\tilde{R}_S] - C_S). \tag{1}$$

However, the independence assumption, between types as well as between licenses of different size, appears somewhat unrealistic given the common nature of the business that will be perused with the licenses. I therefore assume now that $\tilde{R}_L$ and $\tilde{R}_S$ are perfectly correlated in the sense that bidders assume

$$\tilde{R}_L = (1 - \alpha)\tilde{R}_S \tag{2}$$

for some constant $\alpha > 0$. Under this condition, one would have

$$\Delta V_i = \alpha E[\tilde{R}_S] - (C_L - C_S). \tag{3}$$

Given that the license holders operate in the same market, one also expects a strong common value component in the bidders' individual valuations. Under this condition, observing a high price level in the auction would generate a higher conditional valuation for a bidder, so that $E[\tilde{R}_S]$ would be increasing during the auction unless a bidder exits. Since there were only six bidders for five licenses, an exit could not happen during the auction, however. From (3), one can see therefore that the behavioral valuation differential ΔV_i would be increasing over time. But this is the behavior that the author documents in the Dutch UMTS auction.

References

Börgers, T., and C. Dustmann. 2002. "Strange Bids: Bidding Behavior in the United Kingdom's Third Generation Spectrum Auction." Working paper, University College London.

Damme, Eric van. 2001a. "The Dutch UMTS Auction in Retrospect." *CPB Report* 2: 25–30.

Damme, Eric van. 2001b. "The European UMTS Auctions and Next." Mimeo.

Milgrom, P. 2000. "Putting Auction Theory to Work: The Simultaneous Ascending Auction." *Journal of Political Economy* 108(2): 245–272.

Index